D0771831

Prisoner Reentry and Crime in America

Prisoner Reentry and Crime in America is intended to shed light on a critical question that fuels the public's concern about the large number of returning prisoners, shapes the policies of elected officials, and remains largely unaddressed in the research literature: What are the public safety consequences of the fourfold increase in the number of individuals entering and leaving the nation's prisons each year? Many have speculated about the nexus between prisoner reentry and public safety. Journalistic accounts of the reentry phenomenon have painted a picture of a tidal wave of hardened criminals coming back home to resume their destructive lifestyles. Law enforcement officials have attributed increases in violence in their communities to the influx of returning prisoners. Politicians have recommended policies that keep former prisoners out of high-crime neighborhoods in the belief that crime would be reduced. The chapters in this book address these issues and suggest policies that will keep released prisoners from committing new crimes.

Jeremy Travis is President of John Jay College of Criminal Justice in New York. He has written and published extensively on constitutional law, criminal law, and criminal justice policy.

Christy Visher is Principal Research Associate at the Urban Institute, in Washington, D.C. Dr. Visher has published widely on crime and justice topics, including prisoner reentry, crime prevention strategies, criminal careers, the arrest process, youthful offending, incapacitation, and use of drug testing in the criminal justice system.

Cambridge Studies in Criminology

Edited by

Alfred Blumstein, *H. John Heinz School of Public Policy and Management, Carnegie Mellon University*, and David Farrington, *Institute of Criminology, University of Cambridge*

Other books in the series:

Prisoner Reentry and Crime in America

Edited by

JEREMY TRAVIS

John Jay College of Criminal Justice

CHRISTY VISHER

Urban Institute

CAMBRIDGE
UNIVERSITY PRESS

CAMBRIDGE UNIVERSITY PRESS
Cambridge, New York, Melbourne, Madrid, Cape Town, Singapore, São Paulo

Cambridge University Press
40 West 20th Street, New York, NY 10011-4211, USA

www.cambridge.org
Information on this title: www.cambridge.org/9780521849166

© Cambridge University Press 2005

First published 2005

Printed in the United States of America

A catalog record for this publication is available from the British Library.

Library of Congress Cataloging in Publication Data

Prisoner reentry and crime in America / edited by Jeremy Travis, Christy Visher.
    p.   cm. – (Cambridge studies in criminolgy)
Includes bibliographical references and index.
ISBN 0-521-84916-0 (hardback) – ISBN 0-521-61386-8 (pbk.)
1. Criminals – Rehabilitation – United States.   2. Ex-convicts – United States.
3. Recidivism – United States.   4. Crime – United States.   5. Imprisonment – United
States.   I. Travis, Jeremy.   II. Visher, Christy Ann.   III. Title.   IV. Series: Cambridge
studies in criminology (Cambridge University Press)
HV9304.P74   2005
364.8'0973 – dc22   2005008118

ISBN-13   978-0-521-84916-6 hardback
ISBN-10   0-521-84916-0 hardback

ISBN-13   978-0-521-61386-6 paperback
ISBN-10   0-521-61386-8 paperback

Contents

Contributors

Allen Beck, Bureau of Justice Statistics, U.S. Department of Justice

Alfred Blumstein, Carnegie Mellon University

Todd Clear, John Jay College of Criminal Justice

Robert Fornango, University of Missouri at St. Louis

Stefan LoBuglio, Montgomery County Department of Correction and Rehabilitation, Maryland

Shadd Maruna, Institute of Criminology, Cambridge University

Joan Petersilia, University of California at Irvine

Anne Morrison Piehl, Rutgers University, New Brunswick

Richard Rosenfeld, University of Missouri at St. Louis

Kristen Scully, University of Massachusetts, Lowell

Hans Toch, The University at Albany

Jeremy Travis, John Jay College of Criminal Justice

Christopher Uggen, University of Minnesota

Christy Visher, The Urban Institute

Sara Wakefield, University of Minnesota

Joel Wallman, Harry Frank Guggenheim Foundation

Elin Waring, Lchman College, City University of New York

Bruce Western, Princeton University

1

Introduction

VIEWING CRIME AND PUBLIC SAFETY THROUGH THE REENTRY LENS

Jeremy Travis and Christy Visher

Overview

One consequence of the fourfold increase in the per-capita rate of incarceration in America is a parallel growth in the number of individuals released from the nation's prisons. In 2001, approximately 630,000 prisoners were released from the nation's state and federal penitentiaries to return home, 4 times more than the number who made similar journeys 20 years ago (Harrison and Karberg 2003). The increased use of imprisonment as a response to crime has received considerable attention in academic circles, among policymakers, and within the general public. There have been spirited debates over the wisdom of indeterminate sentencing, the value of sentencing guidelines, the abolition of parole boards, the emergence of private prisons, the benefits of "three-strikes" laws, the impact of incarceration on racial minorities, and the cost-effectiveness of the network of state and federal prisons constructed to house over a million inmates. Until recently, however, little attention has been paid to one immutable result of building more prisons, namely the reality that more prisoners will be returning home each year.

Recent years have witnessed an explosion of interest in the phenomenon of "prisoner reentry." Within policy circles, all levels of government have been engaged in sustained examinations of the reentry issue. In his 2004 State of the Union address, President Bush called for a 4-year, $300 million federal initiative to provide jobs, transitional housing, and community support to the nation's returning prisoners, reminding his audience that America is the "land of the second chance" (January 20, 2004). This new program would build upon an existing $100 million federal effort supporting the development of new reentry strategies in all 50 states. The Council

1

of State Governments has created the Reentry Policy Council, representing all three branches of government and drawing on the expertise of a wide assortment of practitioners, with a mission to develop a consensus document recommending policies that will improve outcomes for returning prisoners, their families, and their communities. The National Governors Association has established a Reentry Policy Academy, selecting 7 states to work collaboratively to develop state policies to enhance the reentry process. Asserting that the flow of prisoners back to their cities has harmful effects, particularly on neighborhoods already disadvantaged, mayors of a number of cities, including Chicago, Oakland, Fort Wayne, Houston, Cleveland, and Boston, have announced that improving the reentry process is a priority for their administrations.

Interest in prisoner reentry as a research topic is also high. In August 2001, *Crime and Delinquency* devoted an entire issue to the subject. The Russell Sage Foundation funded research in four states to document the impact of incarceration on employment. A prominent scholar of the U.S. correctional system, Joan Petersilia, wrote the first book devoted to the topic of reentry, *When Prisoners Come Home: Parole and Prisoner Reentry*, published by Oxford University Press. By early 2005, an informal count reveals that close to a dozen other books and edited volumes are in production. The Urban Institute created the Reentry Roundtable, a group of prominent academics, practitioners, and community leaders who explore the intersections between the reentry phenomenon and other policy domains such as housing, health care, employment, policing, and community development. The Institute has also launched a longitudinal study in four states called *Returning Home* to document the reentry experience from the perspectives of the individual prisoner, his or her family, and communities with large concentrations of returning prisoners.

This book is intended to shed light on a critical question that fuels the public's concern about the large number of returning prisoners, shapes the policies of elected officials, and remains largely unaddressed in the research literature: What are the public safety consequences of the fourfold increase in the number of individuals entering and leaving the nation's prisons each year? There has been considerable speculation about the nexus between prisoner reentry and crime rates. Journalistic accounts of the reentry phenomenon have painted a picture of a tidal wave of hardened criminals coming back home to resume their destructive lifestyles. Law enforcement officials have attributed increases in violence in their communities to the influx of returning prisoners. Politicians have recommended policies that keep former prisoners out of high crime neighborhoods in the belief that crime would be reduced.

With generous support from the Harry F. Guggenheim Foundation, we convened a group of scholars to address the public safety dimensions of prisoner reentry. In our deliberations, we quickly realized that the question is not a simple one. For example, a discussion of the characteristics and size of the reentry cohort would be incomplete without an analysis of the changing profile of the entry cohort, the population going into prison. Similarly, an analysis of the contributions of former prisoners to local crime rates would necessarily require an analysis of the crime reduction effects of the imprisonment of those individuals. Furthermore, the substantial increases in rates of incarceration should be understood from the perspective of the communities most affected to determine whether the reality of mass incarceration weakens the local networks of social control that constrain antisocial behavior. Finally, we realized that an analysis of the nexus between prisoner reentry and crime would be incomplete without placing the incarceration experience in the context of the longer processes of desistance from criminal activity and, in turn, examining the role of other factors, particularly family structures and employment experiences, that might influence the behavior of former prisoners. In short, we came to the conclusion that exploring the nexus between prisoner reentry and crime would require a number of distinct intellectual inquiries. To conduct those inquiries, we solicited as partners the distinguished scholars who have written the chapters that make up this book.

Reentry, Recidivism, and Public Safety

This book explores the intersection of three distinct phenomena – the large numbers of individuals leaving prison, their criminal behavior following their release, and the public's sense of safety. These complex phenomena are sometimes captured in the shorthand phrases reentry, recidivism, and public safety. Before proceeding with a preview of the book's chapters, we should consider the contours of these concepts.

Reentry

We define *reentry* as the inevitable consequence of incarceration. With the exception of those who die of natural causes or are executed, everyone placed in confinement is eventually released. Reentry is not a legal status. Indeed, as we shall see, not all state prisoners are released to parole supervision; many are released directly into the community with no continuing obligation to observe special conditions of their release. Nor is reentry a new kind of program. Certainly, the pathways of reentry can be influenced by such factors as the prisoner's participation in drug treatment, literacy classes, religious organizations, or prison industries, but reentry is not a result of program participation. Reentry happens when incarceration ends. In other words, for those who are incarcerated, reentry is not an option.

In this broad definition, reentry is experienced by individuals sent to either jail or prison, federal or state facilities, as adults or juveniles. In the chapters that follow, our focus will be primarily on adults sent to state prisons and the impact of their release from prison on public safety. By adopting this focus, we do not imply that jails, juvenile facilities, and federal prisons have no responsibility for promoting public safety. On the contrary, we believe that an examination of the safety dimensions of reentry from these institutions would be enormously valuable. Far more people leave county jails each year than leave state and federal prisons – nearly 7 million, compared to 630,000 (Hammett, Roberts, and Kennedy 2001; Harrison and Karberg 2003). Given the volume of jail releases, any diminution in their criminal activity could result in significant improvements in public safety. Unfortunately, there has been little research on the impact of jail reentry on public safety. Similarly, although the volume of discharges from juvenile facilities is much smaller (about 100,000 a year), the clear nexus between juvenile justice involvement and adult criminal activity argue for an examination of juvenile reentry from a public safety perspective (Sickmund 2002). We applaud those who have studied juvenile aftercare and have applied some of the new reentry perspectives to the unique challenges of adolescent development (Altschuler and Brash 2004; Mears and Travis 2004). Finally, we focus our attention on state prisons and only occasionally refer to the experiences of federal prisoners. Although federal prisoners are less likely than their state counterparts to be convicted of crimes of violence and be rearrested for crimes of violence, the growth of the federal criminal justice system and the blurred boundaries between federal and state crimes make an exploration of the public safety impact of federal prisoner reentry a compelling research priority.

Our focus on reentry from state prisons has the important benefit of raising profound questions of social policy, questions that apply with equal force to an examination of jails, juvenile incarceration, and the federal justice system. The growth of the state prison population reflects a pronounced policy shift regarding the use of incarceration as a response to crime. State prisoners have been removed in large numbers, from a small number of neighborhoods, for long periods, with uncertain effects on families and communities left behind. While in prison, they frequently participate in programs designed to reduce the likelihood they will return to crime after getting out of prison. Most released prisoners are subject to supervision by agencies that seek to reduce the safety risk they pose to the public. Questions regarding the efficacy of public policies on the use of incarceration, treatment of those incarcerated, and supervision of individuals who have violated the law cut across all system boundaries. In this book, we hope to shed light on policies that have cast a long shadow over the broad landscape of incarceration and reentry in America.

Recidivism

A touchstone performance indicator for the criminal justice system has been the rate of "recidivism" – or reoffending – of individuals whose cases have been processed by the system. Sometimes, entire institutions such as prisons are evaluated by their recidivism rates, as when corrections directors claim credit if recidivism rates are lower this year than last. Similarly, directors of individual programs such as drug treatment, job training, anger management, or parenting classes are frequently asked whether the recidivism rates of their participants are lower than those of a comparison group. And on the broadest scale, the changes in recidivism rates for large samples of released prisoners, marked in studies by the Bureau of Justice Statistics (BJS), are scrutinized by the national press and policy analysts to ascertain whether the individuals coming out of prison today are more or less likely to reoffend than their counterparts from an earlier period of time.

Unfortunately, this key indicator of criminal justice performance is difficult to measure accurately. Whether released prisoners commit crimes is largely unobservable, requiring researchers and practitioners to turn to official records of criminal behavior, primarily police arrest records. Although the chapters in this book most frequently use arrest data as indicators of the criminal behavior of released prisoners, we recognize the limitations of a reliance on arrest records. By encompassing only behavior that is brought to police attention and warrants police action, this definition captures neither unreported crimes nor reported crimes that do not result in arrests. It may also over-count crimes committed by individuals known to the police. Ideally, these official measures would be augmented by self-report surveys in which respondents would report conduct that can be characterized as violating the criminal laws. But these surveys are quite expensive and limited in scope. Notwithstanding these limitations, we rely principally on arrest records as the basis for measuring recidivism.

We recognize that some colleagues embrace definitions of recidivism that are broader or narrower. Some define recidivism as including only those arrests that lead to criminal convictions. Although this construct reflects a high concern for legal accuracy, it significantly understates the level of criminal activity in the community. Defining recidivism as including only those arrests that result in successful prosecutions would superimpose upon our measure of criminal behavior all the vagaries of the criminal justice system that stand between arrest and conviction. Other definitions of recidivism count only those prisoners who return to prison, either on a new arrest or for a parole violation. This metric is highly misleading because it does not include arrests that do not result in a new prison sentence, thereby discounting the reality of crime on the streets. Second, by including returns to prison for parole violations, this definition embraces a category of prison returns that is highly susceptible to policy influence. Compare, for example, State A, which places only half of its released prisoners on parole supervision and returns none of them to prison for technical violations of parole, with State B, which places all released prisoners on parole and aggressively returns them to prison for even minor parole violations. State B will have a higher recidivism rate, not due to differences in the behavior of its former prisoners, but because of policy choices it made. This definition makes cross-state comparisons of recidivism rates virtually impossible. More important, it captures misconduct such as technical parole violations that cannot be considered criminal.

Accordingly, we prefer to define recidivism as an arrest for a new crime. This formulation is particularly valuable for a book on prisoner reentry because it allows us to distinguish between arrests for new crimes, convictions resulting from those arrests, returns to prison for new convictions, and returns to prison for parole violations. In our view, only the first of these constitutes recidivism; the second and third reflect court decisions; the fourth reflects a combination of sentencing policy, parole enforcement practices, and parolee behavior.

Introduction

Public Safety

Although recidivism is clearly an important indicator of criminal justice system effectiveness, we would argue that the broader term *public safety* should be seen as the ultimate measure of the impact of incarceration and reentry. Recidivism is, after all, an individual measure of reoffending. Men and women who are released from prison do, or do not, commit new crimes, and those individual acts, when they result in arrests, are aggregated to create a rate of recidivism. That rate may change over time, may be different for different subgroups, and may vary according to geographic community. But the phrase *public safety* captures a different quality, one that is more integral to the functioning of communities and reflects the collective sense of well-being beyond the aggregation of individual behaviors (Smith 1999).

Some examples may illustrate the difference. The arrest of a rapist may provide peace of mind to his victims and a sense of relief in the community he has terrorized. When he is released from prison, however, those victims and the broader community may feel unsafe, even though, over time, his rate of reoffending is low or even nonexistent. A gang member imprisoned for crimes of violence may return to resume command over a criminal enterprise, harming the safety of the community, even though he is not rearrested for another crime. In these examples, public safety is affected by prisoner reentry in ways not measured by recidivism data. Certainly, policies governing the reentry process would be more effective if they enhanced the sense of safety, even though the yield in recidivism reduction might be negligible.

Public safety can be affected in other ways by a state's reentry policies. For example, a state that adopts a "zero tolerance" policy regarding technical violations of parole conditions may find itself balancing the twin goals of recidivism reduction and safety enhancement. Returning a parolee to prison for minor infractions may have little impact on recidivism rates. But a widespread policy of revoking the parole status of large numbers of parolees for minor infractions and removing them for short, unproductive stints in prison may be highly destabilizing to communities where many parolees live, ultimately creating a sense that the state is capriciously depriving citizens of their liberty without regard for the long-term consequences. In such a scenario, the sense of public safety may be undermined, not enhanced, by the actions of the state.

Finally, the concept of public safety provides a useful framework for understanding the net effects of the current policies that result in the arrest, removal, incarceration, and return of large numbers of individuals, mostly men, from a small number of communities in America. One hypothesis being tested by researchers is that these policies, originally justified in part on their crime reduction effects, are actually having the opposite impact. In this theory, the cycle of removal and return has so weakened the social networks and institutions that prevent crime – such as families, work, and community organizations – that crime rates actually increase (Clear and Rose et al. 2003). Testing this hypothesis requires more than recidivism measures and more than crime analysis. Ultimately, the key measure is the ways that communities and families function and, in large part, their sense of safety in their relationships with each other.

Data Sources

In preparing this book, the chapter authors were fortunate that BJS had just released its analysis of the recidivism rates of a sampled cohort of prisoners released from 15 state prisons in 1994. This study, which parallels a similar study of a cohort released from 11 state prisons in 1983, provided a rich data set that was extremely useful for the research conducted for some of the chapters of this book. We acknowledge our indebtedness to BJS for collecting these data and making them publicly available (Beck and Shipley 1989; Langan and Levin 2002).

In sum, the new BJS recidivism study found that, within 3 years of their release from prison, 68 percent of state prisoners were rearrested for one or more serious crimes, 47 percent were convicted of new offenses, and 52 percent were returned to prison. One headline conclusion reported in the popular media was that, because the recidivism rate had increased from the 63 percent rate found in the 1983 study, prisons were failing in their mission to rehabilitate inmates. Others have concluded that a closer comparison between the two studies yields more similarities than differences. The more salient observation may be that too much had changed in the intervening years to allow either inference. Prison populations had increased significantly, reflecting both increases in sentence length and in new admissions. The profile of incoming prisoners had changed substantially, mostly due to changes in arrest patterns for drug offenses. Between these years, the crack epidemic hit urban America hard, contributing to a sharp rise in violence, and then peaked and declined substantially. When the second BJS recidivism study was conducted, the country was experiencing a substantial economic expansion, raising employment levels of low-skilled

8

workers, an economic climate that, if anything, would result in lower rates of recidivism.

But the most important difference between the two time periods was the growth in the size of the annual reentry cohorts. In 1983, 226,000 state and federal prisoners were released. In 1994, 457,000 were released (Harrison 2000). The rise in the prison population over these years had led to a substantial increase in the reentry population, placing new strains on the system of postrelease supervision. This flow of large numbers of individuals, mostly men, was concentrated in a small number of communities, in essence requiring those burdened service networks and social institutions to take on additional responsibilities of reintegrating large numbers of returning prisoners. In addition, the methods of release from prison had changed, as the nation moved away from discretionary release by parole boards toward mandatory release by operation of law (Travis and Lawrence 2002). Finally, the system of supervision had undergone a gradual shift from a service orientation to a more enforcement orientation, as witnessed by the increase in parole revocations from 59,000 in 1983 to 171,000 in 1994 (Rice and Harrison 2000). In short, the scale, philosophy, and operations of the interlocking systems of sentencing, incarceration, release, and supervision had changed profoundly in little over a decade, making comparisons between the recidivism rates of the two release cohorts nearly impossible.

To understand the impact of these changes in the phenomenon of prisoner reentry, we look at the *flow* of prisoners rather than the *stock* of the prison population. This perspective necessarily presents a different profile of the population. In a flow analysis, prisoners serving short sentences will be represented in greater portions than those who serve longer sentences, whereas in a stock analysis, the longer-term prisoners will figure more prominently. A flow perspective will highlight the phenomenon Lynch and Sabol (2001) aptly call *churning*, namely the large number of prisoners who cycle in and out of prison serving short sentences, getting released, then returning a few months later on another charge or for a parole violation only to be released again in a matter of months. Viewing the prison population through the reentry lens allows researchers and policymakers to focus on the distinctive attributes of the churners who now constitute a large share of those in prison, on supervision, and entering the front doors of the nation's correctional institutions.

In addition to the BJS data on recidivism rates, these chapters draw on two other BJS data series. The Survey of Inmates in State and Federal

Correctional Facilities, based on a nationally representative sample of inmates about every 5 years, provides self-reported data on information about the current and past offenses of inmates, their sentences, prior use of drugs and alcohol, medical and mental health conditions, family background, use of firearms, and characteristics of the victims of their crimes (Bonczar 2003). But, because our interest is in reentry, not simply describing the state of the prison population, the authors configure the data to reflect the movement of prisoners, not a portrait of the prison population. Second, the Annual Probation and Parole Data Surveys collect counts of the total number of persons supervised in the community on January 1 and December 31 and a count of the number entering and leaving supervision during the collection year (Glaze 2003).

These BJS data provide the best systematic information available on characteristics of persons released from state prisons, their supervision conditions, and their success or failure after release. Unfortunately, these data have limitations. First, as discussed, official measures of repeat offending are an imperfect indicator of postrelease criminal activity. Arrest rates are known to be higher among some subgroups who are subject to greater police attention, including young minority men, persons who have previous arrests, and those who reside in high-crime neighborhoods (Sampson and Lauritsen 1997). Second, data describing the population of persons released each year from state prisons are limited to persons incarcerated in 38 states with a sentence length of 1 year or more. Additionally, although the individual-level data include demographics, educational attainment, and incarceration histories, including current offenses and total time served, it does not capture their medical histories, receipt of heath or educational services during incarceration, or the circumstances of their return to the community (e.g., housing or employment) (Hughes, Wilson, and Beck 2001). Additional information about the characteristics of ex-prisoners would seem to be critical for policy purposes, such as informing local law enforcement about recently released prisoners or estimating local demand for mental health and substance abuse treatment for this population. The characteristics of a reentry cohort must be estimated from existing sources, as Joan Petersilia does in her analysis for this book when she uses the BJS Inmate Survey and examines only those prisoners who are to be released within 12 months. Third, for reasons discussed, tremendous variation exists among the states in the population of state prisoners, those released, and those on supervision. Local communities focusing on prisoner reentry issues need current information from their state correctional agencies; national statistics do not always provide the level of detail needed for state and local policy decisions. Finally, official data sources, by definition, cannot present the perspective of the individual who has been released from prison and is reentering society. Some of the chapters in this book, however, include such data from interviews with prisoners and ex-prisoners. More data of this type may be necessary to fully understand the nexus between prisoner reentry and public safety.

National and State Perspectives

It is tempting to make sweeping statements about how sentencing policy and corrections practice affects reentry experiences and crime rates across the nation. But these questions are best addressed at a state, not national, level. The overwhelming reality of the past generation of sentencing reform has been the development of quite different policies by the 50 states (Tonry 1999). Some have abandoned indeterminate sentencing; others still adhere to that model. Some have increased postrelease supervision; others have decreased it. Some corrections departments have continued to provide high levels of program services to their inmates; others have cut back. Of particular interest to the questions addressed in this book is the philosophy of community supervision. Some states have limited the use of revocations for parole violations; others send more people back to prison for parole violations than for new crimes (Travis and Lawrence 2002).

Thus, although criminal behavior may not differ much from state to state, the policies that determine society's response to that behavior differs markedly. For this reason, we hope to call attention to some of the state-level variation in those policies so that the analysis reflected in these chapters can be valuable to state policymakers as they consider new directions for their sentencing and corrections agencies.

Themes of the Chapters

The central focus of the book is how to understand, empirically and conceptually, different facets of the relationship among crime rates, the four-fold increase in the rates of incarceration, and the consequent increases in the cohorts of returning prisoners. The eight chapters that follow examine this problem at multiple levels – state, community, agency, and individual. Together, these chapters provide important insights into how the phenomenon of prisoner reentry affects public safety.

In Chapter 2, Allen J. Beck and Alfred Blumstein present an empirical portrait of incarceration, reentry, and recommitment to prison in the United States over the past 20 years. They conclude that most of the growth in the U.S. prison population is a consequence of how states choose to respond to crime rather than any growth in crime. Furthermore, despite recent decreases in crime, prison populations remain at historically high levels in part because of state policies regarding drug enforcement and recommitments of persons who violate conditions of parole supervision. In Chapter 3, Joan Petersilia describes the characteristics of persons released from prison (relying on a survey of prisoners who report that they will be released within a year). Not surprisingly, she finds that returning prisoners have a wide range of social, psychological, and physical problems, most of which are not addressed in prison. Lack of a high school education (41 percent) and history of illegal drug use (73 percent) are particularly formidable problems that are likely to influence postrelease outcomes. In Chapter 4, Richard Rosenfeld, Joel Wallman, and Robert Fornango estimate the contribution of ex-prisoners to state crime rates. In a provocative analysis with important implications for public safety, the authors show that former prisoners contribute significantly to overall crime rates, and this contribution varies by state, type of postrelease supervision, and crime type. In Chapter 5, Anne Morrison Piehl and Stefan LoBuglio attempt to answer the question, "Does supervision matter?" The authors find existing research on this question to be inconclusive but propose that states critically examine their supervision policies and practices to ensure that the dual goals of supervision and support for returning prisoners are being met. In Chapter 6, Shadd Maruna and Hans Toch review what is known about the effects of incarceration on criminal careers, including whether the prison experience increases or decreases postrelease criminal activity. They conclude with some suggestions for correctional policy and practice that may improve the likelihood that exiting prisoners will desist from crime. In Chapter 7, Todd Clear, Elin Waring, and Kristen Scully explore the effects of prisoner reentry on community life. In particular, they discuss the phenomenon of concentrated *reentry cycling* – a pattern of incarceration, reentry, and reincarceration – which is occurring in many urban neighborhoods and is highly disruptive to these communities. In Chapter 8, Christopher Uggen, Sara Wakefield, and Bruce Western examine the consequences of incarceration and reentry for labor market participation and family formation. They show how these life circumstances of former prisoners can powerfully affect public safety. Finally, in Chapter 9,

Introduction

Jeremy Travis and Christy Visher discuss the implications of the chapters in this volume for improving those policies and practices focused on prisoner reentry and the implications of such attention for enhancing public safety.

Conclusion

It is quite clear that the landscape of punishment in America has changed considerably over the past generation. The use of prisons has increased dramatically, with the result that more Americans than ever before have been arrested, incarcerated, and released from prison. In this volume, the chapter authors, representing a variety of disciplines and perspectives, examine the relationship between the prison buildup, the associated increase in the numbers of individuals leaving prison, and the safety of the broader society to which they return. The question addressed in the pages that follow is not whether the expansion of imprisonment has reduced crime in America, although that question is clearly implicated in this exploration of the impact of incarceration on American life. Rather, this book explores the intersection between the new realities of prisoner reentry, the safety risks posed by the hundreds of thousands of prisoners who now leave prison each year, and the challenges they face – and society faces – in improving the odds that they will not again violate the law. It is our hope that the chapters in this book will illuminate the new landscape of punishment in America so that, in the future, policymakers, practitioners, researchers, community leaders, students, and the general public will have a better understanding of the nexus between prisoner reentry and public safety.

References

Altschuler, D., and R. Brash. 2004. "Adolescent and Teenage Offenders Confronting the Challenge and Opportunities of Reentry." *Youth Violence and Juvenile Justice* 2: 72–87.

Beck, A., and B. Shipley. 1989. *Recidivism of Prisoners Released in 1983*. Washington, DC: U.S. Department of Justice, Bureau of Justice Statistics.

Bonczar, T. 2003. *Prevalence of Imprisonment in the U.S. Population, 1974–2001*. Washington, DC: U.S. Department of Justice, Bureau of Justice Statistics.

Clear, T., D. Rose, E. Waring, and K. Scully. 2003. "Coercive Mobility and Crime: A Preliminary Examination of Concentrated Incarceration and Social Disorganization." *Justice Quarterly* 20: 33–64.

Glaze, L. 2003. *Probation and Parole in the United States, 2002*. Washington, DC: U.S. Department of Justice, Bureau of Justice Statistics.

Hammett, T., C. Roberts, and S. Kennedy. 2001. "Health Related Issues in Prisoner Reentry." *Crime and Delinquency* 47(3): 390–409.

Harrison, P. 2000. *Total Sentenced Prisoners Released from State or Federal Jurisdictions.* Washington, DC: U.S. Department of Justice, Bureau of Justice Statistics, National Prisoner Statistics data series (NPS-1).

Harrison, P., and J. Karberg. 2003. *Prison and Jail Inmates at Midyear, 2002.* Washington, DC: U.S. Department of Justice, Bureau of Justice Statistics.

Hughes, T., D. Wilson, and A. Beck. 2001. *Trends in State Parole, 1990–2000.* Washington, DC: U.S. Department of Justice, Bureau of Justice Statistics.

Langan, P., and D. Levin. 2002. *Recidivism of Prisoners Released in 1994.* Washington, DC: U.S. Department of Justice, Bureau of Justice Statistics.

Lynch, J., and W. Sabol. 2001. *"Prisoner Reentry in Perspective." Crime Policy Report,* vol. 3. Washington, DC: The Urban Institute. September.

Mears, D., and J. Travis. 2004. *The Dimensions, Pathways, and Consequences of Youth Reentry.* Washington, DC: The Urban Institute.

Rice, C., and P. Harrison. 2000. *Conditional Release Violators Returned to Federal or State Jurisdiction, 1977–1998.* Washington, DC: U.S. Department of Justice, Bureau of Justice Statistics, National Prisoners Statistics Data Series (NCP-1). http://www.ojp.usdoj.gov/bjs/dtdata.htm. (Accessed April 8, 2004.)

Sampson, R., and J. Lauritsen. 1997. "Racial and Ethnic Disparities in Crime and Criminal Justice in the United States," Michael Tonry, ed., *Ethnicity, Crime, and Immigration: Comparative and Cross-National Perspectives.* Chicago, IL: The University of Chicago Press.

Sickmund, M. 2002. *Juvenile Offenders in Residential Placement: 1997–1999.* Washington, DC: U.S. Department of Justice, Office of Juvenile Justice and Delinquency Prevention.

Smith, S. 1999. "What Future for 'Public Safety' and 'Restorative Justice' in Community Corrections?" *Sentencing and Corrections: Issues for the 21st Century,* no. 11. Washington, DC: U.S. Department of Justice, National Institute of Justice. September.

Tonry, M. 1999. "Reconsidering Indeterminate and Structured Sentencing." *Sentencing and Corrections: Issues for the 21st Century,* no. 2. Washington, DC: U.S. Department of Justice, National Institute of Justice. September.

Travis, J., and S. Lawrence. 2002. *Beyond the Prison Gates: The State of Parole in America.* Washington, DC: Urban Institute.

2

From Cell to Society

WHO IS RETURNING HOME?

Joan Petersilia

It is estimated that about 630,000 people were released from U.S. prisons in 2002, a number equal to the population of Washington, DC, and greater than that of Wyoming (Harrison and Karberg, 2004). Who exactly are the people coming home? What continuing danger do they pose to their families and communities? How have their prison experiences prepared them for reentry? Understanding offenders' crimes and life circumstances is a necessary precursor to designing successful reintegration programs.

But the seemingly simple question, "Who is coming home?" has no easy answer. In fact, respected analysts have given widely differing answers to it. There are those who argue that returning prisoners are mostly first-time and nonviolent offenders. Austin and Irwin (2001) write: "Our research indicates that most people being sent to prison today are very different than the specter of Willie Horton that fuels the public's fear of crime. More than half of the persons sent to prison committed crimes that lacked any of the features the public believes compose a serious crime." Elsewhere Austin (2001) writes: "A significant number of prison releases will pose little risk to public safety."

Other analysts reach markedly different conclusions. They argue that the vast majority of those in prison and coming home *are* dangerous career criminals. DiIulio and his colleagues write: *"Virtually all convicted criminals who do go to prison are violent offenders, repeat offenders, or violent repeat offenders* (italics in original). It is simply a deadly myth that our prison cells are filled with people who don't belong there. The widespread circulation of that myth is the result of ideology masquerading as analysis" (Bennett, DeIulio, and Walters 1996).

The debate over the seriousness of the prison population is not simply an academic one. If the public perceives returning prisoners as having

15

many needs and posing little risk, they are more likely to be sympathetic to their circumstances and invest in rehabilitation and work programs. But if the public believes most returning inmates are dangerous career criminals, reentry resources will likely be invested in law enforcement and surveillance. In one scenario, we prioritize services to the offender; in the other, we prioritize public safety. So, accurately answering the question, "Who is coming home?" has important policy significance.

Of course, inmates have always been released from prison, and in many ways, their profiles have not changed much. The prison and parole populations are mostly male, although the number of incarcerated females has risen steadily over the past decade. Most prisoners are racial or ethnic minorities. Most have serious work and education deficits, and a disproportionate number have drug- and alcohol-abuse problems. Most prisoners come from single-parent families, and many produce the same experience for their own children.

But other inmate characteristics are changing in ways that pose new challenges. The number of prison releasees who have been convicted of drug trafficking has increased significantly. The drug wars also imprisoned more females and more drug addicts. At the same time, mandatory minimum and truth-in-sentencing laws have increased sentence length, so that prisoners currently being released have served an average of 27 months in prison – 5 months longer than those released in 1990 (Beck 2000). Moreover, about 25 percent of state, and 33 percent of federal, prisoners will have served more than 5 years. This longer time in prison translates into a longer period of detachment from family and other social networks, posing new challenges to reintegration.

But returning inmates are more than simply composites of their demographic and crime profiles, the so-called "hard data." An equally important aspect of understanding who is coming home pertains to their *in-prison* experiences. Clearly, some inmates will use their prison time productively, participating in education, industries, counseling, and other personal development programs. But equally clear, others are made worse or more violent by their prison experiences. Some inmates will have been assaulted or raped. Others will have spent weeks, if not months, in solitary confinement or supermax prisons, devoid of most human contact. Others will hone their criminal skills and develop new networks of criminal contacts, confirming their criminality and convict identity.

This chapter will summarize what is known about the characteristics and experiences of inmates coming home. It is based on the recent book by the author entitled, *When Prisoners Come Home: Parole and Prisoner Reentry* (Petersilia 2003).

Demographic and Crime Profiles of Adults Leaving Prison

Most of what we know about U.S. prisoners and parolees comes from the Bureau of Justice Statistics' (BJS), *Survey of Inmates in State Adult Correctional Facilities*, conducted every 5 years. The *Inmate Survey* interviews a nationally representative sample of inmates about their background and families, criminal histories, drug and alcohol use, infectious diseases, sentence, time served, and participation in prison programs. The *Inmate Survey* relies on the honesty of inmates, because none of their self-reports are validated with official record data. For a detailed description of the sample design and survey methods see Mumola (1999).

The *Inmate Survey* also asks inmates the following question: "In what month and year will you be released?" Using their answer to this question, a "prison release" cohort can be identified. It is important to distinguish the "in-prison" population from the "prison release" population. On average people committed to prison for violent crimes serve longer prison terms than those committed for nonviolent or drug crimes. Violent offenders eventually get out, but not as quickly, and so their proportion in prison release cohorts is less. Nonviolent and drug offenders receive shorter sentences and so they recycle back into the community faster than violent offenders. Hence, their proportion in prison release cohorts is higher. For this reason, analysts studying prisoner reentry examine prison release or parole cohorts when the information is available, as in-prison data overrepresent the seriousness of the inmate population.[1] For this chapter, a "soon-to-be-released" cohort was selected, defined as all state and federal prisoners who reported that they would be released within the next 12 months.[2] According to the 1997 *Survey*, 40.1 percent of state inmates,

---

[1] In fact, it is the difference between in-prison and prison-release cohorts that accounts for some of the discrepancy in the figures cited by those who argue that prisoners are not a particularly serious group (they tend to use incoming or release cohorts), and those who argue that the majority of prisoners are serious career criminals (they tend to use in-prison samples). Another problem is the blending or combining of all types of prior criminal record. Those who argue that inmates are mostly violent offenders and "recidivists" merge the two categories as if they were equally threatening. "Recidivists" might have been only convicted of minor crimes. See Tonry (1995, pp. 24–27) for a full discussion.

[2] The author is indebted to Paula Ditton, former doctoral student at University of California, Irvine, for conducting this analysis.

Table 2.1. *Demographics of Soon-To-Be-Released Inmates (Within 12 Months)*

	Percentage of Inmates	
	State ($n = 375,095$)	Federal ($n = 21,535$)
Gender		
Male	91.4	90.1
Female	8.6	9.9
Race/Hispanic origin		
White non-Hispanic	33.3	36.4
Black non-Hispanic	46.5	26.5
Hispanic	17.1	30.7
Other	3.2	6.4
Mean age	33 yrs.	37 yrs.

and 26.1 percent of federal inmates are expected to be released in the next year, for a total of 396,630 prison releases.

Age, Gender, and Race

Age The average age of exiting prisoners was 33 years for state prisoners and 37 years for federal prisoners (Table 2.1). The age of soon-to-be-released inmates is slightly older than the median age of the in-prison population, which was 32 years for state prisoners and 36 years for federal prisoners. But the average age misses a critical point: there are a greater number of older prisoners now being released. Hughes, Wilson, and Beck (2001) report that in 1999, an estimated 109,300 state prisoners age 40 or older were paroled – 26 percent of all entries to parole. There were about 44,000 parolees aged 55 or older. This number has more than doubled over the past decade, and the majority of these older state prisoners (61 percent) are incarcerated for violent offenses.

The American Correctional Association estimates that the cost of incarcerating older offenders (those over age 55) is $69,000 per year, or 3 times the $22,000 average it costs to keep younger, healthier offenders in prison. Age is also negatively correlated with recidivism: The older an offender is at release, other factors held constant, the lower the rate of recidivism (Gendreau, Little, and Goggin 1996).

Gender Prisoners and parolees are mostly male and always have been. However, women constitute the most rapidly growing, and least violent, segment of the U.S. prison population. Females are 8 to 10 percent of soon-to-be-released inmates. Two thirds of women parolees are minorities, and nearly half were convicted of drug offenses (42 percent in 1999, up from 36 percent in 1990). Almost all female prisoners are classified as low-risk on prison classification instruments (Greene and Schiraldi 2002).

In many ways, the war on drugs has hit females harder than males. Mandatory drug laws were passed in 1986, and during the next decade, the number of women incarcerated for drug crimes rose by 888 percent (Mauer, Potler, and Wolf 1999). Mandatory sentencing laws required judges to sentence men and women who committed the same offense to the same punishment. Extenuating circumstances often could not be fully considered. The federal sentencing guidelines, for example, do not permit judges to consider the role of women in caring for children, the subordinate roles women play in many crimes, or the fact that women are much less likely than men to commit new crimes after being released (Raeder 1993). Three years after full implementation of the federal sentencing guidelines, the absolute number of women in federal institutions nearly doubled (Bureau of Justice Statistics 1993).

Female offenders have different needs than male offenders, as 57 percent of women in state prison report prior physical or sexual abuse, and they have higher rates of drug addiction and infectious disease than their male counterparts (Harlow 1999). Nearly half of all female prisoners ran away from home as youths, and a quarter of them had attempted suicide prior to being incarcerated. Most had never earned more than $6.50 an hour (Donziger 1996). Despite these unique needs, there are fewer prison and parole programs to assist them and their children.

Race Race is a critical dimension of the reentry discussion. About a third of soon-to-be-released state prisoners are white, 47 percent are black, and 17 percent are Hispanic, who may be of any race – hence, about two thirds of all returning prisoners are racial or ethnic minorities. This is approximately 3 times the percentage of minorities in the general population of the United States.

In terms of inmates *in* prison (as distinguished from prison *releases*), Hispanics represent a fast-growing minority group. Hispanics comprise 9.4 percent of the U.S. population, but are 16 percent of the current prison population. In 1985, they were 11 percent of the prison population. These increases reflect a rate twice as high as the increase for black and white inmates (Walker, Spohn, and DeLone 2002). With little information about the number of Asian and Native American prisoners, it appears their representation is not substantially greater than their representation in the general population.

Minority families and their communities are feeling the consequences of imprisonment and release in unprecedented ways. Bonczar and Beck (1997) calculated that in 1991, a black male had a 29 percent chance of being incarcerated at least once in his lifetime, 6 times higher than the chance for white males. Beck and Harrison (2001) estimated that nearly 10 percent of black males, and 3 percent of Hispanic males in their late twenties and early thirties, were in prison at year-end 2000. At the start of the 1990s, there were more young black men (between the ages of 20 and 29) under the control of the nation's criminal justice system (including jail, probation, and parole) than there were in college (Haney and Zimbardo 1998; Mauer 1990).

There are a number of reasons for the overrepresentation of racial minorities in prison, including overt discrimination, policies that have differential racial effects, and racial differences in committing the kinds of crimes that lead to imprisonment. However measured, rates of criminal offending among black Americans for many crime categories are much higher than comparable rates of offending among whites (Blumstein 2001). Especially for the crimes of homicide and armed robbery, black rates of offending have been 8 and 10 times the white rate (Zimring and Hawkins 1998). Blumstein (1993) found that, except for drug crimes and some property crimes, differential black imprisonment rates are explained almost entirely by differential rates of offending.

It is with respect to drug crimes that the United States stands alone in its punitive response and where the minority disproportionality is most evident. Tonry (1995) argues that the war on drugs had a remarkably disproportionate effect on black American males. The rate of prison drug admissions for black persons has escalated sharply over the past 15 years. Although white drug admissions increased more than 7-fold between 1983 and 1998, Hispanic drug admissions increased 18-fold, and black drug admissions increased more than 26-fold.

The differential impact of the War on Drugs is due more to drug-law enforcement and sentencing rather than higher patterns of minority drug use. Critics argue that, whereas the police are *reactive* in responding to robbery, burglary, and other index offenses, they are *proactive* in dealing with drug offenses. Walker and his colleagues conclude: "There is evidence to suggest that police target minority communities – where drug dealing is more visible and where it is thus easier to make arrests – and tend to give less attention to drug activities in other neighborhoods" (Walker et al. 2002, p. 16).

It is also true that although the conviction rate for powdered cocaine is higher for whites and lower for minorities, minorities are much more likely to be convicted for crack-related offenses, which, in the federal system, carry penalties that are 100 times greater than those involving equivalent amounts of powdered cocaine. Many minority inmates, especially in the federal prison system, are serving long mandatory prison terms because they handled crystalline cocaine instead of powder cocaine.

This is not the place to debate the racial disparities issue or the effectiveness of the war on drugs. Suffice to say that for prisoner reentry discussions, race is the "elephant sitting in the living room." It affects every aspect of reentry – including communities, labor markets, family welfare, government entitlements, and program innovations that need to be culturally appropriate. It eventually cuts into our notions of democracy, voting rights, and civic participation. Moreover, involvement with the criminal justice system has been shown to lead to distrust and disrespect for government systems. Greater alienation and disillusionment with the justice system also erodes residents' feelings of commitment and makes them less willing to participate in local activities. This is important, because our most effective crime-fighting tools require community collaboration and active engagement.

Conviction Crime

The inmate characteristic that has changed most dramatically over the past two decades is the crime for which the offender was convicted. From 1980 to 1997, the number of violent offenders committed to state prison nearly doubled (up 82 percent) and the number of nonviolent offenders tripled (up 207 percent), whereas the number of drug offenders increased 11-fold (up 1040 percent) (Greene and Schiraldi 2002). Nonviolent offenders accounted for 77 percent of the growth in intake to America's state and federal prisons between 1978 and 1996 (Blumstein and Beck 1999).

Like the general prison population, the current offense of inmates leaving prison is quite different for state and federal prisons (see Table 2.2). Over

Table 2.2. *Current Offense of Soon-To-Be-Released Prison Inmates*

Offense	Percentage of Inmates	
	State	Federal
Violent	31.0	11.7
Murder	2.9	0.3
Manslaughter	1.0	0.0
Kidnapping	0.7	0.4
Rape	1.3	0.2
Other sexual	4.2	0.5
Robbery	11.4	8.2
Assault	8.7	1.4
Other	0.8	0.6
Property	27.2	13.7
Burglary	11.3	0.5
Larceny	6.2	1.1
Motor vehicle theft	2.6	0.2
Arson	0.6	0.3
Fraud	3.7	10.2
Stolen property	2.1	1.0
Other	0.7	0.3
Drug	27.5	55.3
Drug possession	13.1	11.5
Drug trafficking	13.5	40.0
Other	0.8	3.7
Public-order	14.0	18.5
Weapons	3.4	5.4
Other	10.6	13.1

half (55 percent) of those released from federal prisons are drug offenders, whereas this is the case with just 27.5 percent of state prisoners. Among state inmates, 31 percent of soon-to-be-released inmates were incarcerated for a violent offense (5.5 percent for sexual offenses), whereas this is true for just 11.7 percent of federal inmates (0.7 percent for a sex offense).

Prior Criminal Record and Status at Arrest

Of course, it is not just a prisoner's current conviction that causes us concern, we also care about an inmate's prior criminal record. Repeated criminal convictions not only reflect disdain for the law, but having a prior criminal record is also one of the best predictors of parolee recidivism: the worse the

Table 2.3. *Criminal History of Soon-to-Be-Released Inmates*

	Percentage of Inmates	
	State	Federal
No previous sentence	21.7	43.9
Current violent offense	10.0	4.2
Current drug offense	5.6	24.4
Violent recidivists	38.6	17.7
Current and prior violent	11.4	5.0
Current violent only	12.4	3.2
Prior violent only	14.7	9.6
Nonviolent recidivists	39.8	38.4
Number of prior sentences to probation or incarceration		
0	21.9	44.3
1	16.6	16.1
2	15.9	13.7
3 to 5	25.6	15.0
6 to 10	13.5	8.0
11 or more	6.6	2.8
Criminal justice status at time of arrest		
None	44.7	70.8
Probation	26.7	13.2
Parole	27.9	15.5
Escape	0.7	0.5

offense and the longer the prior record, the greater the recidivism. So, as we consider the public safety risks of releasing inmates to the community, it is useful to consider both their current crime and prior criminal history.

Table 2.3 shows that about 22 percent of those being released from state prison, and 44 percent of those being released from federal prison, have *not* served a prior juvenile, jail, probation, or prison sentence. This is their first criminal sentence and will be their first prison release experience. Conversely, 46 percent of exiting state prisoners, and 26 percent of exiting federal prisoners, will have served three or more prior probation *or* incarceration (jail or prison) terms. Those serving their first prison term may have been subject to mandatory sentencing laws, and those with lengthy criminal histories may have been subject to career criminal and three-strikes laws. Between 1980 and 2001, this combination sent prison populations skyrocketing, increasing from 319,598 to 1,330,019 – a rise of over 400 percent (Bureau of Justice Statistics 2002).

Table 2.3 shows the status of prisoners when they were arrested for the crime that led to their current conviction. This table reveals that over half (55 percent) of those being released from state prison were on conditional status (probation, parole, or escape) when they were arrested for their most recent crime. This was true for just 29 percent of federal inmates.

Education, Marriage, Substance Abuse, and Other Life Circumstances

The *Inmate Survey* also asks prisoners about a variety of life circumstances. Canadian researchers have shown that many of these circumstances are related to recidivism and can be used to identify criminogenic needs (Gendreau et al. 1996). The Correctional Service of Canada has devised a Case Needs Identification and Analysis (CNIA) instrument that records criminogenic needs, grouped into seven domains, with each domain consisting of multiple individual indicators (Dowden, Blanchette, and Serin 1999). Table 2.4 contains the *Inmate Survey* responses, according to the need areas identified in the CNIA. Much of the data needed for the full CNIA index were not available in the *Inmate Survey*; for example, no data were available on attitudes and therefore this domain was eliminated. Nevertheless, the CNIA provides a listing of items that generally predict a new conviction.

Nearly all soon-to-be-released inmates (those who expect to be released within the next 12 months) report a problem in one area of need, and the majority had problems in multiple domains. About 84 percent of state inmates and 65 percent of federal inmates reported problems in three or more of the need domains. Less than 1 percent of state inmates and 3 percent of federal inmates reported no problems in any of the need areas.

Educational and Employment

Although poor academic performance is not a direct cause of criminal behavior, research consistently shows an inverse relationship between recidivism and education – the higher the education level, the less likely the person is to be rearrested or reimprisoned (Gottfredson, Wilson, and Najaka 2002). Table 2.4 reveals that 41 percent of exiting state prisoners, and 26 percent of federal prisoners, do not have a high school diploma or general equivalency degree (GED). In comparison, 18 percent of the general U.S. population aged 18 or older had not finished the 12th grade (Harlow, 2003). About 17 percent of exiting state prisoners had an 8th

Table 2.4. *Life Circumstances of Soon-To-Be-Released Inmates*

	Percentage of Inmates	
	State	Federal
I. Education/employment		
8th grade education or less	17.3	15.5
No high school diploma or GED	40.7	25.6
Learning disability	9.5	5.0
Speech disability	3.1	1.5
Physical disability	10.9	12.3
Unemployed during month before arrest	33.4	26.4
Unemployed 50% or more	12.2	10.1
Never employed	4.8	2.8
II. Marital/family		
Parents incarcerated	18.4	8.8
Children, sibling, or spouse incarcerated	39.9	29.8
Parents abused drugs while growing up	32.4	21.9
Divorced or separated	23.9	27.1
III. Associates/social interaction		
Affiliated with drug organization during year prior to arrest	7.5	14.5
Drug-involved friends	30.5	22.9
Boyfriend/girlfriend incarcerated	4.2	4.3
Childhood friends engaged in delinquent activity	75.9	53.7
Received income from illegal sources in month prior to arrest	27.5	24.7
IV. Substance abuse		
Alcohol		
History		
Started drinking at young age	13.8	7.0
History of drinking on a regular basis	62.1	55.3
History of binge drinking	41.9	31.4
Drinking interfered with employment or school	16.4	9.3
Drinking interfered with marital/family relationships	41.6	29.9
Arrested due to drinking	31.9	22.4
Drinking resulted in detox placement	12.9	4.9
Felt they should cut down on drinking	41.9	31.7
Needed a drink first thing in the morning	23.0	14.8
Had a car accident after drinking	15.3	12.0
Current		
Used alcohol daily during year before arrest	27.8	19.8
Under influence of alcohol at time of current offense	35.4	21.0

(continued)

Table 2.4 (*continued*)

| | Percentage of Inmates | |
	State	Federal
Drugs		
History		
Started using drugs at young age	14.3	6.3
Used drugs on a regular basis	72.6	55.3
Lost a job due to drug use	18.1	9.2
Drug use interfered with marital/family relations	44.6	32.6
Drug use resulted in law violations	34.2	20.8
Had a car accident under the influence of drugs	8.3	5.3
Current or Recent History		
Under influence of drugs at time of current offense	33.9	20.6
Committed current offense to get money for drugs	21.2	15.4
Used drugs in month before offense	59.3	43.1
V. Community functioning		
Unstable housing at time of arrest	4.8	2.2
Homeless in 12 months prior to arrest	10.1	4.9
Health problems	30.3	32.3
VI. Personal/emotional orientation		
History of violence/aggression	48.4	21.9
History of physical abuse	14.1	7.3
History of sexual abuse	7.2	4.3
Mental or emotional condition	8.6	4.9
Overnight admission for a mental condition	9.1	4.8

grade education or less. Harlow (2003) reports that the number of inmates entering state prisons without a high school diploma increased 44 percent between 1991 and 1997.

Employment remains one of the most important vehicles for hastening offender reintegration and desistance from crime, and there is fairly strong evidence to indicate that an individual's criminal behavior is responsive to changes in his or her employment status (i.e., unemployment is associated with higher crime commission rates and more arrests) (Bushway and Reuter 2002). In the *Inmate Survey*, inmates were asked to report whether they were employed in the month prior to their arrest. As expected, soon-to-be-released prisoners in both federal and state facilities have poor employment histories. Thirty-three percent of state prisoners reported that they were unemployed in the month before their arrest, whereas this was true for 26 percent of federal prisoners (Table 2.4). During the year of this survey, just 7 percent of Americans over the age of 18 reported being unemployed. The *Inmate Survey* also revealed that about 5 percent of state prisoners, and 3 percent of federal prisoners, about to be released from prison have *never* been employed.

Empirical evidence demonstrates that prisoners will have an extremely hard time finding employment after release. There is a serious stigma attached to a criminal history – particularly a prison record – in the legal labor market, and ex-offenders are often shut out from legitimate jobs. Surveys of employers reveal a great reluctance to hire felony offenders (Holzer 1996). Kling found that even if ex-prisoners are able to find a job, there is substantial impact on future earnings (about 30 percent lower), and firms willing to hire ex-offenders tend to offer them lower wages and fewer benefits (Kling 2000).

Employment prospects for ex-prisoners are further complicated by the fact that many of them have already developed behavior patterns that make holding a job quite difficult. Criminologists have documented that over time, ex-offenders become "embedded" in criminality and they gradually weaken their bonds to conventional society (e.g., attachment to parents and commitment to jobs and school). After years of engaging in a criminal lifestyle, reestablishing these bonds becomes very difficult.

Marriage, Family, and Delinquent Associates

Legal employment and marriage are the two most prominent ties to conventional society for adults. A solid marriage can give a prisoner emotional support upon release, an immediate place to live, motivation to succeed, and possibly financial assistance until they get their feet on the ground. Conversely, marriage can also produce family dynamics that contribute to family violence, substance abuse, and economic pressure. Strained marriages often end during imprisonment. Table 2.4 shows that 24 to 27 percent of exiting prisoners are separated or divorced. The data do not reveal whether the divorce occurred prior to or during imprisonment. Interestingly, the table also shows that fully 40 percent of state, and nearly 30 percent of federal, prisoners have a child, sibling, or spouse also incarcerated. About 4 percent report that their current boyfriend or girlfriend is also incarcerated.

Reviews of prisoners' family relationships yield two consistent findings: male prisoners who maintain strong family ties during imprisonment have higher rates of postrelease success, and men who assume husband and parenting roles upon release have higher rates of success than those who do not (Shapiro 2001). Presumably female family relationships are similarly important, but there exist no data on that.

In a recent study of people's experiences during the first 30 days after release from jail or prison, the Vera Institute of Justice found that families provided critical support early on. A majority of the offenders lived with family and ate with them, and some received financial support as well. Family members helped locate work and encouraged abstinence from drugs and compliance with treatment. The Vera study also found that people with strong family support had lower levels of recidivism. Offenders whose families accepted and supported them also had a higher level of confidence and were more successful and optimistic for their future (Nelson and Allen 1999).

Some states (e.g., New York) have begun to realize the critical role that families can play in rehabilitation and are trying to include families as natural supports in rehabilitation and parole programs. For a review, see Shapiro (2001). Unfortunately, at the same time, we are also seeing policies that serve to sever ties between family members and inmates (e.g., greater restrictions on visitation). As Hairston recently concluded: "The correctional policies and practices that govern contact between prisoners and their families often impede, rather than support, the maintenance of family ties" (Hairston 2002, p. 49).

Part of the move to make prisons "tougher" has included reducing the visits of children and family members. Of course, this is also done for security reasons, as family visits are one of the main ways that drugs and contraband enter the prisons. But in terms of reentry, limiting family visits has significant implications for cutting the very contacts the inmate needs to succeed on the outside. As one parolee told the author, "If you come out of prison without a real support system of family and friends, nine out of ten times, you won't make it." Given what we know about the positive impacts of family members on recidivism, we should be encouraging rather than discouraging family visitation.

Drug and Alcohol Use and Abuse

There are different ways to define drug and alcohol use, abuse, and involvement. There are no studies to systematically measure the prevalence of alcoholism, drug abuse, and drug addiction disorders in correctional facilities, as defined by the American Psychological Association's *Diagnostic Statistical Manual of Mental Disorders*. Nevertheless, there can be no doubt that substance abuse disproportionately affects prisoners, that sustained treatment is rare, and that continued use contributes to recidivism.

Inmates were asked to self-report their involvement with various substances, and these reports were used to compile the information in Table 2.4. Nearly two thirds of state inmates (59 percent) reported using drugs in the month before they committed their current crime, more than a third (34 percent) said they were under the influence of drugs at the time they committed their crime, and over a fifth (21 percent) reported committing crime to get money for drugs. Fewer state prison inmates reported using alcohol daily during the year before their arrest (28 percent), but 36 percent said they were under the influence of alcohol at the time of the commission of their crime.

Alcohol is linked more closely with violent crimes than are drugs. The National Center on Addiction and Substance Abuse reports that over 20 percent of inmates in state and federal prisons for violent crimes reported they were under the influence of alcohol – and no other substance – when they committed their crimes. In contrast, at the time of their crimes, only 3 percent of violent offenders were under the influence of cocaine or crack alone, and only 1 percent were under the influence of heroin alone. Continued criminality is also highly related to substance use and abuse. Over 40 percent of first-time offenders have a history of drug use. The proportion increases to over 80 percent among offenders with five or more prior convictions (National Center on Addiction and Substance Abuse 1998).

Physical Impairment, Mental Conditions, and Prison Assaults

By any indicator, prison inmates are less healthy – both physically and mentally – than the population at large. Some felons are born with conditions that increase their probability of becoming involved with crime (e.g., attention deficit disorder). For others, their risky lifestyles, poor access to health care, and substance-abuse histories take a heavy toll on their physical and mental health. As shown in Table 2.4, fully a third of soon-to-be-released prisoners report having health problems.

The *Inmate Survey* asked, "Do you have . . . a learning disability, such as dyslexia or attention deficit disorder?" Similar questions were asked for other health-related conditions, including mental illness. The accuracy of the estimates in Table 2.4 therefore depends on the ability of inmates to recognize and report such problems. Yet, for most of these conditions, inmate self-reports are the only source of information, because most prison systems lack comprehensive and accessible data on the health status of their inmates. BJS's recent publication, *Medical Problems of Inmates*, reports that nearly a third of all state inmates and a quarter of federal inmates report having some physical impairment or mental condition. Ten percent of state inmates and 5 percent of federal inmates reported a learning disability, such as dyslexia or attention deficit disorder (Maruschak and Beck 2001). These figures are identical for those about to be released (see Table 2.4).

Maruschak and Beck compared the rates of some physical impairments in the prison population with that in the general population and found the prevalence of speech disabilities among state inmates (3.7 percent) is more than 3 times higher than that in the general U.S. population (1.0 percent). The percentage with impaired vision among inmates (8.3 percent) is more than twice as high as that in the U.S. population (3.1 percent). The percentage with impaired hearing is lower among inmates (5.7 percent) than in the U.S. population (8.3 percent) (Maruschak and Beck 2001). Yet because some of these differences result from differing age and gender distributions (e.g., a higher percentage of inmates are middle age and male), Maruschak and Beck further compared these conditions with U.S. population figures, standardizing for differences in age and gender. Even with these controls, they found that prisoners had higher rates of speech and vision impairments and slightly lower rates of hearing impairments.

The BJS *Survey* also asked inmates if any of these conditions limited their ability to work and then compared the prisoner estimates with similar estimates from the National Adult Literacy Survey (NALS). Twenty-one percent of state and federal inmates reported having some condition that limited their ability to work (compared to 12 percent of the general U.S. population). This is an important consideration for reentry practices, because getting a job is one of the common requirements of parole release.

Researchers have long noted that inmates with disabilities have a harder time adjusting to prison, and their disability makes them easy prey for other inmates. The BJS *Survey* also asked inmates whether they had been injured in a fight since their admission to prison. Based on these self-reports, BJS concluded that 7 percent of state inmates reported being injured in a fight while in prison. The risk of being in a fight while in prison increases with time served: inmates serving 5 years or more have a 16 percent chance of being injured in a fight while in prison (Maruschak and Beck 2001). Wiebe and Petersilia (2000) also found that inmates who reported having various physical and mental conditions were more likely to be injured while incarcerated. After controlling for a number of factors previously found to be related to the risk of prison injury and victimization (e.g., age, race, criminal history, past physical and sexual abuse, institutional factors, and work assignment), they found that inmates reporting a mental disability were 1.4 times more likely to be injured while in custody. With regard to sexual assault, inmates reporting physical or mental disabilities were 3 times more likely to be sexually assaulted while incarcerated. Both of these results were statistically significant.

Mental Illness

Persons with mental illness are increasingly criminalized and processed through the corrections system instead of the mental health system. In 1955, the number of mental health patients in state hospitals had reached a high of 559,000. New antipsychotic drugs were developed in the 1950s, and by prescribing them to people with mental illness, many could remain in the community rather than being placed in mental hospitals. This community-based alternative seemed more humane and less expensive than committing people to state hospitals. This fundamental change in mental health policy, known as desinstutionalization, shifted the focus of care of persons with mental illness from psychiatric hospitals to local communities. As a result, states closed many of their mental hospitals, and by 2000, fewer than 70,000 persons remained in such facilities (Lurigio 2001).

Unfortunately, persons with mental illnesses living in the community sometimes stop taking their medication. Without the medication, the symptoms of mental illness return. If these people begin committing crimes, they come to the attention of law enforcement. Because there are now fewer mental health hospitals, and we have more stringent criteria for involuntary commitment, many of these people wind up in prison. Prison is not the place for a seriously mentally ill criminal. By and large, most everyone agrees with this proposition in principal but not in practice. In recent years, a growing number of seriously mentally ill have been sent to prison. Ultimately, most of them are also released back into the community.

Few studies have directly measured the number of persons with mental illness in prison, and estimates vary widely on the proportion of inmates having various mental illnesses. Part of the problem in estimating prevalence rates results from differences in defining serious mental illness and in using assessment tools for research purpose. The *Inmate Survey* asked inmates to self-report whether they ever felt they had a a mental or emotional problem or ever had experienced an overnight stay in a mental hospital or

Table 2.5 *Prevalence of Mental Illness in State Prisons versus U.S. Population*

	Percentage of Inmates	
Disease	Lifetime Prevalence, State Prisoners	Lifetime Prevalence, U.S. Population
Schizophrenia/Other Psychotic Disorders	2.3–3.9%	.8%
Major Depression	13–19	18
Anxiety Disorders	22–30	Not Available
Bipolar (Manic) Disorder	2–4	1.5
Post-Traumatic Stress Disorder	6–12	7
Dysthymia (Less Severe Depression)	8–13	7

Source: National Commission on Correctional Health Care, 2002.

mental health facility. Ditton (1999) reported that more than 16 percent of all state prison inmates report a mental condition or overnight stay in a mental health facility. This is greater than the number who report mental conditions in the soon-to-be-released cohort: about 9 percent of state, and 5 percent of federal, prisoners report mental or emotional problems (Table 2.4).

Because of the methodological issues involved in using inmate self-reports to establish the prevalence of mental health conditions, the National Commission on Correctional Health Care commissioned an article from Veysey and Bichler-Robertson (2002) to establish the prevalence of psychiatric disorders in correctional settings. This article concludes that the prevalence of certain mental health disorders in inmate populations is remarkably greater than that of the overall U.S. population. Their results are contained in Table 2.5, contained in the report *The Health Status of Soon-To-Be-Released Inmates*.

Despite the high prevalence of mental disorders in persons released from prisons, 75 percent of the parole administrators responding to a 1995 national survey reported that they do not have special programs for mentally ill clients (Boone 1995). Administrators also note that mental disorders in parolee populations are likely to be ignored unless offenders' psychiatric symptoms are an explicit part of their offense, are specified in their release plans, or are obvious at the time of discharge.

There are also relatively few public mental health services available, and studies show that even when they are available, mentally ill parolees fail to access available treatment because they fear institutionalization, deny that they are mentally ill, or distrust the mental health system (Schoeni and Koegel 1998). A recent review of the topic concludes that, overall, persons with mental illness on parole are an underidentified and underserved population, and most parole officers are unable to handle the problems of these new offenders successfully (Lurigio 2001).

One point deserves mentioning: people with mental illness have no higher incidence of violent and nonviolent serious crime than those in the general population with the same age and socioeconomic circumstances. But people who are *both* mentally ill and are also abusing drugs or alcohol (the "dually diagnosed") *do* have a higher incidence of committing violent and serious crimes (Monahan 1996). Treating them at release is a particularly high priority.

Interestingly, a period of incarceration sometimes has positive consequences for the health status of a prisoner – in part because adequate health care is constitutionally required and also because the food and living environment are more conducive to better health outcomes than many situations in the community. Yet the consequences for a prisoner's mental health may be adverse. Haney, an expert on the psychological effects of imprisonment, notes that prisons do not, in general, make people "crazy." However, psychologists agree that for some people, prison can produce negative, long-lasting change. Prisoners who are mentally ill have a tougher time adjusting to prison life, and their symptoms may become more bizarre and threatening. Ultimately, they are often placed in segregation or, increasingly, supermax conditions. Haney says for persons who are mentally ill or developmentally disabled, "the rule-bound nature of institutional life may have especially disastrous consequences. Yet, both groups are too often left to their own devices to somehow survive in prison and leave without having had any of their unique needs addressed" (Haney 2002, p. 21).

Prisoners with mental illness often refuse to take their medication (or are not prescribed the right dose or medication) and then enter a vicious cycle in which their mental disease takes over, often causing hostile and aggressive behavior to the point that they break prison rules and end up in segregation units as management problems (Streeter 1998). The result, increasingly, is placement in punitive isolation, or so-called supermax facilities, where they are kept under conditions of unprecedented levels of social deprivation for exceptional lengths of time. Kurki and Morris (2002) estimate that in the United States 1.2 percent of all prisoners (about 17,000) are now held in supermax-type units, and the number is increasing. Haney (2002) concludes that such confinement creates its own set of psychological pressures that, in some instances, uniquely disable prisoners for free-world reintegration. Many of these prisoners are released directly from long-term isolation into free-world communities.

As the proportion of prisoners with mental illness grows, in combination with the increasing use of maximum-security facilities, more prisoners with mental illness will surely find themselves in supermax conditions – and eventually be released to the community. The human and public safety consequences are severe, and serious thought should be given to mobilizing community resources to better support people with mental illness who return to the community from prison.

Parenting and Contacts with Children

One of the most dramatic effects of the increase in the number of prisoners, particularly women, is the impact of incarceration on their children. There were about 72 million minor-age children living in the United States in 1999, and it has been determined that 2.1 percent of them had at least one parent in state or federal prison at year-end 1999 (Mumola 2000). This means that on any one day an estimated 1.5 million minor-age children have a parent in prison, a 50 percent increase since 1990.

As expected, there are more minority parents in prison than white non-Hispanic parents. In terms of minor-age children living in the United States, on any given day nearly 7 percent of African American children, 3 percent of Hispanic children, and 1 percent of white children had an incarcerated parent (Mumola 2000). Importantly, this is an estimate of the number of children with parents incarcerated on any *one* day. If one considered the lifetime probability of children having a parent in prison, the figure is much higher. Over 10 million children in the United States have parents who were imprisoned at some point in their children's lives (Hirsch, Dietrich, Landau, Schneider, and Ackelsberg 2002). In some ways, children are the unseen victims of the prison boom and the war on drugs.

The Bureau of Justice Statistics reports that in 1997, 65 percent of women in state prison and 59 percent of women in federal prison had minor-age children. The majority were single mothers, with an average of two children, and prior to their arrests were the custodial parents (Mumola 2000). According to these parents, the children they left behind were young – nearly 60 percent were under 10 years old. Most commonly, grandparents become the caregivers (53 percent of the time for state prisoners). Approximately 10 percent of children of mothers in state prisons, and

4 percent of the children of mothers in federal prisons, are in foster care.

Certainly, sometimes children are better off separated from a parent who commits a crime, especially if the parent had been abusive or involved with illegal substances. We know that children who grow up with parents who are criminally involved have a high probability of engaging in delinquent behavior. In their meta-analysis of 34 prospective longitudinal studies of the development of antisocial behavior, Lipsey and Derzon (1998) found that having an antisocial parent or parents was one of the strongest predictors of violent or serious delinquency in adolescence and young adulthood. So, certainly, removing the negative influence of a parent can result in both positive and negative outcomes for the children, but we have virtually no data on this.

Most imprisoned mothers plan to reunite with their children at release and cite separation from their children as one of the most difficult aspects of imprisonment (Hairston 2002). A parent's imprisonment is also a traumatizing event for most children. Studies have indicated that children may suffer from separation anxiety and depression, are preoccupied with their loss, and experience a pervading sense of sadness. Boys are more likely to exhibit externalizing behavior problems, whereas girls are more likely to display internalizing problems (Parke and Clarke-Stewart 2001).

AIDS, HIV, and Other Infections Diseases

Prisoners have significantly higher rates of infectious diseases than those of the general population, because of lifestyles that often include crowded or itinerant living conditions, prior IV drug use, poverty, and high rates of substance abuse. Some 2 to 3 percent of prisoners are HIV positive or have AIDS; a rate 5 times higher than that of the general population. However, there is considerable variation in prisoners' rates of HIV infection across states: 50 percent of all known prison cases are concentrated in New York, Florida, and Texas (Maruschak and Beck 2001). Eighteen percent of all U.S. prisoners are infected with hepatitis C, 9 to 10 times the rate of the general population. The Centers for Disease Control (1997) found the rate of prison inmates with tuberculosis to be 6 times that of the general population.

Rates of communicable diseases grow faster among prisoners because they live in close living quarters, and there have been recent outbreaks that cause public health officials to worry (e.g., tuberculosis in three Alabama state prisons in 1999 and in South Carolina in 2000). Public health experts

Table 2.6 *Percentage of Total Burden of Infectious Disease among People Passing through Jails and Prisons*

Condition	Est. Number of Jail and Prison Releases with Condition, 1997	Total Number in U.S. Population with Condition	Releases with Condition as Percentage of Total Population with Condition
AIDS	39,000	247,000	16%
HIV Infection	112,000–158,000	503,000	22–31
Total HIV/AIDS	151,000–197,000	750,000	20–26
Hepatitis B Infection	155,000	1–1.25 million	12–16
Hepatitis C Infection	1.3–1.4 million	4.5 million	29–32
Tuberculosis Disease	12,000	32,000	38

Source: Hammett 2000.

predict that these rates will continue to escalate within prisons and eventually make their way to the streets, particularly as we incarcerate more drug offenders, many of whom engage in intravenous drug use, share needles, and/or trade sex for drugs.

According to analysis conducted for Congress by the National Commission on Correctional Health Care, between 20 and 26 percent of the nation's individuals living with HIV or AIDS, 29 to 32 percent of the people with hepatitis C, and 38 percent of those with tuberculosis disease were released from a correctional facility in 1997 (Table 2.6). In a given year most inmates with infectious diseases pass through jails, rather than prisons.

HIV/AIDS is rising rapidly among women, and women in state prison are now more likely than men to be infected with HIV (3.4 percent of female inmates compared to 2.1 percent of male inmates). HIV infection rates among females are predominately related to injecting drugs, crack use, and prostitution for drugs. Female crack smokers tend to have more sex partners, are more likely than other female drug users to exchange sex for drugs, and have a higher prevalence of HIV infection in comparison to other female drug users. Officials report, however, that HIV rates in prison have leveled off, and AIDS-related prison deaths have declined (Hammett, Harmon, and Maruschak 1999)

As noted under the section on mental illness, incarcerated inmates may have greater access to medical care than those with similar sociodemographic characteristics not serving time in a correctional facility. Prison inmates have access to free health care as result of the 1976 U.S. Supreme

Court case, *Estelle v. Gamble* (1975). *Estelle* concluded that inmates have a constitutional right to reasonable, adequate health services for serious medical needs.

On average, prisoners draw heavily on available health care services while incarcerated. One reason for this is that prisoners are generally in worse health than nonincarcerated persons. The cost of providing health care services in the prisons has been increasing rapidly in recent years. A survey by the National Commission on Correctional Health Care found that state departments of correction budgeted $2.3 billion in 1995 to support inmate health care services, or approximately $2,308 per inmate. This is an increase of 160 percent in the per-prisoner expenditure over that in 1982 (estimated at $883 per prisoner). A recent survey found that this per-inmate cost is increasing and is now closer to $3,300 per inmate (American Correctional Association 2000). Medical budgets comprised, on average, 10 percent of corrections agencies' total operating budget in 1999 (Camp and Camp 2000). But in states where inmates have higher health care needs, the costs are much greater. For example, California spends 16 percent of its entire corrections budget on health care.

Prisoners are the only U.S. citizens with a constitutional right to health care. But upon release, most are unable to access programs to maintain many health benefits accrued during imprisonment or to access some of the medications they previously were prescribed. Many return to unhealthy lifestyles and have the potential for spreading disease (particularly tuberculosis, hepatitis, and HIV). Public health experts have begun to work more closely with corrections officials to collaborate on health-related reentry programs. Whether this capacity exists and whether criminal justice supervision could increase the likelihood of healthy outcomes are open questions.

What Happens in Prison?

Of course, answering the question, "Who is coming home?" cannot rely solely on a description of preexisting inmate characteristics. Inmates will have spent, on average, about 2½ years incarcerated. That time period might be beneficial to some inmates, those who choose to participate in programs or use the time for personal reflection and growth. But for others, the pains of imprisonment will take a horrendous personal and psychological toll. These inmates will return to society more socially isolated, embittered, and committed to a criminal lifestyle.

Prison Programs: Need for Treatment versus Prison Program Participation

Nearly all prisons operate treatment and work programs. The latest *Census of State and Federal Correctional Facilities* shows that 97 percent of all confinement facilities have inmate-counseling programs, 90 percent have drug and alcohol counseling, 80 percent have secondary education programs, and 54 percent have vocational training programs (Stephan 1997). Some of these programs are excellent. But the prison population has expanded so rapidly that prison administrators cannot meet the expanding demand. Lynch and Sabol (2001) compared prison program participation rates during the past decade and found that in 1997, approximately a third of the inmates about to be released participated in vocational (27 percent) or educational (35 percent) programs – down from 31 percent and 43 percent, respectively, in 1991. Of the entire prison population, an estimated 24 percent are altogether idle – never participating in any prison program during their entire prison stay (Austin and Irwin 2001).

Virtually all existing data on prison program participation come from the *Inmate Survey*. Prison administrators usually cannot tell researchers the number of prisoners who need different types of programs or the extent to which they are participating in programs of various types. Even when we know the counts of inmate participants, we seldom have the details about the nature (e.g., intensity and duration) of the programs. Moreover, most prison education, substance abuse, and work programs are never evaluated. It is quite telling that such little data exist about prison programs: we measure what matters most to us.

The *Inmate Survey* asked each prison inmate the question, "Since your admission, have you ever been in __ (program type specified)?" Table 2.7 contains the results for soon-to-be-released prisoners. Prison program participation rates are distressingly low for all programs and for both state and federal prisoners. About 10 percent of state or federal inmates report participating in alcohol treatment, and about 12 percent report participating in drug treatment (e.g., in-patient, unit-based program, individual or group counseling). Approximately one in four inmates report participating in a drug or alcohol program (e.g., peer group or self-help group since admission to prison). Among both state and federal prisoners, the highest participation rate was in educational programs. It is important to note also that, among those expected to be released in the next 12 months, 36 percent of federal inmates versus 12 percent of state inmates had participated in a prerelease program.

Table 2.7. *Treatment and Program Participation Since Admission to Prison for Soon-To-Be-Released Inmates*

	Percentage of Inmates	
	State (n = 375,096)	Federal (n = 21,535)
Treatment		
Alcohol	10.4	9.5
Drugs	12.5	12.1
Mental health	14.3	9.8
Programs		
Alcohol	22.4	19.6
Drugs	23.3	22.5
Educational	34.5	42.5
Vocational	27.7	25.9
Religious study groups	28.5	26.4
Other religious programs	31.1	29.9
Prisoner assistance groups	6.9	6.9
Other Personal improvement groups	11.6	12.5
Life-skills classes	17.9	17.2
Pre-release	11.9	35.8

Of course, not all prisoners need all types of programs. So, a better question to ask is: "What percentage of those who have been identified as in need for treatment will receive it while in prison?" Table 2.8 presents these results. Using the inmate responses shown in Table 2.4, the author created a very simple "need for treatment" index for four programs: alcohol, drug, mental health, and education. Inmates who answered yes to five or more of the alcohol questions and inmates who answered yes to three or more of the drug, mental health, or education/vocational questions were judged as having a "high need" for treatment in that program area. The author then cross-tabulated the need index (high, medium, none) with whether they had participated in the relevant type of treatment program during their current incarceration. Four areas were analyzed by need indices: drug treatment, alcohol treatment, mental health treatment, and educational or vocational programs. These results are shown for soon-to-be-released prisoners in Table 2.8.

As expected, in all program types, inmates with the most severe problems reported considerably higher rates of treatment and program participation

Table 2.8. *Treatment and Program Participation by Need of Soon-To-Be-Released Inmates*

	Percentage of Inmates with Need Participating in Relevant Program	
	State (*n* = 215,545)	Federal (*n* = 21,533)
Alcohol index		
History of problem		
None (0)	11.2	8.2
Moderate (1 to 2)	15.1	18.3
High (5 or more)	**36.5**	**38.3**
Drug index		
History of problem		
None (0)	7.0	8.3
Moderate (1 to 2)	21.9	28.6
High (3 or more)	**39.6**	**48.8**
Mental health need index		
None (0)	4.4	4.3
Moderate (1 to 2)	15.5	18.0
High (3 or more)	**63.1**	**74.6**
Education/employment need index		
None (0)	45.3	50.3
Moderate (1 to 2)	47.7	55.0
High (3 or more)	**52.4**	**54.1**

than those with more moderate problems. Table 2.8 shows that just 36 to 38 percent of soon-to-be-released state or federal prisoners with a "high" need for alcohol treatment will have participated in a treatment or alcohol-related program during the current prison term. It is important to recall that program participation in this analysis includes *all* types of programs, including Alcoholics Anonymous, individual and group counseling, and/or drug education or awareness programs.

For those reporting a severe drug problem, relevant treatment or program participation was slightly higher. For state inmates, about 40 percent of those with a high need for drug treatment participated in relevant programs. For federal inmates, the percentage is higher at 49 percent. In analysis not shown here, the author also examined whether program participation rates increased if the sample included only those prisoners released within 6 months (rather than 12) of the interview. In no program did the results increase more than a few percentage points. Thus, it is safe to say that more than half of those who admit to having a severe alcohol or drug problem prior to prison fail to participate in a relevant treatment program while incarcerated.

The highest rate of treatment among a population with a severe need was in the mental health domain. Among inmates released in 12 months, 63 percent of state inmates and 74 percent of federal inmates with a severe mental health need reported they had received some form of mental health treatment since admission to prison.

Finally, we found that about half of those with high educational and vocational needs participated in relevant programs. But in the education/ vocational area, unlike the other program areas, those with a high need were not participating in programs much more than those who reported none or moderate needs. About 45 to 55 percent of all released inmates had participated in a vocational or education program. These programs seem to be utilized more freely by those who did not report a strong need.

The data suggest that U.S. prisons today offer fewer services than they did when inmate problems were less severe, although history shows that we have never invested much in prison rehabilitation. It is not that inmates do not want to participate in these programs. On the contrary, virtually all prison programs today have long waiting lists. Prison programming not only helps prepare inmates for the outside, but also provides an important element of keeping prisons safe, the subject to which we now turn.

The Culture of Confinement

There are two popular and competing images of American prisons. One suggests that prisons are country clubs, where inmates lounge around in collegelike settings. The other says that prisons are always violent hellholes and that no one is made better by participating in prison programs. Both images are equally wrong. Each image fits some prisons, but not the vast majority of them. Many American prisons do a pretty decent job of protecting inmates from each other and providing them with basic amenities (decent food, clean quarters), and do so in a way that ensures prisoners' constitutional and legal rights. Of course, many others do not. In fact, research has shown that quality of life behind bars varies dramatically by state and even within a state, and is primarily a function of how a prison is organized, led, and managed (DiIulio 1987).

Inmate narratives attest to the wide variation among prison environments. Ex-convict Charles Terry compares his California and Oregon prison experiences as follows:

The Oregon State Penitentiary (OSP) was different from any California prison I had ever seen. When I first stepped onto the yard I thought they might have sent me to the wrong place. To my surprise, I found myself in an institution where violence was almost nonexistent. Compared to California prisons, the Oregon State Penitentiary was a relatively safe place to be. (2003, p. 103)

Terry also recalls how it was possible for him to pursue a college education while in prison. For two years, he attended classes as a full-time student. "During this period my self-concept and ideas about life began taking a radical shift. Ultimately, I began to question my own way of thinking. My perception of others became noticeably different. Just as my initial use of heroin propelled me into an alien social world, the new ideas and thoughts I was exposed to in school were, in effect, altering my reality and preparing me for a future I never imagined." At parole, Terry recalls, "my parole plans were vague. Unlike times in the past, I did not feel anxious about getting out. Somehow, I sensed that I would never have to spend more time behind bars. Yet, how this would be possible was unclear. One day a thought crossed my mind: I know I am institutionalized. School is an institution. I like school. Maybe I will get out of prison and go to college. I will just switch institutions" (Terry 2003, p. 104).

Terry did pursue a college degree – eventually earning a Ph.D. at UC-Irvine in Criminology, where the author had the pleasure of working with him. Granted, Charles Terry is an exception. But one third of exiting prisoners never return to prison, and prison programs often encourage crime desistance.

But for many inmates, prison is a painful, traumatic, and possibly criminogenic experience. Prisons often serve as schools for criminal learning. Another ex-convict, Manny, describes this process as follows:

The convict learns new techniques of criminal behavior. This learning process comes about naturally in the prison environment. As in groups anywhere, talk commonly turns to shop. Each type of con describes those techniques with which he is best acquainted. The forger talks forgery; the burglar refines his methodology for breaking and entering unobtrusively. So, a whole lot of inmates who would like to make it on the outside society are systemically confronted with refined methodologies for doing just the opposite. (Rettig 1999, p. 106)

Sexual assault and rape are also serious problems in prison. Although there are no reliable national data on prison rape, Human Rights Watch (2001) cites research estimating that roughly 20 percent of all prisoners were coerced into inmate-on-inmate sex while incarcerated. The Bureau of Justice Statistics recently reviewed the existing studies on prison rape and concluded that the studies being used to estimate the prevalence of prison rape are methodologically flawed and overestimate the incidence. They note that although prison rapes are certainly higher than what most correctional systems officially report, they are likely to be substantially lower than the 20 percent rate referred to in the Human Rights Watch report, and may be between 3 and 6.5 percent, depending on the assumption of the level of victimization among nonresponding inmates (Beck 2003).

Victims of prison rape tend to be young, physically small, first-timers, and/or gay, have feminine characteristics, and have been convicted of sexual offenses against a minor. Not only are such attacks traumatic, but they also make the victim a target for further exploitation. Most prison assaults go unreported to authorities, and if reported, few prisons provide medical or psychological care for the victim. Certainly, the very real pains of imprisonment – psychological and well as physical – affect the prospects of successfully transitioning to the free community.

As a matter of survival, all inmates adhere more or less to the "convict code." There is a large literature detailing the convict code and subculture, which has it own set of rewards and behaviors. There is a consensus among convicts that the contemporary prison is more violent than in years past and that changes in prison life have come about as a result of the use of drugs, prison crowding, and demographic changes in prisoners. Young drug dealers and users, most from inner-city ghettos, have swelled prisons and increased prison fear and violence. Loic Wacquant (2001, p. 97) writes, "The 'convict code', rooted in solidarity among inmates and antagonism towards guards, has in effect been swamped by the 'code of the street.' Accordingly, 'the old hero' of the prison world – the 'right guy' – has been replaced by outlaws and gang members. These two types have raised toughness and mercilessness to the top of the prisoners' value systems. Ethnically based street gangs and supergangs ... have taken over the illicit economy of the prison and destabilized the entire social system of inmates, forcing the latter to shift from 'doing your own time' to 'doing gang time.'"

Victor Hassine, an inmate serving life without parole in Pennsylvania, describes the impact these newer inmates had on prison life in Graterford Prison:

Soon, the mentally ill were commanding too much of the staff's attention. Drug addicts, many of them going through withdrawal, were doing anything they could to get high. Juveniles were being raped and causing havoc trying to attract some attention. Because of all this, instead of changing people, Graterford itself was changing. The new prison subcultures with their disrespect for authority, drug addiction, illiteracy, and welfare mentality had altered the institution's very character. Much of the violence that invaded Graterford in the 1980s was actually imported from the streets by the social misfits who were now being called convicts. They were criminals before – the only change in their identity is that now they're incarcerated. For many of these newcomers, prison violence was simply life as usual. (Hassine 1996, p. 31)

Hassine writes that prison survival now depends on the ability of the new prisoners to learn to adapt to the violent lifestyle of the hard-core convict. John Irwin (1980), a widely regarded expert on the culture of prisons, agrees that prisons have changed. He writes that today's convict code differs from the old code in three ways: it emphasizes toughness, primacy of loyalty to one's ethnic or racial group, and willingness to go to extremes, including murder, to prove oneself.

Several prisoner narratives have documented how inmates have to transform themselves to do time in today's prisons. Silberman (1995) describes how some convicts, with bandanas around their heads and covered with tattoos such as "born to lose," project a tough biker image to those around them. Still others are feared by other inmates because of their reputation as ruthless killers on the street or in prison. Over time, accounts reveal, the private self may be transformed by the public expressed self-identity. In other words, eventually we become what we do. We are taken in by our own performance as we come to believe in the role we are playing. This orientation, although presumed necessary within the prison, ultimately backfires in postrelease adjustment.

In his best-selling book, *In the Belly of the Beast*, Jack Abbott, who killed another prisoner when he was 21 years old, explains "you are not killing in physical self defense . . . but in order to live respectably in prison." He wrote, "you must either kill or turn the tables on anyone who propositions you with threats of force" (Abbott 1991, p. 79). Abbott was imprisoned at the federal penitentiary in Marion, Illinois, when Norman Mailer, the well-known author, wrote a strong letter to the parole board on Abbott's behalf, not only saying he was fit for release but that Mailer could guarantee him gainful employment. Just six weeks after being released, and while living in a halfway house, Abbott stabbed a waiter to death. In February 2002, Jack Abbott hanged himself with a bedsheet in Wende Correctional Facility.

JoAnne Page, a prison teacher, recounts a story told to her by an ex-convict after his release. One man who had served almost 20 years described to her what it was like for him to step into a subway and be shoved by another rider. He began swinging to attack in an automatic move that he learned behind bars, only to stop short upon seeing that the person who had shoved him was a little old lady with shopping bags. Had the person been male and anywhere near his age, violence would have resulted, and he would have viewed his actions as self-defensive, based on the conduct code he had learned behind bars. Another man, also released after many years, described to her how he was walking down the street and heard running footsteps behind him. Swinging around to attack or defend, he saw a jogger coming at him and put his fists down in embarrassment. She concludes, "Incarceration breeds and fosters 'global rage,' an impulsive and explosive anger so great that a minor incident can trigger an uncontrolled response" (Page 2000, p. 140).

Conclusions

The chapter reveals a consistent portrait of prisoners coming home. Many, if not most, are people who did not have much to begin with, and have been born with, or have developed, serious social, psychological, and physical problems. Most of those problems will go unaddressed in prison, because prison program capacity is limited, the programs offered are of insufficient quality to make a difference, or the inmate chooses not to participate. For many, the years spent in prison will be lived in an atmosphere of fear, violence, and racial tension. Increasingly, inmates sit idle in their cells or talking to other inmates in the yard, often honing their criminal skills and developing further allegiances to the convict code and identity.

Eventually, 93 percent of all of these prisoners return home. Some, welcomed by families and aided by agencies, will make a successful transition. More often than not, however, they will be released to poor inner-city communities with few services and little public sympathy for their plight. Their prison record will have created new barriers to work, housing, and social relationships. Now more embittered, alienated, and prone to violence than before, many ex-convicts return to crime. The result is that the convict code, increasingly characterized by a willingness to use violence to prove oneself, gets transferred over and over again to the street.

New crimes by ex-convicts further fuel public fear, encouraging legislatures to pass even tougher sentencing policies. In turn, more criminals are sent to prison and budgets are stretched, resulting in fewer programs and even worse conditions for inmates, again creating a ripe environment for increased violence at release. It becomes a self-fulfilling prophecy, and the multiplier effect – returning more than five million prisoners to communities over the next decade – is certain to exact a staggering, but as yet unmeasured, future toll.

References

Abbott, Jack Henry. 1991. *In the Belly of the Beast: Letters from Prison*. New York: Vintage Books.

American Correctional Association. 2000. *Vital Statistics in Corrections*. Lanham, MD: American Correctional Association.

Austin, James. 2001. "Prisoner Reentry: Current Trends, Practices, and Issues." *Crime & Delinquency* 47: 314–334.

Austin, James, and John Irwin. 2001. *It's About Time: America's Imprisonment Binge*. Belmont, CA: Wadsworth.

Beck, Allen. Personal correspondence with author, June 18, 2003. Washington, DC: Bureau of Justice Statistics.

Beck, Allen J., and Paige M. Harrison. 2001. *Prisoners in 2000*. Washington, DC: Bureau of Justice Statistics.

Beck, Allen J. 2000. "Prisoners in 1999." *Bureau of Justice Statistics Bulletin*. Washington, DC: U.S. Department of Justice.

Bennett, William J., John J. DiIulio, Jr., and John P. Walters. 1996. *Body Count*. New York: Simon & Schuster.

Blumstein, Alfred. 1993. "Racial Disproportionality of U.S. Prison Populations Revisited." *University of Colorado Law Review* Vol. 64:743–760.

Blumstein, Alfred. 2001. "Race and Criminal Justice," Neil Smelser, William Julius Wilson, and Faith Mitchell, eds., *American Becoming: Racial Trends and Their Consequences*, pp. 21–31. Washington, DC: National Academy Press.

Blumstein, Alfred, and Allen J. Beck. 1999. "Population Growth in U.S. Prisons: 1980–1996," M. Tonry and J. Petersilia, eds., *Prisons: A Review of Research*, pp. 17–62. Chicago: University of Chicago Press.

Bonczar, Thomas P., and Allen J. Beck. 1997. *Lifetime Likelihood of Going to State or Federal Prison*. Washington, DC: Bureau of Justice Statistics.

Boone, H. B. 1995. "Mental Illness in Probation and Parole Populations: Results From a National Survey." *Perspectives* 19: 14–26.

Bureau of Justice Statistics. 1993. *Prisoners in 1992*. Washington, DC: U.S. Government Printing Office.

Bureau of Justice Statistics. 2002. *Prison and Jail Inmates at Midyear 2001.* Washington, DC: U.S. Department of Justice.

Bushway, Shawn, and Peter Reuter. 2002. "Labor Markets and Crime," J. Q. Wilson and J. Petersilia, eds., *Crime: Public Policies for Crime Control*, pp. 191–224. San Francisco, CA: ICS Press.

Camp, Camille, and George Camp. 2000. *The Corrections Yearbook 2000.* Middletown, CT: Criminal Justice Institute, Inc.

Centers for Disease Control. 1997. *Reported Tuberculosis in the United States, 1996*, p. 19. Atlanta, GA: Centers for Disease Control.

DiIulio, John. 1987. *Governing Prisons: A Comparative Study of Correctional Management.* New York: Macmillan.

Ditton, Paula. 1999. *Mental Health and Treatment of Inmates and Probationers.* Washington, DC: Bureau of Justice Statistics.

Donziger, Steven R. 1996. *The Real War on Crime.* New York: HarperCollins.

Dowden, C., Kelley Blanchette, and Ralph C. Serin. 1999. "Anger Management Programming for Federal Male Inmates: An Effective Intervention." *Research Reports: Correctional Service of Canada.* http://www.csc-scc.gc.ca/text/rsrch/reports/r82/er82.pdf, accessed June 18, 2003.

Gendreau, Paul, Tracy Little, and Claire Goggin. 1996. "A Meta-Analysis of Adult Offender Recidivism: What Works?" *Criminology* 34: 575–607.

Gottfredson, Denise, David B. Wilson, and Stacy Najaka. 2002. "The Schools," J. Q. Wilson and J. Petersilia, eds., *Crime: Public Policies for Crime Control*, pp. 149–190. San Francisco, CA: ICS Press.

Greene, Judith, and Vincent Schiraldi. 2002. *Cutting Correctly: New Prison Policies for Times in Fiscal Crisis.* Washington DC: Bureau of Justice Statistics.

Hairston, Creasie F. 2002. "Prisoners and Families: Parenting Issues During Incarceration." *From Prison to Home.* Washington, DC: U.S. Department of Health and Human Services.

Hammett, Theodore M., Patricia Harmon, and Laura M. Maruschak. 1999. *1996–1997 Update: HIV/AIDS, STDs, and TB in Correctional Facilities.* Washington DC: Bureau of Justice Statistics.

Haney, Craig. 2002. "The Psychological Impact of Incarceration: Implications for Post-Prison Adjustment." Prepared for the *From Prisons to Home Conference*, held on January 30–31, 2002 at the National Institutes of Health. Washington, DC: U.S. Department of Health and Human Services.

Haney, Craig and Philip Zimbardo. 1998. "The Past and Future of U.S. Prison Policy: Twenty-five Years After the Stanford Prison Experiment," *American Psychologist*, Vol. 53, No. 7 (July), p. 716.

Harrison, Paige and Jennifer C. Karberg. 2003. Prison and Jail Prisoners at Midyear 2002. Washington, DC: U.S. Department of Justice, Bureau of Justice Statistics.

Harlow, Caroline Wolf. 1999. *Prior Abuse Reported by Inmates and Probationers.* Washington, DC: Bureau of Justice Statistics.

Harlow, Caroline Wolf. 2003. *Education and Correctional Populations.* Washington, DC: Bureau of Justice Statistics.

Hassine, Victor. 1996. *Life without Parole: Living in Prison Today.* Los Angeles, CA: Roxbury.

Hirsch, Amy E., Sharon Dietrich, Rue Landau, Peter Schneider, and Irv Ackelsberg. 2002. *Every Door Closed: Barriers Facing Parents with Criminal Records*. Washington, DC: Center for Law and Social Policy.

Holzer, H. J. 1996. *What Employers Want: Job Prospects for Less-Educated Workers*. New York: Russell Sage Foundation.

Hughes, Timothy A., Doris J. Wilson, and Allen J. Beck. 2001. *Trends in State Parole, 1990–2000*. Washington, DC: U.S. Department of Justice, Bureau of Justice Statistics.

Human Rights Watch. 2001. "No Escape: Male Rape in U.S. Prisons." New York: Human Rights Watch. http://www.hrw.org/reports/2001/prison/report.html, accessed June 18, 2003.

Irwin, John. 1980. *Prisons in Turmoil*. Boston: Little, Brown.

Kling, Jeffrey. 2000. "The Effect of Prison Sentence Length on the Subsequent Employment and Earnings of Criminal Defendants." *Princeton University Discussion Paper in Economics*. Princeton, NJ.

Kurki, Leena, and Norval Morris. 2002. "The Purposes, Practices, and Problems of Supermax Prisons," M. Tonry and N. Morris, eds., *Crime and Justice*, pp. 385–450. Chicago, IL: University of Chicago Press.

Lipsey, M. W., and J. H. Derzon. 1998. "Predictors of Violent or Serious Delinquency in Adolescence and Early Adulthood: A Synthesis of Longitudinal Research," R. Loeber and David P. Farrington, eds., *Serious & Violent Juvenile Offenders: Risk Factors and Successful Interventions*, Pp. 86–105. Thousand Oaks, CA: Sage.

Lurigio, Arthur J. 2001. "Effective Services for Parolees with Mental Illnesses." *Crime & Delinquency* 47: 446–461.

Lynch, James P., and William J. Sabol. 2001. *Prisoner Reentry in Perspective*. Washington, DC: Urban Institute.

Maruschak, Laura, and Allen J. Beck. 2001. *Medical Problems of Inmates, 1997*. Washington, DC: Bureau of Justice Statistics.

Mauer, Marc. 1990. *More Young Black Males Under Correctional Control in U.S. Than in College*. Washington, DC: The Sentencing Project.

Mauer, Marc, Kathy Potler, and Richard Wolf. 1999. *Gender and Justice: Women, Drugs and Sentencing Policy*. Washington, DC: The Sentencing Project.

Monahan, John. 1996. *Mental Illness and Violent Crime*. Washington, DC: NIJ Research Review.

Mumola, C. 1999. *Substance Abuse and Treatment, State and Federal Prisoners, 1997*. Washington, DC: Bureau of Justice Statistics.

Mumola, C. 2000. *Incarcerated Parents and Their Children*. Washington, DC: Bureau of Justice Statistics.

National Commission on Correctional Heath Care. 2002. *The Health Status of Soon-to-Be-Released Inmates: A Report to Congress*, vol. 1. Washington, DC: National Institute of Justice, Office of Justice Programs, U.S. Department of Justice.

Nelson, Marta, Perry Deess, and Charlotte Allen. 1999. *The First Month Out: Post-Incarceration Experiences in New York City*. New York: Vera Institute of Justice.

Page, JoAnne. 2000. "Violence and Incarceration: A Personal Observation," John P. May, ed., *Building Violence: How America's Rush to Incarcerate Creates More Violence.* Thousand Oaks, CA: Sage.

Parke, Ross, and Alison Clarke-Stewart. 2001. "Effects of Parental Incarceration on Young Children." *From Prison to Home.* Washington, DC: U.S. Department of Health and Human Services.

Petersilia, Joan. 2003. *When Prisoners Come Home: Parole and Prisoner Reentry.* New York: Oxford University Press.

Raeder, Myrna. 1993. "Gender and Sentencing: Single Moms, Battered Women and Other Sex-Based Anomalies in the Gender-Free World of the Federal Sentencing Guidelines." *Pepperdine Law Review* 20: 905–990.

Rettig, Richard P. 1999. *Manny: A Criminal-Addict's Story.* Prospect Heights, IL: Waveland Press.

Schoeni, Robert F., and Paul Koegel. 1998. "Economic Resources of the Homeless: Evidence from Los Angeles." *Contemporary Economic Policy* XVI: 295–308.

Shapiro, Carol. 2001. "Coming Home: Building on Family Connections." *Corrections Management Quarterly* 5: 52–62.

Silberman, Matthew. 1995. *A World of Violence: Corrections in America.* Belmont, CA: Wadsworth.

Stephan, James J. 1997. *Census of State and Federal Correctional Facilities, 1995.* Washington, DC: Bureau of Justice Statistics.

Streeter, P. 1998. "Incarceration of the Mentally Ill: Treatment or Warehousing?" *Michigan Bar Journal* 77: 167.

Terry, Charles M. 2003. "From C-Block to Academia: You Can't Get There From Here," Jeffrey Ian Ross and Stephen C. Richards, eds., *Convict Criminology*, pp. 95–119. Belmont, CA: Wadsworth.

Tonry, Michael. 1995. *Malign Neglect: Race, Crime, and Punishment in America.* New York: Oxford University Press.

Veysey, Bonita M., and Gisela Bichler-Robertson. 2002. "Prevalence Estimates of Psychiatric Disorders in Correctional Settings." In Health Status of Soon-to-Be Released Inmates: Report to Congress. Chicago, IL: National Commission on Correctional Health Care.

Wacquant, Loic. 2001. "Deadly Symbiosis: When Ghetto and Prison Meet and Mesh," David Garland, eds., *Mass Imprisonment: Social Causes and Consequences*, pp. 121–137. Thousand Oaks, CA: Sage.

Walker, Samuel, Cassia Spohn, and Miriam DeLone. 2002. "Corrections: A Picture in Black and White," Tara Gray, ed., *Exploring Corrections*, pp. 13–24. Boston, MA: Allyn & Bacon.

Wiebe, Doug, and J. Petersilia. 2000. *The 1996 Survey of Jail Inmates: A Comparison of the Victimization of Persons With and Without Disabilities.* Irvine, CA: University of California, Irvine.

Zimring, Franklin. E., and Gordon Hawkins. 1998. *Crime Is Not the Problem: Lethal Violence in America.* New York: Oxford University Press.

3

Reentry as a Transient State between Liberty and Recommitment

Alfred Blumstein and Allen J. Beck

Introduction and Background

Between 1980 and 2001 the incarceration rate in state and federal prisons grew by nearly 240 percent. This growth far exceeded any growth in crime rates and diverged markedly from the trendless and stable pattern of incarceration that prevailed for the previous half-century.[1] Growth in incarceration is attributable first to the 10-fold increase since 1980 in incarceration rates for drug offenses. Beyond drugs, no contribution to that increase is associated with increases in crime rate or increases in police effectiveness as measured by arrests per crime. Rather, the entire growth is attributable to sentencing broadly defined – roughly equally to increases in commitments to prison per arrest (an increase in prosecutorial effectiveness and judicial sanctioning) and to increases in time served in prison, including time served for parole violation.[2] It is this last factor, the role of parole, involving both release from prison (reentry) and recommitment to prison, which provides the focus for this chapter. Indeed, reentry can be seen as an inherently transient state that individuals occupy for only a limited time, whereby a prisoner moves to either full liberty in the community or recommitment back to prison. Analysis of these flows and their impact on public safety are our major concern.

Prior to the mid-1970s, it was common for parole boards to have unchallenged authority to decide when an offender would be released from prison

---

[1] Blumstein, Alfred, and Jacqueline Cohen. 1973. "A Theory of the Stability of Punishment." *Journal of Criminal Law, Criminology, and Police Science* 63(2), 198–207.

[2] Blumstein, Alfred, and Allen J. Beck. 1999. "Population Growth in U.S. Prisons, 1980–1996," Michael Tonry and Joan Petersilia, eds., *Crime and Justice: Prisons*, vol. 26, pp. 17–61. Chicago: University of Chicago Press.

prior to the expiration of the offender's maximum sentence. In that era of *indeterminate sentencing*, the courts typically prescribed sentence length as a minimum and a maximum range (e.g., 2 to 5 years) and prisoners were not eligible for parole until they had served the minimum sentence.[3] Although parole boards could not hold prisoners beyond the maximum length of their sentences, they had considerable discretion to release prisoners prior to that maximum.

The possibility of parole facilitated a balanced flow into and out of state prisons for decades, thereby contributing to the stable incarceration rate. As crime rates began their upward climb beginning in the late 1960s, crime and sentencing policy became more politicized as legislatures, responding to public concerns, imposed their own pressure on sentencing policies. Judges were challenged for "excessive leniency" whenever an offender was given a probation sentence that affronted the public's sense of appropriateness – or, more commonly, that of the mass media. The result of this concern was the introduction of the mandatory-minimum sentence, which imposed the legislature's judgment as a constraint on all the judges in its jurisdiction. When an offender on parole committed a newsworthy crime, that incident often gave rise to public pressure on the entire parole system, blaming it for permitting the offender to endanger the public.[4] Repeated incidents of reoffending by parolees led to a movement to "eliminate parole," restricting the right of parole authorities to release prisoners prior to the expiration of their maximum sentences. In some states, the movement focused on establishing presumptive sentences established by the legislature; if that turned out to be unsatisfactory, then the legislature retained the authority to increase those presumptive sentences. Some states established sentencing commissions to develop a coherent schedule of sentence ranges based on seriousness of the current offense and the offender's prior conviction record.

All of these efforts at parole reform were targeted at the release decision and not at the decision to recommit an offender to prison for violating the conditions of parole. However, all the political pressure to limit the release decision also worked to harden the recommitment decisions.

---

[3] The minimum could also be reduced by adjustments such as granting credit for good behavior in prison, for participating in rehabilitative programs, and so on.

[4] The infamous murder committed by Willie Horton while he was on parole from the Massachusetts prison system raised enough of a public outcry that it was a significant factor in electing George H. W. Bush as president over Michael Dukakis, then the governor of Massachusetts.

Recommitment could be for commission of a new crime[5] or for a technical violation involving violation of one or more of the conditions of the parole release, such as avoiding certain places or contact with certain individuals, avoiding use of alcohol or illegal drugs, not possessing firearms, and, of course, not committing further crimes. These conditions of release were intended to insulate the parolee from the environments and situations that gave rise to his crime in the first place. Most of these conditions were general and applied to all offenders (e.g., the drug prohibition applied whether or not the parolees had previously been drug users) and some were specific (related to the circumstances surrounding the offender's earlier crimes or special needs).

The discretion afforded the parole authorities to recommit, whether for technical violations or for new crimes, differed across the states regarding the prescribed duration of the recommitment term. In some states, parole authorities could impose a new recommitment term; in others, they could only return the offender for at most the remainder of the original maximum sentence.

The right to recommit is typically accompanied by a broader range of postrelease supervision functions. These include periodic required meetings with a parole officer for counseling to help in the postrelease adjustment in home life, employment, drug treatment, or other individual needs. The parole authorities also have a surveillance right, including search authority, that would not be available to police more generally. Parolees are required to report any changes in residence or employment and in their activities more generally. However, parole officers' high caseloads often preclude consistent and careful monitoring of the parolees and limit the degree of support or surveillance that can be provided. An active caseload of 80 parolees is not uncommon and permits at most one 15-minute meeting per parolee every 2 weeks.[6]

---

[5] States differ in the degree to which the parole authorities have autonomy on recommitment for a new crime without having to go through the court. In some, only a court may convict and sentence for a new crime, whereas in others the parole authorities can exercise that discretion.

[6] In 1976, the average adult caseload per full-time supervisory employee ranged from 50 in adult parole agencies to 67 in combined parole and probation agencies. (State and Local Probation and Parole Agencies," LEAA Report No. SD-P-1, February 1978.) In 1991, the average formal caseload per probation or parole officer was 69 for all agencies nationwide. (Census of Probation and Parole Agencies, Bureau of Justice Statistics, August 2003.)

In any examination of recidivism rates, parolees' rates were typically quite high. A comprehensive study of releasees in one year[7] found that 62 percent of state prison releasees were rearrested for a felony or serious misdemeanor within 3 years, 47 percent were reconvicted, and 41 percent were re-incarcerated.[8] These high rates of recidivism provided a strong argument for keeping prisoners incarcerated and incapacitated longer. These results were also not surprising. With little effort devoted to rehabilitation or to facilitating prisoners' reentry into the community, and with the inherent selectivity involved in who is sent to prison in the first place, further involvement in crime was almost expected, especially at a time when drug use and addiction were widespread among the offender population. Perhaps more surprising was the large number of releasees not rearrested within 3 years.

Aside from the criticism about the leniency of parole release decisions, there was also concern that indeterminate sentencing caused unjustifiable *disparity* in sentencing because of inconsistent and arbitrary enforcement of sentences. Many questioned whether parole authorities, who are often political appointees rather than professionally trained staff, should be endowed with the power to determine individual liberty and doubted the quality of their judgments. Challenges to the seeming arbitrariness of the varying lengths of time served in prison for similar offenses generated this concern about disparities in sentencing.

By 1975, the movement to abolish parole saw *determinate sentencing* as its principal solution. California passed its Uniform Determinate Sentencing Act in 1976, eliminating discretionary parole release for all offenses except for some violent crimes with a long sentence or a life sentence. By 2000, 19 other states had enacted similar legislation.[9]

The movement toward increased severity in sentencing grew in the early 1980s as states developed *mandatory-minimum sentences* to counteract

---

[7] Beck, Allen, and Bernard E. Shipley. 1989. "Recidivism of Prisoners Released in 1983." Washington, DC: Bureau of Justice Statistics Special Report, NCJ 116261, April.

[8] A follow-on BJS study of releasees eleven years later (Patrick A. Langan and David J. Levin, "Recidivism of Prisoners Released in 1994," Bureau of Justice Statistics Special Report, NCJ 193427, June 2002, Washington, DC) found strikingly similar results. Within three years after their release in 1994, 67 percent of released prisoners in 15 states were rearrested, 47 percent were reconvicted, and 25 percent were sent back to prison on new sentences, with a total of 52 percent sent back on new sentences or on technical violations.

[9] Hughes, Timothy, Doris Wilson, and Allen J. Beck. 2001. "Trends in State Parole, 1990–2000." Washington, DC: Bureau of Justice Statistics Special Report, NCJ 184735, October.

judicial leniency and toughen penalties. These sentencing changes targeted drug offenses, weapons offenses, and repeat offenses. Federal programs that offered grants to states to build or expand correctional facilities provided further incentives to increase the severity of sentencing laws (primarily for violent offenders) by enacting restrictions on the possibility of early release.[10] At the same time, states mandated prison terms instead of probation or short sentences through mandatory minimum sentencing statutes that specified the minimum sentence length for various offenses.

Another variant of the determinate-sentencing movement in the early 1980s was the move toward *sentencing guidelines*. These were established initially as a means of reducing disparity by creating a state-level commission that would establish categories of offenses and promulgate appropriate sentencing ranges for each category. By 1996, 19 states had sentencing commissions. Ten states had presumptive guidelines, and seven had voluntary or advisory guidelines.[11] In some states the ranges were narrow and in others much broader.[12] Most commissions took account of a prior record by moving the sentencing range upward for those with a more serious prior record. Judges usually had discretion to sentence outside the prescribed range, but were usually required to explain the aggravating or mitigating circumstances that warranted going outside the prescribed range. Some states adopted aggravating and mitigating ranges outside the normal guideline range. In some states, there was a right of appeal for sentences outside the range.

Washington State enacted the first "truth-in-sentencing" law in 1984, so-called for its effective restriction of the possibility of early release. Although

---

[10] The Violent Offender Incarceration and Truth-in-Sentencing (VOI/TIS) Incentive Grants Program administered by the U.S. Department of Justice, for example, provided more than $2.7 billion to states between 1996 and 2001 for prison construction. States were eligible for half of the funds if they adopted laws that increased the percentage of violent offenders sentenced to prison, increased prison time actually served, or increased the percentage of sentence served prior to release. In addition, states that required violent offenders to serve at least 85 percent of their sentence were eligible for the other half of the funds.

[11] "1996 National Survey of State Sentencing Structures," Bureau of Justice Assistance Monograph, NCJ 169270, September 1998.

[12] In the Sentencing Reform Act of 1984 (Public Law No. 98-473), Congress established the United States Sentencing Commission with a similar mandate. In light of the much more complex federal criminal code, the guideline structure is more elaborate than that of any of the states. In addition, the federal guideline ranges are typically much narrower, leading to objections by many federal judges. The Act, which took effect on November 1, 1987, also established a series of mandatory penalties, most notably for various drug types and quantities and for using a weapon to commit an offense.

the details of truth-in-sentencing laws vary from state to state, they are largely focused on making violent offenders serve a greater portion of their maximum sentence. Such laws restrict or eliminate the ability of prisoners to earn early release. By year-end 2001, 30 states and the District of Columbia met the federal standard of requiring violent offenders to serve not less than 85 percent of their prison sentence. Other states had adopted laws that required violent offenders (Maryland and Texas) or all inmates (Indiana and Nebraska) to serve at least 50 percent of their sentence. Still others targeted truth-in-sentencing statutes to certain types of offenders (such as repeat violent offenders or those convicted of drug manufacturing).[13]

Consistent with the adoption of truth-in-sentencing and determinate sentencing policies, mandatory parole releases – with postrelease parole supervision specified by statute – have steadily increased, from 26,735 in 1980 to 116,857 in 1990 to 229,110 in 2001. As a percentage of all releases from state prisons, mandatory parole releases increased from 19 percent in 1980 to 39 percent by 2001. Discretionary releases, based on parole board decisions, dropped from 55 percent in 1980 to 25 percent in 2001. In addition, the number of inmates serving their entire prison sentence before release has increased sixfold, from 20,460 in 1980 to 124,053 in 2001. More than one in every five state prisoners released in 2001 had served their entire sentence or "maxed out" and were released without any parole supervision.[14]

In many states, parole boards or their functional equivalent – established when the boards were "abolished" – still set the conditions and monitored postrelease supervision. Such supervision often emphasizes deterrence by increasing parolees' vulnerability to recommitment and on maintaining control by means such as frequent drug testing. The now ubiquitous drug testing is a significant factor in technical violations. One of the perplexing ironies here is the difficulty of expecting a drug-addicted individual to display the rational sanction-avoidance behavior inherent in the deterrence model. At the same time, much of the casework supposed to occur in community supervision has been limited by an inadequate number of parole officers. As a result, many states have shifted their conception of parole supervision from service delivery to surveillance and punishment through recommitment.

---

[13] States that met the federal standard included 29 states (which qualified in FY 1999–2000) and Oklahoma (which qualified in FY 2001). See Hughes et al. 2001.

[14] National Prisoners Statistics, 2001, and Hughes et al., October 2001.

The number of commitments to state prisons because of parole violation has increased steadily, with an increase of 61 percent between 1990 and 2001. This is a result of the growth in the prison population and the consequent growth in the parole population. The decline of crime rates since the early 1990s has contributed to a slowing of the growth in new court commitments, which increased by only 13 percent between 1990 and 2001.[15] The toughening of parole recommitment decisions – reflecting increasing court convictions for new crimes, recommitments for technical violations, and returns to prison in lieu of adjudication for new offenses – has been an important factor in the growing number of parole violators returned to prison. As a result, flows into and out of parole supervision have become an increasingly salient factor accounting for trends in the prison population.

Our intent here is to explore the trends in prison release and recommitment between 1980 and 2001. In this discussion, we define *release* as any form of release from prison confinement, which may be conditional or unconditional and may be supervised by postrelease authorities or unsupervised. We define *recommitment* to characterize return to prison of anyone on any form of release, either for a technical violation or for a new crime, because of a decision of postrelease authorities or a court. We first examine the importance of trends in release and recommitments to the growth of state prison populations.

Increasing Importance of Release and Recommitment in Prison Population Growth

The incarceration rate that had remained stable for the 50 years preceding 1973 more than quadrupled to 470 inmates per 100,000 U.S. residents by 2001. This occurred despite a decline in crime rates through the 1990s, resulting in crime rates that had not been seen since the 1960s.[16]

---

[15] Harrison, Paige M., and Jennifer C. Karberg. 2003. "Prison and Jail Inmates at Midyear 2002." Washington, DC: Bureau of Justice Statistics Report NCJ 198877, April.

[16] There are some who view these two trends in the 1990s and argue that the rise in incarceration caused the drop in crime. But this argument fails to reconcile the fact that an even larger growth in incarceration during the late 1980s was associated with an *increase* in crime. There is obviously a complex relationship between crime contributing to prison growth by providing more convicted offenders and prison contributing to crime decline through incapacitation and deterrence. There has undoubtedly been an incapacitation effect due to the growth of incarceration, but the crime–punishment relationship is more complex than can be addressed by this simplistic one-sided analysis. Two carefully developed articles (Rosenfeld 2000 and Spelman, 2000) independently estimate that about 25 percent of the violent crime drop of the 1990s was attributable to the growth of incarceration.

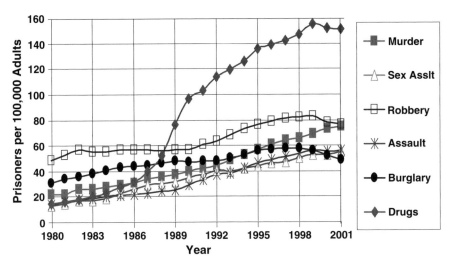

Figure 3.1 Incarceration Rates by Crime Type

In an earlier article examining the growth of prison populations from 1980 to 1996 (Blumstein and Beck, 1999), we attributed this increase in incarceration to the rapid growth in incarceration for drug offenses and also to increases in sentencing broadly defined: increased commitments per arrest and increased time served. The growth was not attributable to increases in crime nor to more effective policing as measured by arrests per crime.

This article's focus on parole must start with the prison population, the source of parolees. We extend the earlier analysis 5 years to 2001. An examination of prison population growth allows us, first, to assess the degree to which the earlier trends continued or have shifted and, second, to provide a basis for examining in more detail the relationship between the prison and parole populations and the flows between these two forms of correctional supervision.

The continued sharp growth in incarceration has slowed since 1999, reaching 470 sentenced inmates per 100,000 U.S. residents by year-end 2001. An examination of how the adult incarceration rate has varied for the crime types[17] displayed in Figure 3.1 shows a general continuation of the upward trends first identified through 1996. However, rates have begun to

---

[17] The crime types considered here are murder, robbery, assault, burglary, drugs, and sexual assault. Collectively, these six account for about two-thirds of state prison populations.

Table 3.1. *Partitioning the Growth in State Incarceration Rates, 1980–2001*

	Single Period		Two Periods	
	1980–1996*	1980–2001	1980–1992	1992–2001
All 6 offense types				
Crime trends	11.5%	–	22.1%	–
Police effectiveness	0.5	–	–	–
Commitments per arrest	51.4	52.8	62.9	40.1
Time served	35.6	47.2	15.0	59.9
5 offense types, excluding drugs				
Crime trends	–	–	13.1%	–
Police effectiveness	0.8	–	–	–
Commitments per arrest	41.5	45.1	46.3	50.1
Time served	57.7	54.9	40.6	49.9

* Entries in this column are based on Blumstein and Beck (1999).
– No contribution to growth.

level off – a trend that was not at all evident in 1996. Incarceration for drug offenses and for robbery reached a peak in 1999 and declined in each of the next 2 years. Burglary peaked earlier, in 1997, and by 2001 had dropped to 15 percent below its peak. The other offense types (murder, sexual assault, and aggravated assault) continued their steady upward trajectories.

In our earlier article on prison population (Blumstein and Beck, 1999), we partitioned the factors contributing to incarceration growth into four parts: (1) increased crime rate, (2) increased police effectiveness as measured by the number of arrests per crime, (3) increased "front-end" sentencing as measured by prison commitments per arrest, and (4) increased "back-end" sentencing as measured by time served in prison, including time served on recommitments from parole. The trends in each of these factors were measured[18] for each of the six crime types depicted in Figure 3.1.

The results of these analyses are presented in Table 3.1, where we compare our earlier estimates[19] for the 1980–1996 period to the updated

[18] Each of the factors other than time served can be measured directly from available statistics. Time served is much more complicated to measure, and we estimate it by the ratio of the prison population to the number of new commitments by crime type in each year. Other approaches are possible, each with its own form of bias. For an overview of the sources of distortion in measuring average time served in prison. (See Biderman 1995.)

[19] To generate the contribution of each of the component factors, we measure the linear time trend for each crime type over each period considered and then aggregate by weighting each of these components by the mean contribution of that crime type to the growth in total incarceration rate.

1980–2001 period. Because the growth trend has not at all been linear, we examine the trend in two periods, 1980–1992 and 1992–2001.[20] This partition will demonstrate the major shift in the role of time served, to which policies of parole release and recommitment were major contributors. We also distinguish the trends associated with all six crime types (including drugs, for which we are limited to measuring arrests because we have no independent measure of drug crimes) and the other five crime types (for which there are separate measures of crimes and arrests).

We can first dismiss police effectiveness as a significant factor in any of the analyses as the number of arrests per reported crime did not increase at all during this period. Police effectiveness contributes at most 1 percent to the growth in incarceration rate. This is somewhat surprising in light of the growing sophistication of many aspects of policing and police management over this 21-year period, but the flatness of the trend was consistent for all the crime types (except for drugs, for which there is no measure of arrests per crime).

The contribution of the other factors to prison population growth changed between 1980 and 2001. When we consider all six crime types over the entire 21-year period, we find that 53 percent of the growth in incarceration rate is attributable to front-end sentencing and 47 percent to back-end sentencing, with no contribution associated with crime trends.[21] When we partition into the periods before and after 1992, however, the crime rise of the 1980s becomes meaningful, accounting for 22 percent of the growth (including the substantial rise in drug arrests during the early period). In the early period, the role of time served is diminished considerably (dropping from 47 percent to 15 percent), and the dominant contributor is front-end sentencing, commitments per arrest (63 percent). In the later period (1992–2001), the effects are substantially reversed: there is no effect of crime trends on incarceration growth during the period of the crime drop; the effect of front-end sentencing drops from 63 percent to 40 percent; and the effect of back-end sentencing increases fourfold from 15 percent to 60 percent, making it the dominant factor. Changes in parole release and recommitment policies contributed in important ways to these shifts.

When we omit the drug offenses, we find that 45 percent of the growth in prison population over the 21-year period for the other five crimes

---

[20] The 1992 break point was chosen to best represent the break in the upward trends.

[21] The increase in crime in the early part of the period was offset by the drop in crime during the later part of the period.

was attributable to growth in commitments per arrest and 55 percent to increases in time served. In the examination of the two periods, we find that crime trends contributed 13 percent of the growth in the crime-rise period (1980–1992) and not at all in the later crime-drop period. The role of time served grew from 41 percent in the earlier period to 50 percent in the later period. This was undoubtedly the result of state sentencing changes, prompted by federal incentives that keep offenders – especially violent offenders – in prison for longer periods. We find that there was no major difference in the contribution of front-end sentencing in the two periods. Finally, although the growth in prison population has begun to moderate, growth since 1992 is equally divided between front-end and back-end sentencing, including additional time served by recommitments from parole.

Trends in the Parole and Recommitment Populations

With the growth in prison population, there has also been a steady growth in the parole population. It rose faster than the prison population through the 1980s and more slowly during the 1990s. As a result of sentencing changes, offenders were spending more time in prison, thereby slowing their movement to parole release. Figure 3.2 displays the rapid rise through the 1980s in both the annual entries to parole and the total year-end parole

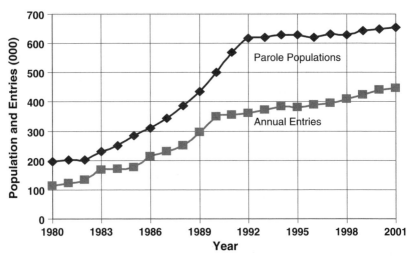

Figure 3.2 State Parole Populations and Annual Entries

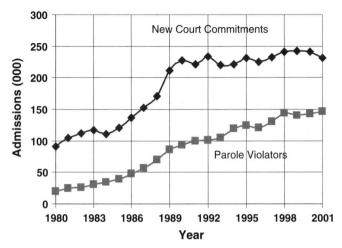

Figure 3.3 State Prison Admissions: New Court Commitments and Parole Violations

population. Between 1990 and 2001, however, the growth rate dropped significantly. The rate of growth in the prison and parole populations both declined in the 1990s, though the parole growth rate declined to a much greater extent. State prisoners increased by 132 percent from 1980 to 1990 and by 76 percent from 1990 to 2001. In contrast, state parolees grew by 155 percent in the 1980s (even faster than prisoners), but only by 33 percent from 1990 to 2001 (less than half the growth of prisoners). At year-end 2001, there were 312 state parolees per 100,000 adult U.S. residents, up from 271 in 1990 and 123 in 1980.

With more parolees, we can also expect to see more parole recommitments. This trend is displayed in Figure 3.3, which shows the steady growth of the parole recommitments to prison and contrasts sharply with the recent flat trend in new court commitments. In 1980, parole violators were only 17 percent of admissions, but by 2001, this fraction had more than doubled to 36 percent.

We can look separately at the new court commitments and the parole violators by crime type. The growth of new court commitments in the 1980s shown in Figure 3.4 was dominated by offenders convicted of drug-law violations; any trend in the other crime types was of minor influence. The growth by a factor of 10 essentially stabilized in about 1990 and has stayed around 100,000 per year, albeit with some recent growth of about 10 percent. During the 1990s, adult arrests for drug-law violations rose by

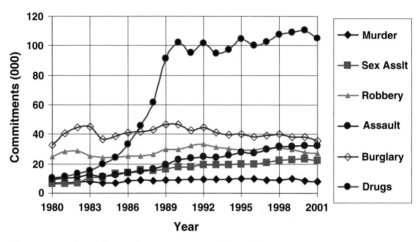

Figure 3.4 New Court Commitments to State Prison

37 percent, reaching nearly 1.4 million in 2001. At the same time, the likelihood of incarceration dropped from 101 commitments per 1,000 arrests in 1990 to 76 per 1,000 in 2001. Had it not been for this drop in the use of incarceration for drug offenders, state prison populations in the 1990s would have grown even faster.

With the dramatic growth in the drug commitments in the 1980s, it is not surprising that drug offenders[22] also constitute the bulk of the parole violators sent back to prison, as can be seen in Figure 3.5. In the early 1980s, parole violators were predominantly burglars and robbers, two high-recidivism offenses. By 2001, the number of drug offenders in the parole violation population had climbed steadily to the point where they represent 34 percent of the recommitments for the year. This is a consequence of their relatively short prison sentences and their dominating presence among entries to parole. In 2001, drug offenders represented 21 percent of state prisoners, but 34 percent of releases to parole. The mean time served by drug offenders in 2001 was 2.3 years, less than the 3 years associated with burglary and the shortest of the crime types being considered here.

---

[22] We use the term *drug offender* to indicate those prisoners or parolees whose most serious charge is violation of a drug law. These include street sellers who may be serious drug users as well as individuals who are simply workers in the drug trade, perhaps as sellers or couriers, but not users. In many cases, their charge may be possession, but few offenders are sent to a state prison without some basis for suspicion of their involvement in the drug trade.

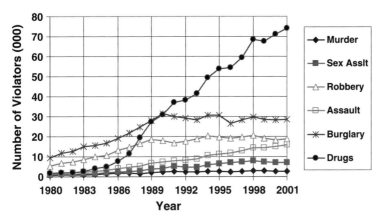

Figure 3.5 Parole Violators Admitted to State Prison

Combined with their particular vulnerability to relapse when they return to the community, drug offenders constitute a major portion of the recommitments. At a minimum, those drug offenders who are also continuing users are particularly vulnerable to a technical violation because of failing a urinalysis test.[23] Their need for money also makes them likely to engage in a property crime or robbery. Even the nonusing drug dealer may have limited income opportunities other than returning to drug dealing.

Figure 3.6[24] provides an indication of the low average time served by drug offenders sent to prison. After declining from 1.9 years in 1980 to 1.3 years in 1989, the average time served by drug offenders began to rise, reaching a peak of 2.3 years by 1999 before leveling off. The figure also highlights the sharp growth in time served for all the crime types during the 1990s. In particular, between 1990 and 2001, the time served for robbery grew from 3.3 to 5.6 years, for sexual assault from 3.6 to 5.3 years, and for aggravated assault from 2.4 to 3.7 years. The time served for these violent crimes rose by 70, 47, and 54 percent, respectively. The time served for burglary also rose 53 percent from 1.9 to 2.9 years, reflecting a steady

---

[23] Among parole violators in a state prison in 1997 serving time for a drug law violation, more than half (54 percent) had been recommitted for a new offense, 29 percent had a drug-related technical violation, 17 percent had absconded, and 14 percent had other technical violations. (Survey of Inmates in State Adult Correctional Facilities, 1997, Bureau of Justice Statistics, August, 2003.)

[24] Figure 3.6 is a graph of the growth of time served over the 1980–2001 period. Because the time served for murder is so much larger than the others, we excluded murder from the graph to provide greater differentiation among the other crime types.

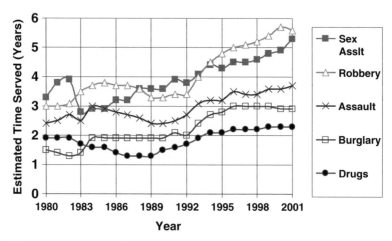

Figure 3.6 Estimated Time Served

increase in the ratio of burglars in state prison relative to new admissions for burglary.

Effect of Changes in Sentencing and Release Policies on Parole Flows

There was considerable growth in entries to parole across the states between 1985 and 2001. This growth is reflected in Table 3.2, which notes the trends in entries to parole by crime type. The striking observation here is how dominant a role the drug offenders play in the growth of the parole entries. They comprise half of the growth in releases to parole over that period even though they account for only 34 percent of the releases in 2001.

The method of release – discretionary or mandatory – has also been changing significantly. These changes are displayed in Table 3.3. Over the 1985–2001 period, the number of discretionary releases rose by a net of 57,500, whereas the number of mandatory releases rose by 166,300, nearly 3 times as much. This was clearly a consequence of the reduced discretion of parole authorities to make release decisions.

Offenders convicted of drug-law violations dominate the growth among the discretionary parole releases. Drug offenders comprised 37 percent of those released by parole authorities in 2001, but they accounted for 78 percent of the total growth since 1985. The reduction of discretion is most evident among the violent offenses, with a decline in all violent offense

Table 3.2. *Growth in State Parole Entries, by Crime Type, 1985–2001*

	Number of Entries				Total	Percentage
	1985	1990	1995	2001	Growth	of Total
All offenses	175,490	349,030	381,878	437,251	261,761	100%
Murder	5,100	6,300	5,100	6,500	1,400	0.5
Sex assault	8,000	13,300	15,100	16,300	8,300	3.2
Robbery	30,800	39,800	39,200	37,900	7,100	2.7
Assault	10,900	22,500	25,100	34,200	23,300	8.9
Burglary	45,200	65,100	55,700	54,400	9,200	3.5
Larceny	19,300	40,000	33,500	31,100	11,800	4.5
Drugs	19,400	95,200	122,800	149,100	129,700	49.5
Other	36,800	66,900	85,400	107,900	71,100	27.2

Note: Estimates were based on data from the National Prisoner Statistics and National Corrections Reporting Program, 1985, 1990, 1995, and 2001 and then rounded to the nearest 100.

categories except assault, which accounted for only 5 percent of all releases by parole boards in 1985. When we examine mandatory releases, we see that all offense types increased since 1985. Drug offenses still made up more than 40 percent of the growth, much more than any other single crime type.

As the number of parole recommitments to prison have grown, so too have the number of rereleases to a second or subsequent entry to parole supervision. As shown by the data on Table 3.4, in 1985, at an early stage of the growth of the prison population, there were 2.8 times (126,300/45,200) as many new releases as rereleases. As a percentage of all parole releases, rereleases rose from 26 percent in 1985 to 41 percent in 2001. This is an indication of a more seasoned population of parole entries, a population more likely to fail while under parole supervision.

Table 3.4 also highlights the growing saliency of the drug offenders among the releases and the rereleases. The drug offenders were 5.5 times as numerous in 2001 compared to 1985 among the new parole entries but 15.7 times as numerous among the rereleases. Once again, these differences indicate drug offenders' high failure rate on parole and their overrepresentation among parole revocations and recommitments. More than any other type of offender, released drug offenders cycle between prison and parole supervision. This situation may well be a result of the problem of the drug-dependent offenders controlling their addiction and their likely return to crime to finance their addiction. It may also be an indication of the

Table 3.3. *Growth in State Parole Entries, by Release Type and Crime Type, 1985–2001*

	Discretionary Releases				Mandatory Releases			
	1985	2001	Growth	Percentage of Net Growth	1985	2001	Growth	Percentage of Net Growth
All offenses	88,000	145,500	57,500	100%	62,900	229,100	166,300	100%
Murder	3,100	2,800	−300	−0.5%	1,500	3,300	1,800	1.1
Sex assault	3,700	3,300	−400	−0.7%	3,300	9,900	6,600	4.0
Robbery	17,000	15,600	−1,400	−2.4%	10,800	17,600	6,800	4.1
Assault	4,600	7,800	3,200	5.6%	4,700	21,500	16,800	10.1
Burglary	22,400	19,000	−3,400	−5.9%	16,500	27,100	10,600	6.4
Larceny	8,700	9,100	400	0.7%	7,400	17,600	10,300	6.2
Drugs	9,500	54,300	44,800	72.9%	6,700	76,400	69,700	41.9
Other	19,000	33,600	14,600	25.4%	12,000	55,700	43,700	26.3

Note: Estimates based on data from National Prisoner Statistics and National Corrections Reporting Program, 1985 and 2001. Excludes releases to probation and other conditional releases.

Table 3.4. *Growth in State Parole Entries, by Release Type and Offense, 1985–2001*

	New Releases			Percentage of	Ratio
	1985	2001	Growth	Total Growth	2001/1985
All offenses	126,300	252,600	126,200	100%	
Murder	3,900	4,300	400	0.3	1.10
Sex assault	6,600	11,300	4,700	3.7	1.71
Robbery	20,500	21,500	1,000	0.8	1.05
Assault	8,200	20,900	12,700	9.9	2.55
Burglary	30,300	28,900	−1,400		0.95
Larceny	13,900	15,600	1,700	1.3	1.12
Drugs	15,200	83,800	68,600	53.7	5.51
Other	27,700	66,200	38,500	30.2	2.39

	Rereleases			Percentage of	Ratio
	1985	2001	Growth	Total Growth	2001/1985
All offenses	45,200	176,800	131,600	100%	
Murder	1,200	2,100	900	0.7	1.75
Sex assault	1,300	4,900	3,600	2.7	3.77
Robbery	9,500	15,700	6,200	4.7	1.65
Assault	2,500	13,100	10,600	8.1	5.24
Burglary	13,600	24,200	10,600	8.0	1.78
Larceny	5,000	14,800	9,800	7.4	2.96
Drugs	4,000	62,700	58,700	44.6	15.68
Other	8,200	39,500	31,200	23.7	4.82

Note: Estimates based on data from National Prisoner Statistics and National Corrections Reporting Program, 1985 and 2001.

sensitivity of urinalysis in detecting continued use among released drug offenders. Moreover, the nonaddicted drug sellers may have difficulty finding other employment opportunities for earning income, and so are at high risk of recidivism for drug offenses.

Trends in Recommitment Rates

The growth in the number of parole violators being sent back to prison (displayed in Figure 3.5) could simply be attributed to the growth in the number of individuals under parole supervision, without any change in rates of success or failure. Alternatively, there may have been a toughening of the conditions of parole, which would lead to an increase in technical violations, or to an increase in the commission of new crimes by parolees.

Table 3.5. *Number of Returns to State Prison per 100 Parole Entries, by Crime Type,*
1985–2001

Crime Type at Parole Entry	Number of Parole Violators Returned to Prison per 100 Entries to Parole				Percentage Change, 1985–2001
	1985	1990	1995	2001	
All offenses	32.0	38.4	45.9	49.3	53.9
Murder	26.5	36.1	52.5	39.8	50.6
Sex assault	25.4	30.2	42.5	42.4	67.4
Robbery	37.1	45.4	50.5	49.7	33.8
Assault	29.4	32.1	44.1	46.7	59.1
Burglary	38.0	48.1	54.8	52.3	37.6
Drugs	21.3	32.5	43.9	49.7	134

Note: The number of violators returned per 100 entries to parole by crime type is a ratio calculated based on annual flows

Table 3.5 addresses the latter issue by documenting trends in the number of parole violators returned to state prison relative to the number of prisoners entering parole each year. For all crime types combined, there were 49 recommitments for every 100 parole entries in 2001; in 1985, this ratio was 32 recommitments per 100 parole entries, and so the recommitment rate rose by 54 percent over the 21-year period.

Ratios of prison recommitments relative to parole entries varied across crime type and year. For most of the crime types, 1995 was the year of highest return, with a slight decline in 2001. For two crime types, drug offenses and assault, the return rate increased over the entire period. However, because of the increasing number of drug offenders on parole, the return rate for all parolees combined showed a steady increase. The crime types displaying the highest recommitment rate in 2001 were burglary, assault, and drugs. The crime type displaying the largest growth in recommitment was drugs, which more than doubled from 21 recommitments per 100 parole entries in 1985 to nearly 50 per 100 entries in 2001.[25] The smallest change was associated with robbery, increasing from 37 per 100 entries in 1985 to nearly 50 in 2001.

---

[25] The rise in recommitment/parole entry ratios among drug offenders is confirmed in the 1983 and 1994 Bureau of Justice Statistics recidivism studies. Comparing recidivism measures for the 1983 and 1984 release cohorts, the percentage of drug offenders rearrested within 3 years of prison release rose from 50 percent to 67 percent, the percent reconvicted rose from 35 percent to 47 percent, and the percent returned to prison rose from 30 percent to 49 percent. (See Beck and Shipley 1989 and Langan and Levin 2002.)

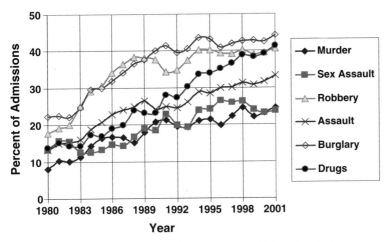

Figure 3.7 Parole Violators as a Percent of State Prison Admissions

As the recommitment rates have risen, parole violators have become an increasing part of annual admissions to state prison. This is clearly reflected in Figure 3.7, which depicts the percentage of admissions for each crime type that are parole violators. There is a clear upward trend in these percentages. Parole violators comprised 44 percent of admissions of burglars in 2001 (up from 22 percent in 1980), 41 percent of admissions for drug offenses (up from 14 percent), and 41 percent of robbers (up from 18 percent). Understandably, parole violators for murder represented a very low fraction of murderers admitted to prison (25 percent) and yet experienced a sharp increase from 1980 (when they were only 8 percent).

Patterns of Release and Recommitment

The process of release and recommitment can be analyzed as a stochastic flow process tracking individuals released from prison: some never return to prison and others violate parole – for either a technical violation or a new crime – and are sent back to prison. This process can then be repeated any number of times.

It is of interest to characterize the specifics of this process in terms of the probability of flow along the various possible paths and the time spent in the various states of liberty, either on parole or in the community, and in prison. We anticipate that the details of this process will differ among the states, but we begin with a single state to develop the process. We choose

Table 3.6. *Release and Recommitment of California Prisoners Released in 1995 and Followed through 2001*

	Number	Percentage	Mean time (in months)
Number released in 1995	92,977		
1st recommitment	62,042	66.7%	9.3 free
1st rerelease	59,752	96.3	7.9 prison
2nd recommitment	44,554	74.6	7.4
2nd rerelease	42,766	96.0	7.0
3rd recommitment	32,147	75.1	6.3
3rd rerelease	30,551	95.0	6.4
4th recommitment	22,303	73.0	5.6
4th rerelease	20,963	94.0	5.9

Note: Data are based on unique persons and their first release during 1995, including parole violators released and recommitted. All recommitments and rereleases exclude transfers, escapes, AWOLs, and deaths.

California for that purpose, partly because the flows in California comprise such a large portion of the national total (nearly a quarter in 1995), but also because the fullness of those flows allows for richer characterization of the process. Using that generic background, we can then examine features of the process to compare a number of different states. We then compare features of this flow process in California with those in New York, Illinois, and Florida. These four states are among the five largest[26] states in number of releases; together, they accounted for 39 percent of all releases in the nation in 1995 and 28 percent of all prisoners at year-end 2001. Because the states differ considerably in the degrees to which parolees are recommitted for technical violations and in the time served by inmates upon recommitment, we can then focus specifically on offenders recommitted for new sentences, typically associated with new crimes.

Process of Release and Recommitment

The flow from prison to parole (or the equivalent) or liberty in the community and return to prison is an important feature of the reentry process. The data for that process in California is presented in Table 3.6. The table

[26] Texas, the other one of the five (with more than 43,000 releases in 1995 and with 13 percent of state prisoners at year-end 2001), was not included in the analysis because of missing data on prison recommitments.

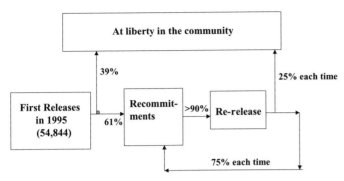

Figure 3.8 Flows of California's first releases in 1995 tracked through their multiple recommitments and re-releases until 2001

shows that 92,977 distinct individuals were released from California prisons in 1995.[27] These released prisoners were followed through 2001, a period of 6 to 7 years. Of the releasees, 66.7 percent had at least one recommitment to prison. A subset of these releasees were 54,844 individuals experiencing their first release; of these, a lesser fraction (60.8 percent) experienced one or more recommitments.

The 1995 releasees spent an average of 9.3 months free in the community before recommitment and then averaged an additional 7.9 months in prison. The other 33.3 percent were never recommitted during the 6- to 7-year observation period – and so are very unlikely ever to be recommitted.

Of those recommitted, almost all (96.3 percent) were rereleased some time before the end of 2001. Of those 59,752 individuals released after their first recommitment, 74.6 percent were recommitted a second time. Interestingly, the recommitment fraction is about the same on each subsequent release – about 75 percent being recommitted and 25 percent released to liberty in the community – until the end of the observation period in 2001, which somewhat limits the opportunity for multiple releases. Thus, it is reasonable to approximate the probability of recommitment to be 75 percent for those on a second or subsequent release. This repeated flow process is depicted in Figure 3.8, which shows the repeated sequence following each rerelease. Figure 3.8 depicts the flow pattern for the first releases (54,844 of

[27] These were drawn from the 126,091 prisoners present on January 1, 1995, and 77,366 offenders admitted in 1995 (who were not in prison at the end of 1994), for a total of 203,457 individuals potentially released. (Based on data from the National Prisoner Statistics Program, 1994, and National Corrections Reporting Program, 1995.)

the 92,977 releases) in particular. For them, the probability of not returning following that first release is nearly 40 percent, whereas individuals on a second or subsequent release have a lower probability (25 percent) of not returning within the 6- to 7-year observation period, and that same probability prevails for each subsequent rerelease.

The estimates of time free on release and time in prison for each release cohort are also presented in Table 3.6. The mean time free (9.3 months) and the time spent in prison before the next release (7.9 months) are both quite short compared to other states, providing the opportunity for multiple passes at the release and recommitment cycle.[28] The censoring process also affects these mean times, which is a likely explanation for the reduced time on successive releases. Alternatively, it could be that individuals with multiple recommitments could be sent back for less serious violations that could occur more frequently and would result in shorter recommitment times.

State-Specific Variations on the Process of Release and Recommitment

As indicated earlier, the release and recommitment process in California is particularly frequent and not representative of other states. These differences are reflected in Table 3.7, which presents recommitment statistics for New York, Illinois, and Florida as well as California for the same 1995 release cohorts followed for 6–7 years. In contrast to California's high recommitment rate of 67 percent, New York and Illinois are close to 50 percent. Florida's rate is still lower (47 percent), largely because the majority of Florida's prisoners are released unconditionally, and so are not subject to technical violations.

These differences are reflected in the number of recommitments over the 6- to 7-year period. In California, 9.4 percent of the initial 1995 releasees accumulated six or more recommitments. In New York, Illinois, and Florida, very few of the released prisoners had more than three recommitments.

The diverse frequencies of release and recommitment are also reflected in the time to first recommitment. In California, nearly 58 percent of the

---

[28] Based on data from Bureau of Justice Statistics National Corrections Reporting Program, times served in prison and parole in California are significantly shorter than in other states. Among successful parole discharges in participating states in 2000, the average time on parole before return to prison was 20 months. Among prisoners rereleased after serving time for a parole violation, the average time served in prison was 14 months.

Table 3.7. *Recidivism Patterns of Prisoners Released in Four States in 1995 and Followed through 2001*

	California	New York	Illinois	Florida
Number of inmates				
Held at year-end 1995	135,646	68,486	37,658	63,879
Released during 1995	92,997	28,665	21,598	19,163
Returned to prison				
Yes	66.7%	51.5%	54.1%	47.4%
No	33.3	48.5	45.9	52.6
Number of times recommitted				
0	33.3%	48.5%	45.9%	52.6%
1	18.7	30.6	26.7	32.6
2	13.4	14.6	17.0	11.5
3	10.7	4.8	7.1	2.8
4	8.5	1.3	2.4	0.5
5	6.2	0.2	0.6	0.0
6 plus	9.4	0.1	0.3	0.0
Year of first recommitment				
1995	29.8%	5.6%	5.7%	5.1%
1996	27.8	21.3	17.1	14.0
1997	6.8	11.0	13.3	10.6
1998	1.7	5.7	7.6	6.6
1999	0.4	3.6	4.9	5.2
2000	0.2	2.6	3.2	3.5
2001	0.1	1.6	2.3	2.4
Year of any recommitment				
1995	29.8%	5.6%	5.7%	5.1%
1996	43.3	22.0	17.8	14.4
1997	33.4	14.7	16.8	12.5
1998	25.8	11.2	14.0	9.8
1999	18.1	9.7	12.6	9.2
2000	12.5	8.9	12.5	7.9
2001	9.9	7.3	14.0	6.4
Number of recommitments				
Total	194,119	23,082	21,027	12,632
Per 100 releases	209	81	97	66

Note: Analysis is based on unique persons released in 1995, excluding releases to custody/detainer, deaths, transfers, appeals, and escapes/AWOLs. Recommitments exclude transfers, returns from appeal, and returned escapes and AWOLs.

initial releasees (86 percent of those recommitted) are first recommitted in the first 2 years (in 1995, the year of initial release, and in 1996), whereas an average of 23 percent of the releases in the other states combined are recommitted in the first 2 years (46 percent of those recommitted). Obviously, recommitment occurs at a much higher frequency in California than in the other three states. These different frequencies are also reflected in the intensity of recommitment over the 6- to 7-year follow-up period. As displayed by the total number of recommitments per initial 100 releasees, California had more than twice as many recommitments (209) as the other states (which averaged 81). Over the follow-up period, inmates released from California in 1995 experienced over 194,000 recommitments, more than 3 times the number of recommitments in the other states combined (56,741).

It is evident that California moves releasees through their parole release very quickly with a high likelihood of and short interval until recommitment. The other states move them through at a much lower frequency; this could reflect a lower level of surveillance and supervision so that violations are less likely to be detected or perhaps a much higher threshold of seriousness of violation before recommitment is invoked. Also, the other states keep them in prison longer when they are recommitted. This raises the question of whether one or the other of these release and recommitment policies is more effective in enhancing community safety.

Patterns of Reoffending

The previous section has highlighted the striking variation across these four states in patterns of release and recommitment. Although there may well be some preventive and deterrent effect of technical conditions of parole, and some incapacitative effect of the subsequent time spent in prison as a result of a recommitment decision, our concern with issues of public safety most directly should focus on recommitments just for new offenses. As an approximation to this, we look at recommitments from court with new sentences. These sentences are for new crimes but also include offenders previously sentenced to probation who are subsequently sent to prison as probation violators. This does omit the large number of recommitments for technical violations of parole, which may include failure to report to the parole officer, failure to participate in required drug or alcohol treatment programs, testing positive for drug use, possessing a firearm, or having

Table 3.8. *Court Recommitment for New Offenses among Prisoners Released in Four States in 1995 and Followed through 2001*

	California	New York	Illinois	Florida
Returned to prison				
Yes	30.2%	32.2%	51.6%	41.6%
No	69.8	67.7	48.4	58.4
Number of times recommitted				
0	69.8%	67.7%	48.4%	58.4%
1	20.8	29.4	31.1	32.4
2	7.3	2.9	15.1	8.0
3	1.8	0.0	4.1	1.0
4	0.3	0.0	1.0	0.1
5	0.0	0.0	0.4	0.0
Year of first recommitment				
1995	6.4%	1.9%	4.4%	2.7%
1996	10.4	7.3	15.1	9.7
1997	6.0	7.1	13	9.3
1998	3.3	5.4	7.9	6.9
1999	1.6	4.3	5.2	5.9
2000	0.6	3.8	3.5	4.2
2001	0.4	2.5	2.5	2.8
Year of any recommitment				
1995	6.4%	1.9%	4.4%	2.7%
1996	10.7	7.3	15.5	9.8
1997	7.4	7.1	15.4	10.0
1998	5.4	5.7	13.0	8.4
1999	3.8	4.9	11.3	8.2
2000	2.7	4.7	9.8	7.1
2001	2.1	3.6	9.0	5.5
Number of recommitments for new offenses				
Total	39,239	10,098	17,140	9,951
Per 100 releases	42	35	79	52

Note: Recommitments for new offenses are based on prison admissions with a new sentence, including new court commitments and parole, mandatory parole, or probation revocations with a new sentence.

contact with known offenders, all of which are issues at the discretion of the parole authorities.

Table 3.8 presents the same information as contained in Table 3.7 but only for new court commitments. The rates and frequency of recommitment are obviously lower in Table 3.8 because only a subset of the recommitments are counted – those for new crimes and presumably for the more serious crimes that warrant a new court hearing and a new sentence. The most striking observation here is the similarity among the states in their recommitment patterns for new crimes. The sharp differences between California and the other states seen in Table 3.7 are attributable primarily to differences in their use of technical violations. California uses technical violations extensively (nearly 80 percent of recommitments in California are for technical violations) with rapid recommitment and rerelease. In contrast, about 56 percent of recommitments in New York, 21 percent in Florida, and 18 percent in Illinois were for technical violations. Indeed, the column of entries for Florida and Illinois in Table 3.8 are quite close to their entries in Table 3.7.

Among the four states, the numbers of new court recommitments are quite similar, and average 52 per 100 releases, with 42 per 100 in California, 35 in New York, and 52 in Florida. Illinois stands out with 79 recommitments per 100 releases. The number of distinct individuals returned to prison average 35 per 100 releases, so that 12 percent of the recommitments are of releasees returned multiple times. This is reflected in the small numbers of individuals recommitted for two or more times, ranging from 2.9 percent in New York to 20.6 percent in Illinois.

Comparison of Tables 3.7 and 3.8 raises the question of the relative effectiveness for crime control of extensive use of technical violation, as in California, compared to its more restricted use in the other states. There is no clear indication that either approach results in any meaningful difference in the criminal activity of the released prisoners, at least to the extent that the recommitments for new offenses in Table 3.8 provide an indication on that issue. If that lack of a difference is found to be the case even when the other crime-preventive aspects of technical conditions of parole are taken into account, then that must raise the question of the value of technical violations. Technical violations involve significant cost and effort for the parole system, frequent admissions to prison, even if for a short time, and frequent disruption to the lives of parolees and their attempts to reintegrate into society. This is an important question requiring more careful investigation than is possible here. Further investigations should focus on the characteristics of the individuals sent back on technical violations, whether they are the same or different from those of individuals sent back for new crimes, and assessment of the differences in the time served under technical violations compared to the time served for new crimes. Addressing these issues requires more carefully controlled comparisons to assess the strengths and weaknesses of the differing approaches represented by California and the other states.

The State of Parole

We have examined in this chapter the growing importance of parole release and recommitment as factors affecting the population of prisons and crime in the community. The number of parole violators has grown from 17 percent of admissions to prison to 36 percent over a 21-year period. Their recommitment rate has also grown over this 21-year period but not so dramatically. With the flatness of growth in new court commitments associated with the crime drop of the 1990s, recommitted parolees have become a burgeoning part of the prison population.

It is hard to consider any aspect of crime or incarceration over the past two decades without seeing the importance of drugs and drug policies. That is certainly the case with parole. We have seen a steady increase in drug offenders' failure rate on parole. Drug offenders constitute a dominant portion of state parole populations, and their success on parole is strongly affected by the support services available to them in the community, particularly for dealing with their addiction.

However, reducing the flows to and from parole supervision is not simply about diverting drug offenders from being sent to prison in the first place. Since 1990 the number of new court commitments to prison of drug offenders has remained stable, at about 100,000 per year. Between 1990 and 2001, there has been an increase of over 376,000 adult arrests for drugs. If incarceration of drug-law violators had followed the patterns of the 1980s, prison populations would have skyrocketed beyond their already record levels. But responses to drug offenders have moderated, partly because of the growing recognition by prosecutors and judges of the limited potential of incarceration to reduce drug offending; partly because of political initiatives such as California's Proposition 36, which mandates treatment in preference to incarceration; and partly as a result of budgetary pressures on the states. Diversion and alternative sanctions for convicted drug offenders have averted even greater increases in the numbers of prisoners.

The flow of drug offenders from prison to parole supervision and back again represents at least half of the growth in entries to parole and half of the subsequent growth in prison recommitments since 1980. Combined with the flow of drug offenders was the release of other prisoners, 59 percent of whom were active drug users in the month prior to their imprisonment.

This combined flow of drug-involved offenders has resulted in parole supervision that is dominated by drug testing and surveillance. With increased surveillance comes greater likelihood of detection of misconduct – including technical violations as well as a return to criminal behavior. Prison recommitments have grown by more than 60 percent since 1990 – drug-law violators account for over half of this growth.

The growth in prison and parole populations is not entirely a story of drug use and offending. Growth in state prison populations has been the consequence of changes in front-end sentencing as evidenced by increasing rates of imprisonment relative to arrest (especially for violent crimes) and changes in back-end sentencing as measured by time served, including time served by recommitments from parole. These changes have largely driven the dramatic increases in violent offenders in prison. As a result, almost two thirds of the growth (63 percent) in the state prison populations since 1995 is attributed to growth in prisoners sentenced for violent offenses and less than 15 percent for drug offenses. Even if all of the nearly 250,000 drug offenders were released from state prisons, the level of incarceration would surely fall, but only to the level that prevailed in 1995. The rate of prison incarceration without drug offenders (378 per 100,000 residents) would still be more than triple that of the pre-1970 stable incarceration rates.

States have the ability to control the flow of prison recommitments from parole. The four large states considered – California, New York, Illinois, and Florida – varied significantly in their patterns of release and recommitment. Independent of policies related to the likelihood of arrest and prosecution of parolees for new offenses, states varied in their parole supervision policies and practices. California, with an incarceration policy of "catch and release" and a parole policy of "violate and recommit," generates a high volume of the nation's prison releases and recommitments. New York, Illinois, and Florida have policies that result in longer terms of imprisonment followed by longer times free under parole supervision. Although the volume and timing of prison recommitments may differ, there is no clear link to variations in community safety.

When we look at recommitments for new crimes, the variation across the states diminishes considerably. Interestingly, California, at 30 percent, has the lowest rate of the four states; this could be a result of the preventive effects (through prevention of precursors of offending, deterrence, and incapacitation) of its intensive use of technical violations. It could be also be that California deals with new crimes through the parole authorities, and so parolees with new crimes do not show up as new court commitments. New

York, however, has a comparably low 32 percent rate of new crimes, raising the question of the distinctive strength of California's intensive approach. The rates for the other states are somewhat higher, 42 percent for Florida and 52 percent for Illinois. We know that Illinois has emphasized a field-based surveillance model of parole supervision, and so that raises the question of whether that approach has led to its having the highest rate of reoffending among these four states. Florida, which has a low level of post-custody supervision and thus limits the return flow of technical violators, has intermediate levels of recommitment for new offenses.

These data raise the question of to what degree a policy of aggressive use of technical violations provides any clear-cut advantage in enhancing public safety. The abandonment of the former policy that emphasized a service and treatment model of parole, and its replacement by a predominant model of surveillance and control has been a major factor in stimulating the steady increase in recommitments that underlies the dramatic growth in state prison populations.

Parolees, having been selected from all offenders to spend some time in prison, are generally at high risk for further offending. Thus, they are a population needing support services, both in prison before release and after they are in the community, to diminish their recidivism risk. As high-risk individuals, they are also a population that is reasonably suspect of being involved in further criminal activity, and so warrant special surveillance in the community. A better mixture of support and surveillance may work together to diminish further recidivism.

We have seen that prison population growth is the result of sanctioning policies, reflecting how states choose to respond to crime rather than underlying growth in crime. The growing volume of prison recommitments reflects similar policy considerations – how states choose to respond to violations of parole supervision. The challenge for states is to effectively direct resources that ultimately break the current cycle of incarceration, release and recommitment, without compromising public safety. An optimum balance of surveillance and support services for inmates returning to the community is required. Further research comparing different states' practices should be able to provide guidance on that appropriate balance.

4

The Contribution of Ex-Prisoners to Crime Rates

Richard Rosenfeld, Joel Wallman, and
Robert Fornango

The quadrupling of the prison population since the 1970s and the precipitous drop in crime rates beginning in the early 1990s are two of the most striking recent trends in crime and punishment in the United States (see Blumstein and Wallman 2000; Hughes and Wilson 2003). The possible connection between the growth in imprisonment and the decline in crime has generated considerable popular and scholarly debate, the key issue being how much, if any, of the crime drop can be ascribed to prison growth through the incapacitation of criminals, deterrence of would-be offenders, or both.

Prison growth has resulted from an increase in both the number of offenders sentenced and the length of time they serve in prison (Blumstein and Beck 1999). The extension of prison time, though, has not been great enough to prevent what, in the absence of permanent incarceration, would be expected to ensue from the quadrupling of the prison population: a burgeoning number of people returning from prison. Attention to massive "prisoner reentry" coincides with signs that the crime drop of the 1990s may be bottoming out or even reversing in the first years of the 21st century. And, just as many observers credited the prison boom for the crime drop, some see a causal connection between recent upturns in crime and either the volume of prison releases or the nature of those returning. Recent articles in *Time* (Ripley 2002), the *Christian Science Monitor* (Axtman 2002),

For comments on an earlier draft of this chapter, we are grateful to Allen Beck, Alfred Blumstein, Todd Clear, Shadd Maruna, Joan Petersilia, Ann Piehl, Jeremy Travis, and Christy Visher. Pat Langan and Tim Hughes of the Bureau of Justice Statistics provided valuable technical assistance. Any remaining errors are the responsibility of the authors.

the *Los Angeles Times* (Landsberg and Casillas 2000), and the *New York Times* (Rashbaum 2002), quoting police authorities and criminologists, attribute the rising crime rates in some cities to massive numbers of released convicts or to the return from prison of "a particularly violent cadre of criminals" (Rashbaum 2002, p. 1).

Although there is little doubt that ex-prisoners make a disproportionate contribution to crime, those who invoke prisoner reentry as an explanation for rising crime rates typically fail to consider that the growth in released prisoners has been accompanied by a commensurately large increase in the number of offenders being sent to prison, a process that tends to counterbalance the crime contribution of the returnees. Of course, even if more persons are admitted to than released from prison, differences in the offending rates of those going in and those coming out could offset any crime reductions associated with prison growth. So, popular concern with the violent histories of returning prisoners is not necessarily misplaced. It is not only the ratio of intake to outflow that matters but also who is going in and who is coming out. The conditions of release should matter as well.

In this chapter, we assess the effect of released prisoners on state crime rates through estimates of the fractional contribution to violent, property, and drug crimes of the following:

- the number of released prisoners (the "how many" question);
- differences among them in reoffending risk (the "who" question); and
- the effects on reoffending of postrelease supervision (the "conditions" question).

Whatever the ex-prisoner share of crime turns out to be, the variables that govern it – at least the ones that are modifiable – should be of interest to those who formulate corrections policies. Correctional populations, by virtue of their captivity and (possible) supervision within the community, are available for treatments and services that may reduce their rate of offending and, in turn, overall levels of crime in the community.

The accuracy of our analysis of the contribution of released prisoners to crime rates depends on the size and direction of the errors associated with three simplifying assumptions underlying our analysis:

1. Those factors influencing crime in the general population (e.g., economic conditions, law enforcement practices, drug markets, and other

criminal opportunities) will influence released prisoners to more or less the same extent. We do not offer separate estimates of those effects.

2. Ex-prisoners do not influence the crime rates of other potential offenders.

3. Arrest rates are a valid proxy for the crime rates of both released prisoners and others.

Like all simplifying assumptions, these three clearly introduce a measure of error into the analysis, although the size and direction of the error is difficult to gauge. For example, released prisoners may be especially vulnerable to the general conditions that determine crime rates (see Lynch and Sabol 2001; Travis, Solomon, and Waul 2001). In addition, the crime rates of ex-prisoners and other potential offenders may not be independent. Released prisoners could potentiate the offending of others by reactivating former criminal networks or creating new ones, by propagating criminal norms in the community, and by increasing the pool of attractive crime targets (persons with criminal records have high rates of victimization).

Finally, several defensible measures of crime exist, each with virtues and drawbacks, including arrests, specific arrest charges, convictions, crimes reported to the police, crimes reported in victimization surveys, and crimes divulged by active or incarcerated offenders, as well as combinations of these measures. We use arrests to represent crimes. This choice, like the other options, introduces errors into our estimate of crimes, although some of these errors are offsetting. Not all criminal offenses result in an arrest, some arrests are unfounded (the charges are dropped or the individual is later found not guilty), and the arrest process is influenced by police practices and public policies uncorrelated with crime rates. Assuming that this imperfect mapping of crimes on arrests affects former prisoners and others roughly to the same extent, our estimates of the *proportion* of crimes accounted for by released prisoners should not be greatly distorted, even if the *level* of crimes committed by released prisoners and others is not accurately estimated.[1]

---

[1] See Petersilia and Turner (1993) for experimental evidence of no significant difference in the arrest rates of offenders under intensive and routine supervision in the community.

Data and Methods

Our analysis, like others in this volume, is crucially indebted to the landmark 2002 study by the Bureau of Justice Statistics (BJS) of the recidivism patterns of inmates released in 1994 and tracked for three years (Langan and Levin 2002). This investigation is an expanded replication of an earlier BJS study of state prisoners released in 1983 (Beck and Shipley 1989). The 2002 study is based on criminal histories and demographic information for a sample of inmates released in 1994 from prisons in 15 states.[2] The sample, numbering 38,624 cases, represents a population of more than 300,000 individuals, or two thirds of all U.S. prisoners released in that year. The sample was constructed by randomly selecting released prisoners from each state in 13 imprisonment-offense categories. The number of cases in the sample compiled for a given offense varied across states, but each state's cases were weighted to reflect the full number of releasees in that offense category. Criminal histories and correctional records for each case were compiled from multiple sources and used to track the recidivism of the released prisoners over a period of 3 years.

Langan and Levin (2002) retained a sample of 33,796 cases, representing a population of 272,111 released prisoners, for their analysis of recidivism. We have excluded additional cases from our analysis due to missing or non-comparable data, for a final sample of 30,431 cases, weighted to represent a population of 243,334 prisoners from 13 states.[3]

The outcome variables in the study are the number of arrests for violent, property, and drug crimes during 1- and 3-year periods following release. Following standard Uniform Crime Reports crime classifications, violent crimes include homicide, rape and other sexual assaults, robbery, and aggravated assault. Property crimes include burglary, larceny, and auto theft. Drug crimes include drug possession, drug trafficking, and other illicit drug offenses.

---

[2] Arizona, California, Delaware, Florida, Illinois, Maryland, Michigan, Minnesota, New Jersey, New York, North Carolina, Ohio, Oregon, Texas, and Virginia. Inmates from federal facilities were not included in the study.

[3] Delaware was dropped from the analysis due to missing data on release type (e.g., mandatory vs. parole-board release). Maryland was excluded because the crime types of a large majority of its released prisoners were recorded as "unknown." Other cases were excluded due to missing data on sex, race, age, prior arrests, release type, and other variables in our analysis.

We employ as predictors of arrest recidivism[4] dichotomous measures of the sex and race (black/white) of released prisoners and a continuous measure of age at time of release. The conviction offense resulting in imprisonment is represented by three dummy variables for violent, property, and drug crimes, defined as in the previous paragraph. We also incorporate the number of prior arrests, number of months served in prison under the current sentence, and a dichotomous (yes/no) indicator of whether the release was the first release under the current sentence. Release type is represented by four dichotomous variables: parole-board decision, supervised mandatory release, other conditional release, and unconditional release.[5] Finally, to capture sources of variation in arrest recidivism that vary among states, we include in our models dummy variables representing the state of release.

All of our models were estimated by negative binomial regression, a technique suitable for analyzing the relationship between predictor variables and an outcome variable that is not strictly continuous but in the form of counts, in this case the number of arrests. Tests of overdispersion indicated that the negative binomial model was preferable to the Poisson, which constrains the variance to equal the mean value of the outcome variable (Long 1997, pp. 217–250).

Our assessments of the impact of released prisoners on crime rates are performed on data aggregated to the state level. Although it might be preferable to study the impact of release cohorts on smaller population units, such as cities or even neighborhoods, available data sources do not provide the city or county into which prisoners are released but only the county in which they were sentenced. The BJS data contain the state of release for each prisoner and also record rearrests that occur in other states during

---

[4] We use the term "arrest recidivism" throughout this chapter to refer to the *incidence* of arrests accumulated by released prisoners (the total number of arrests) and not to the *prevalence* of rearrest (the proportion of ex-prisoners rearrested).

[5] Parole board decisions may include probation and shock-probation releases as well as other types of conditional release except mandatory supervised release. Unconditional releases include expirations of sentence, commutation or pardon, and other unconditional release types. In cross-checking the release-type data with data from the National Corrections Reporting Program (NCRP), we determined that values for California, Delaware, Michigan, and North Carolina had been misreported. Cases from Delaware were dropped from the analysis for the reasons presented above. All cases in California marked as released by parole board were recoded as mandatory supervised releases. Finally, the release-type data for North Carolina required a case-by-case re-analysis to correct the data and ensure consistency with other sources. We are grateful to Allen Beck and Tim Hughes of BJS for bringing these problems to our attention and to Patrick Langan of BJS for performing the case-by-case re-analysis of the North Carolina data.

the 3-year observation window. Approximately 7 percent of all rearrests occurred in states other than the one in which the prisoner was released. These cases are not included in our analysis, which thus underestimates released prisoners' full contribution to crime.

States are meaningful, albeit heterogeneous, "communities" for purposes of determining the effect of corrections policies on recidivism rates. Corrections policy is formulated at the state level and applied statewide. Moreover, marked differences exist among states in imprisonment rates, size of release cohorts, recidivism rates, prison programming, and release policies, even after adjusting for differences in population size and composition. Still, because our results are limited to the state level of analysis, extensions to other population units should be made with caution.

Results

We begin our analysis with estimates of the impact of prisoners released in 1994 on the crime rates of 13 states. We then present the results of our assessment of arrest recidivism, focusing on the effects on recidivism of conditions of release from prison. Based on these results, we engage in hypothetical "policy experiments" that assess the impact on state arrest rates of changes in the number of prisoners exposed to specific release conditions. Finally, we estimate the "net" impact on crime rates of the changing ratio of annual prison admissions to releases between 1994 and 2001, with projections to 2010.

Ex-Prisoners' Contribution to Crime

Released prisoners commit crimes, as measured by arrests, at rates far higher than the general population. The 243,334 ex-prisoners represented in our sample generated 61,323 arrests for violent crimes, 94,239 arrests for property crimes, and 113,959 arrests for drug crimes during the 3 years after their release from prison in 1994. Those arrest frequencies amount to an average annual arrest rate for violent, property, and drug offenses of 8,400, 12,909, and 15,611 per 100,000 released prisoners. These rates, in turn, are between *30 and 45 times higher* than those for the general population in the 13 states in our analysis.

Even when the general population arrest rates are adjusted for race and age differences with released prisoners, the rates for releasees remain many times greater than those of others in the community. Table 4.1 compares

85

Table 4.1. *Violent, Property, and Drug Arrest Rates (per 100,000) for Released Prisoners and U.S. Adult Population, 1994–1997*

	Violent	Property	Drug
All Adults			
Released prisoners	8400.4	12909.4	15610.6
General population	322.6	701.5	678.8
Ratio	**26:1**	**18:1**	**23:1**
Whites			
Released prisoners	6140.1	10341.0	13484.5
General population	209.2	506.7	476.7
Ratio	**29:1**	**20:1**	**28:1**
Blacks			
Released prisoners	10812.6	15650.5	17879.7
General population	1146.2	2115.1	2145.5
Ratio	**9:1**	**7:1**	**8:1**

the arrest rates of U.S. adults, partitioned by race, with those of the released prisoners in our sample.[6] Released prisoners have arrest rates between 18 and 26 times those of the general population of adults. The ratios among whites are roughly similar to those for the total populations of the released prisoners and U.S. adults, but they are only about one third as large for blacks, whose general population arrest rates are 4–5 times greater than those among whites. Nonetheless, arrest rates among black released prisoners are at least 7 times higher than those for the general population of black adults in the United States. There is no question that, regardless of race, ex-prisoners pose a substantially elevated risk to the communities in which they are released, as measured by crimes per capita.

What, then, is the contribution of released prisoners to overall levels of crime? Given their elevated arrest probabilities, the proportion of crimes they contribute depends crucially on their numbers. In 1994, about 500,000 prisoners were released from state prisons in the United States; the number now exceeds 600,000 (Bureau of Justice Statistics 2000; Travis et al.,

---

[6] The rates for the released prisoners are the average annual arrests per 100,000 during the 3-year follow-up period. The rates for the general population represent the average annual arrests per 100,000 U.S. residents ages 18 and over for the period 1994–1997. We could not obtain race-specific adult arrest rates for the 13 states in our sample. However, because the total arrest rates for the 13 states in the sample are very close to those for the nation as a whole, it seems reasonable to compare the race-specific rates for U.S. adults with the corresponding rates for the released prisoners in the 13 states. The U.S rates are from the Uniform Crime Reports and are adjusted to account for non-reporting agencies.

Table 4.2. *Percentage of 1994–1995 State Violent, Property, and Drug Arrests Attributable to Prisoners Related in 1994*

	Violent		Property		Drug	
	All	Adult	All	Adult	All	Adult
Arizona	2.1	2.8	2.1	3.2	2.0	2.5
California	7.3	8.6	6.5	9.6	10.3	11.3
Florida	5.5	7.5	3.9	6.1	4.7	5.3
Illinois	13.9	17.9	6.3	9.7	5.1	6.0
Michigan	2.0	2.5	1.7	2.7	1.0	1.1
Minnesota	3.3	4.8	1.4	3.0	1.2	1.5
New Jersey	4.4	6.0	3.5	5.2	5.5	6.7
New York	3.7	5.0	6.3	8.5	5.9	6.6
North Carolina	6.5	7.5	7.4	9.7	6.6	7.4
Ohio	12.7	16.4	7.7	12.3	8.8	10.2
Oregon	8.1	10.8	2.0	3.3	6.0	7.0
Texas	2.3	3.0	1.3	2.1	1.7	2.0
Virginia	2.2	2.5	2.7	3.9	2.6	2.9
TOTAL	**6.1**	**7.6**	**4.5**	**6.8**	**6.5**	**7.3**

Note: State arrests are 1994–1995 average. Totals are population-adjusted percentages.

Source: Rearrest data from Bureau of Justice Statistics. State arrests from Uniform Crime Reports, Illinois Criminal Justice Information Authority, and Florida Department of Law Enforcement.

2001). During the 1990s, the average state received about 11,000 returning prisoners each year. The 13 states in our sample received a higher average number of released prisoners, over 22,000, reflecting the presence in the sample of several large states, including New York and California. Table 4.2 displays the proportion of violent, property, and drug crimes contributed by those returning prisoners during the first year of release.

Released prisoners on average accounted for about 4–6 percent of all arrests for violent, property, and drug crimes in the 13 states.[7] These figures increase to 7–8 percent when adult arrests are used as the base. Substantial variation exists across the states in the fraction of arrests attributable to released prisoners. For example, they account for nearly 14 percent of arrests for violent crime in Illinois compared with roughly 4 percent in

[7] The BJS study includes prisoners released at any point during 1994, and so the first year after release extends to the end of 1995 for some of them. For that reason, we averaged the general population arrests for 1994 and 1995 to create the base of the 1-year percentages presented in Table 2.

87

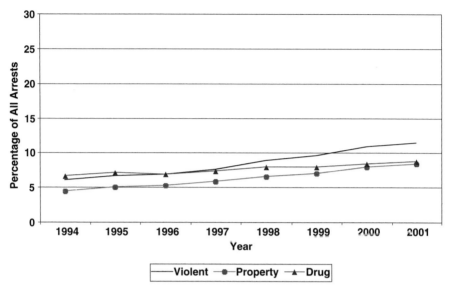

Figure 4.1 Released Prisoners' Estimated Share of Total Arrests, 1994–2001: Released within 1 Year

New York, 3 percent in Minnesota, and 2 percent in Michigan. Not surprisingly, these state differences correspond closely with both the number of returning prisoners and their average arrest rate.

Table 4.2 suggests that during the first year after release, ex-prisoners have a nontrivial but small impact on the crime rates of the states to which they return. As mentioned earlier, however, their crime share depends not just on their numbers and their arrest rate but also on the arrest rate of the population as a whole, which consists overwhelmingly of nonreturnees. All else equal, the lower the general population's crime rate, the greater will be the proportion of all crime attributable to ex-prisoners. It happens that the year depicted in Table 4.2, spanning 1994 and 1995, was the beginning of a marked national crime decline (Blumstein and Wallman 2000). Looking only at 1994–1995, then, might not yield a representative picture of the ex-prisoner contribution to crime in recent years.

Figure 4.1 shows this contribution, for the 13-state sample as a whole, for each year from 1994 through 2001. As in Table 4.2, the ex-prisoner share for each year was derived by multiplying the 1994 cohort's observed first-year rate of arrest – by default, our best initial estimate of this rate for *all* cohorts – by the size of that year's cohort. This predicted number of arrests was then divided by total Uniform Crime Reports (UCR) arrests in the 13 states for that year to yield the aggregate ex-prisoner contribution.

It can be readily seen in Figure 4.1 that the ex-prisoner share of total crime in 1994 was the lowest of any year in the period. Their share grew steadily thereafter. By 2001, the fraction of arrests attributable to released prisoners had nearly doubled for violent and property crimes and increased by a third for drug crimes.

The growth in ex-prisoners' share of crime could be due to an increase in the rate of offending of successive cohorts of ex-prisoners, growth in the size of each cohort, a drop in the crime rate of the general population, or some combination of these factors. We are not aware of any evidence suggesting a progressive increase in the rate of offending of prison release cohorts during the period of the crime decline. Therefore, it seemed reasonable to start from the assumption that roughly the same rate applies to all cohorts.

As a second estimate of the trajectory of released prisoners' violent and property arrest rates after 1994, we adjusted those rates *downward* by the rate at which overall arrest rates fell each year for violent and property crimes. (Aggregate drug arrests, by contrast, did not show this downtrend over the period, instead fluctuating slightly up and down around a remarkably stable rate.) This adjustment is consonant with the assumption, stated at the outset, that the criminality of released prisoners is subject to the same crime-promoting and -suppressing conditions that influence the general population.

Conversely, the contrary argument has been made that the individual crime rates (*lambda*) of the population of persistent offenders may be relatively invariant with respect to the factors influencing general crime rates (Blumstein and Cohen 1979; Blumstein and Graddy 1982). Given reasonable arguments for both change and constancy in the arrest trends of released prisoners during the 1990s, then, we also computed an estimated rate for each release cohort that is midway between an invariant rate (that of the 1994 cohort) and a rate that is adjusted each year to the same degree that the general rate changed. It proved to make little difference which of the estimates is used: The estimated share of crimes contributed by ex-prisoners differs by only about 5 percent each year between the invariant and full-adjustment methods.

Assuming, then, that whether or not released prisoners' arrest rates decreased over this period, they did not *increase*, the explanation for the growth in ex-prisoners' share of all arrests must lie with the increasing size of release cohorts, declining aggregate crime rates, or both. The crime drop

Table 4.3. *Estimated Percentage of 1994–1995 State Violent, Property, and Drug Arrests Attributable to Prisoners Released in 1992, 1993, and 1994*

	Violent		Property		Drug	
	All	Adult	All	Adult	All	Adult
Arizona	4.6	6.0	5.7	8.5	6.5	8.0
California	16.3	19.0	12.6	18.5	22.0	24.1
Florida	16.1	22.0	9.2	14.4	13.4	15.0
Illinois	30.9	39.6	14.2	21.8	11.6	13.5
Michigan	6.4	7.7	4.2	6.8	3.3	3.7
Minnesota	7.6	10.9	3.7	7.7	2.7	3.5
New Jersey	11.1	15.2	9.4	14.0	13.0	15.8
New York	11.3	15.0	15.0	20.2	14.6	16.2
North Carolina	15.0	17.1	15.0	19.8	19.1	21.5
Ohio	44.9	57.9	17.5	27.9	19.8	22.8
Oregon	23.0	30.7	6.2	10.0	20.5	23.8
Texas	9.9	12.9	3.7	6.0	5.5	6.5
Virginia	5.9	6.9	7.0	9.9	8.5	9.6
TOTAL	**15.6**	**19.5**	**10.1**	**15.3**	**15.5**	**17.5**

Note: State arrests are 1994–1995 average. Totals are population-adjusted percentages.

Source: Rearrest data from Bureau of Justice Statistics. State arrests from Uniform Crime Reports, Illinois Criminal Justice Information Authority, and Florida Department of Law Enforcement.

accounts for somewhat more of the trend. From 1994 to 2000 in our sample of states, the size of prison release cohorts grew by 23 percent, whereas aggregate violent and property arrest rates declined by 30 percent.[8]

An argument can be made that focusing only on arrest levels of those released from prison in the past year underestimates the role of ex-prisoners in crime trends, because released prisoners continue to produce arrests beyond their first year of release. Using the second- and third-year arrest rates derived from the BJS study, we can estimate the cumulative effect on 1994–1995 state crime rates of three successive cohorts of released prisoners. To do this, we must assume that prisoners released in 1992 have the same arrest rates during their third year of release (i.e., 1994–1995) as the 1994 cohort during its third year of release and that those released in 1993 have the same arrest rates during their second year of release as the 1994 cohort during its second year since leaving prison. By applying these

[8] We exclude 2001 from the present discussion because that year showed a slight uptick in arrests rates for violent and property crimes. We are also excluding drug crime here because, as discussed above, it did not decline over the period.

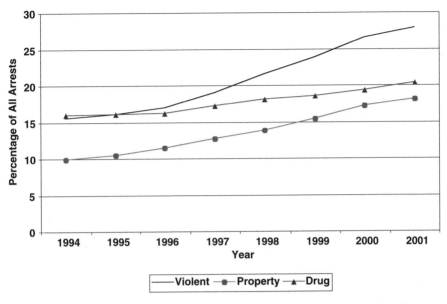

Figure 4.2 Released Prisoners' Estimated Share of Total Arrests, 1994–2001: Released within 3 Years

rates to the release cohorts for 1992, 1993, and 1994, we can estimate the cumulative effect of 3 years of successive prison releases on state crime rates during a single year.[9] The results of this exercise are presented in Table 4.3.

Three successive cohorts of released prisoners have a sizable effect on the crime rates of the states to which they return. Between 10 percent and 16 percent of all arrests for violent, property, and drug crimes in the 13 states during 1994–1995 are accounted for by prisoners released during the previous 3 years. As expected, released prisoners contribute a larger percentage, about 15 percent to 20 percent, of the arrests among adults. In California, ex-prisoners account for nearly one-quarter of all arrests for drug crimes and 16 percent of all violence arrests. In Ohio, ex-prisoners account for roughly 45 percent of all violence arrests. By sharp contrast, even three successive cohorts of released prisoners make only a small cumulative contribution to arrests in Michigan and Minnesota.

As with the 1-year analysis, we can look beyond 1994–1995 to construct a picture of recent yearly changes in the relative importance of ex-prisoner recidivism in overall crime. As Figure 4.2 indicates (and as would

[9] Data on the size of state prison release cohorts are from Harrison (2000) and Rice and Harrison (2000).

be expected from the 1-year analysis), the contribution of recently released prisoners grew steadily over the years of the crime decline, reaching nearly 30 percent of the arrests for violent crime, 18 percent for property, and 20 percent for drugs.

These results arguably are more relevant to public concerns about the crimes committed by ex-prisoners than those limited to the first year of release. They suggest that such concerns are not wholly unrealistic. Released prisoners do make a difference in a community's crime problem, even if they cannot be held directly responsible for most serious crimes. The difference ex-prisoners make is a function of their elevated levels of offending. During periods of declining general crime rates or growing release cohorts, their relative contribution rises. We now turn to an assessment of the characteristics of released prisoners and conditions of their release that are associated with their rate of reoffending, as measured, again, by arrests.

The Correlates of Recidivism

Prior research has consistently shown that three attributes of ex-prisoners are associated with higher rates of recidivism, whether measured by violations of the conditions of release, arrests for new crimes, or returns to prison: age, imprisonment offense, and prior record. Younger persons, property offenders, and those with longer criminal records have higher rates of recidivism than older persons, those sentenced to prison for a violent crime, and those with fewer prior arrests or convictions (Petersilia 2002). More limited evidence suggests that participation in prison programs reduces recidivism (Petersilia 2002, p. 491). Our assessment of arrest recidivism includes the first three factors. We do not have adequate data from the BJS study to reliably measure the effects of participation in rehabilitation programs on recidivism rates.[10] However, we are able to examine more fully the effects on recidivism of the single most widespread postrelease "program": supervision of released prisoners in the community.

Table 4.4 presents estimates of the effects on rearrests over 3 years of several characteristics of prisoners and conditions of release, including sex, race, and age of released prisoners; imprisonment offense (violent, property,

---

[10] Only a few states reported data on participation in education, vocational, alcohol, or drug rehabilitation programs, and among those with data on program participation or completion, large fractions of cases were coded as "unknown."

The Contribution of Ex-Prisoners to Crime Rates

Table 4.4. *Percentage Change in 3-Year Rearrests Associated with Prisoner Demographics, Conviction Offense, History, and Type of Release*[a]

	Violent	Property	Drug
Prisoner demographics			
Male	101**	11	15
Black	72***	39***	36
Age	−5***	−2**	−3***
Imprisonment offense[b]			
Violent	31***	2	−11*
Property	−7	126***	1
Drug	−22***	−15*	72***
History			
Prior Arrests	3***	4***	4***
Time Served	0*	0	0
First Release	−25***	−18***	−22***
Release type[c]			
Parole Release	−36***	−31***	−17*
Mandatory Supervised	−19	−19*	6
Other Release Type	−35**	−44*	−11
State fixed effects[d]			
Arizona	−51***	14***	−45***
California	35*	−35***	−5
Florida	103***	−4	−22***
Illinois	121***	24**	−30***
Michigan	−2	−50***	−75***
Minnesota	10	3	−69***
New York	43***	34***	22***
North Carolina	−10	−21***	−52***
Ohio	58***	−31***	−53***
Oregon	66***	8	18
Texas	12	−37***	−60***
Virginia	−57***	−26***	−57***
Log Likelihood	−141992	−180709	−206533

[a] Standard errors adjusted for clustering within states.
[b] Contrast is public order and other crimes.
[c] Contrast is unconditional release.
[d] Contrast is New Jersey.
*** $p < .001$, ** $p < .01$, * $p < .05$.

drug);[11] number of prior arrests, time (months) served in prison under the current sentence; whether the release is the first release under the current sentence; and type of release (parole, mandatory supervised release, and other release type). Also shown are the "fixed effects" of the 13 states, which capture sources of between-state variation in rearrests not associated with the other covariates in the model (New Jersey is the contrast state).

Table 4.4 shows the percentage change in the number of arrests accumulated by ex-prisoners 3 years postrelease associated with a one-unit change in a given predictor, holding constant the other variables in the model. For example, rearrests for violent crime are reduced by about 5 percent for each additional year of age and increased by about 3 percent for each additional prior arrest. Both of these effects are highly significant ($p < .001$). In the case of categorical predictor variables, such as type of release, the figures in the table indicate the percentage increase or decrease in the outcome variable associated with a given category compared to the outcome value associated with the category used as the contrast in the model. For example, controlling for other variables in the model, males accumulate twice as many rearrests for violent crimes as females.[12]

Younger ex-prisoners have a higher incidence of arrest for property and drug crimes, in addition to violent crimes. Black ex-prisoners are rearrested more often than whites for all three crime types, although the race effect is only marginally significant for drug crimes ($p < .10$). Males are arrested significantly more often than females for violent crimes, but not for property or drug crimes, holding constant the other variables in the model. Our analysis shows evidence of crime-type specialization, with violent offenders rearrested more often for violent offenses, property offenders more often for property crimes, and drug offenders more often for drug crimes. This result is consistent with the findings of Langan and Levin (2002). In light of the dramatic growth in the incarceration of drug offenders over the past two decades (Blumstein and Beck 1999), it is noteworthy that persons imprisoned for drug crimes have significantly lower rearrest rates for violent and property crimes than those imprisoned for public order and other offenses (the contrast). These results are supportive of criticisms of sentencing

---

[11] We substituted a conviction offense typology consisting of 26 crime types for the aggregate violent/property/drug/other classification in this analysis, and found no substantively important differences in results.

[12] The percentage change scores reported in the table were derived by exponentiating the coefficients from the negative binomial model, subtracting 1, and multiplying the result by 100.

policies that focus on drug offenders for purposes of more general crime control (Boyum and Kleiman 2002).

The number of prior arrests significantly increases rearrests for all three crime types. By contrast, the number of months served in prison under the current sentence is not significantly associated with the incidence of rearrest.[13] This result, also obtained by Langan and Levin (2002), carries an important policy implication: Reducing time served in prison evidently would not elevate recidivism, as measured by arrests for new crimes. (However, increasing the length of time served, by reducing the number of released prisoners at any given time, other things equal, would reduce the *aggregate impact* of released prisoners on community crime rates.[14])

Those individuals for whom release from prison in 1994 was their first release under the current sentence have significantly fewer rearrests than those who had been released from prison prior to 1994 under the current sentence, reincarcerated, and released again in 1994. This is an interesting result and not easy to explain given the fact that age and prior arrests are included as predictors in the models. It implies that prior *recidivism* as distinct from prior arrests (or prior incarceration; see note 11) influences subsequent arrests. If many persons were returned to prison under the current sentence on a technical violation of their terms of supervision in the community rather than for an arrest on a new charge, which seems likely because they were reincarcerated under the current rather than a new sentence, then this result could reflect an association between the frequency of technical violations and the frequency of arrests. Persons with multiple releases from prison under a single sentence evidently fare less well under community supervision than those released for the first time (see Piehl, this volume). Therefore, it is important to include an indicator of first versus multiple releases in any analysis concerned with the effects on recidivism of type of release to the community.

Discretionary parole release has a consistent and strong effect on the incidence of rearrest in our sample, especially for violent and property offenses. Prisoners released on discretionary parole accumulate 36 percent fewer arrests for violent crime than those released unconditionally with

---

[13] We also included a squared term to test for a non-linear relationship between time served in prison and recidivism. We found no substantive difference in the results from those reported here and dropped the term from the equations.

[14] We also included a measure of prior incarceration in our rearrest models. It is highly correlated with prior arrests and has little independent influence on recidivism. Therefore, it has been excluded from the models discussed here.

no supervision in the community (the contrast category). Discretionary parole release is associated with 30 percent fewer arrests for property crime and 17 percent fewer arrests for drug crime during the 3-year observation period. Mandatory supervised release (community supervision without discretionary release) is associated with a lower incidence of arrests only for property crime. Compared with unconditional release, the effect of mandatory supervision is not significant for violent or drug crime. Finally, the "other release type" category, which includes prisoners released to halfway houses, boot camps, and other facilities, is associated with a sizable and significant reduction in arrests for violent and property crime, but has no significant effect on drug arrests.

The final set of covariates presented in Table 4.4 are the so-called fixed effects of factors that vary across the states but have not been specifically included in the model. Fixed effects can be interpreted as sources of between-state variation in recidivism that remain when compositional differences in sex, race, age, prior arrests, time served, and conditions of release are held constant. Prisoners released to Arizona, for example, have a significantly lower incidence of rearrest for violent crime, and significantly higher incidence of rearrest for drug crime, than those released to New Jersey (the contrast in the equation), controlling for their demographic characteristics, imprisonment offense, history, and release type. Of course, adding the state variable does not complete the list of plausible predictors of recidivism. The state effects do not capture the influence on recidivism of other characteristics of released prisoners, not included in the model, that vary *within* states (e.g., employment status, family attachments, or social services).

Although in principle the unmeasured sources of between-state heterogeneity in recidivism are accounted for by the fixed effects in the model, the differences in state policies or other conditions represented by those effects remain to be determined. One such condition may be the crime rate in the state. If prisoners returning to states with high crime rates are subject to the conditions that produce those rates, other things equal, they will have higher recidivism rates than those who return to low-crime states. To examine this possibility, we included in the models shown in Table 4.4 the 1994–1997 average violent and property crime rates for each releasee's state of release. Doing so reduces the state fixed effects, on average, by about 25 percent for violent and property crime, and in some instances for drug crime (results not shown). Nonetheless, significant state effects remain even after entering the state crime rates, indicating that other differences across the states also are associated with the incidence of rearrest among released prisoners. Such conditions may include state policies governing the release and subsequent supervision of ex-prisoners in the community.

A Closer Look at Type of Release

The vast majority of prisoners released in 1994 in the 13 states in our sample experienced some level or form of supervision in the community. About one third of the prisoners were released on discretionary parole, and well over half were subject to mandatory supervised release. Only 7 percent of the sample were released unconditionally.[15] The percentage of prisoners released unconditionally is quite a bit lower in our sample than in other states at about the same time. Roughly 16 percent of prisoners nationwide were released unconditionally in 1995, and that figure grew to 22 percent by 1998 (Beck 2000). Between 1990 and 1999, the percentage of prisoners released under discretionary parole supervision dropped from 39 percent to 24 percent (Bureau of Justice Statistics 2003). As the fraction of prisoners released without supervision in the community continues to grow, it is important to know what effect this may have on public safety. We can use our models of recidivism to shed some light on this question.

Consider the following policy experiment. Suppose we were to shift 10 percent of the prisoners in our sample who would have been released on discretionary parole to the category of unconditional release. What effect would this have on the overall incidence of rearrest? What if we were to move 25 percent or 50 percent of the prisoners from parole to unconditional release? We provide the results of this exercise in Table 4.5.

These results were obtained by reducing the number of prisoners released on discretionary parole by a specified percentage and increasing the number of prisoners in the unconditional release category by the number of persons removed from parole. All other variables in the models were set to their mean values. The results show that a 10% shift in prisoners from discretionary parole to unconditional release would produce small increases in the percentage of rearrests. Naturally, the effects of this policy experiment become more pronounced as the ratio of unconditional releases to discretionary parolees increases. Were one half of those subject to discretionary parole in our sample released unconditionally, arrests for violent

---

[15] The remainder of releasees were subject to "other" release. These prisoners comprise about 3% of the sample and are concentrated in just two states, New York and Texas.

Table 4.5. *Percentage Increase in Rearrests from Hypothetical Shifts of Prisoners from Parole to Unconditional and Mandatory Supervised Release*

	Violent	Property	Drug
From parole to unconditional release			
10%	1.6	1.5	0.8
25%	4.1	3.7	2.1
50%	8.4	7.5	4.2
100%	17.6	15.6	8.6
From parole to mandatory supervised release			
10%	0.9	1.0	0.9
25%	2.2	1.6	2.4
50%	4.5	3.2	4.8
100%	9.2	6.5	9.8

Note. All results significant at $p < .05$ except parole to mandatory supervised release for violent crime ($p = .08$).

crimes would increase by just over 8 percent, arrests for property crimes would increase by almost 8 percent, and drug arrests would increase by roughly 4 percent. Under the increasingly common case of a state's abolition of discretionary parole,[16] appreciable increases in recidivism would occur, especially for violent and property crime.

The hypothetical substitution of unconditional for discretionary parole release is not the only policy experiment we can perform with the BJS data. It also is worth examining the effects of shifting discretionary parolees to the condition of mandatory supervised release. This option is increasingly favored by policymakers who want to retain supervision of ex-prisoners in the community but are concerned with the discretionary biases inherent in the decision to grant parole, doubt that parole authorities are able accurately to predict success, or believe (mistakenly – see Hughes, Wilson, and Beck 2001, p. 7) that elimination of discretionary parole will increase time served in prison. The results of shifting prisoners from discretionary parole to mandatory supervised release are presented in the bottom panel of Table 4.5. The effects of this experiment are smaller than those we observed when parole is replaced by unconditional release, except for drug arrests, in which case they are slightly larger. The effects for violent arrests are only marginally significant ($p = .08$) and should be viewed with caution.

---

[16] By 2002, 15 states had abolished discretionary parole release for all prisoners (Bureau of Justice Statistics 2003).

In general, the results in Table 4.5 lend support to the continued use of discretionary parole release for purposes of reducing recidivism. Parolees not only fare somewhat better than prisoners released without supervision, they also accumulate significantly fewer arrests (for property and drug crimes) than those ex-prisoners who are released mandatorily after a specified term and then supervised in the community.

It might be objected that crediting one release system (discretionary parole) with a reduction in arrest rates compared to another release system (mandatory release) fails to recognize that prisoners granted release by a parole board are chosen precisely because they are assessed to have relatively good prospects for success. According to this argument, comparing such a regime with one in which prisoners are released after serving a prescribed fraction of their sentence, without regard to readiness, may be unsound, because the comparison is not of systems that differ in their release mechanism but of groups of prisoners differing in their propensity to recidivate (see Piehl, this volume).

We believe that this criticism of system comparisons, which invokes the differing bases for release, actually supports the validity of such comparisons. Prisoners in a discretionary regime are filtered for release, whereas those in a mandatory regime are not. Under discretion, prisoners deemed ill prepared for success will be kept in prison, in some cases as long as their maximum sentence. This may account for the finding that time served in discretionary systems is greater than in mandatory systems (Hughes et al. 2001, p. 7). If parole boards are reasonably competent, release cohorts from the former should contain proportionately more "better bets" (prisoners with lower expected risk of recidivism) than those from the latter, which will be a relatively heterogeneous mix of good and poor prospects. The results of our comparison are consonant with this reasoning. They suggest that the selection of better bets associated with parole decision making reduces recidivism beyond the reductions associated with community supervision alone.

The "Net" Impact of Incarceration on Crime Rates

We can use the BJS recidivism data to perform a final policy exercise relevant to the question of incarceration and public safety. Thus far, our analyses have been one sided in their exclusive attention to the effect of *released* prisoners on crime rates. However, as discussed at the beginning of this chapter, community safety is also affected by the crimes averted through prison *admissions*. If we assume that the aggregate characteristics of persons admitted to prison during a given time period are the same as those who are released during that period, we can estimate the net impact of both processes on arrests for violent, property, and drug crimes in our sample of 13 states.

This simplifying assumption carries with it at least two sources of possible error, which are to some extent counterbalancing. On the one hand, as states have toughened their response to crime over the past two decades, an increasing proportion of convicted offenders are sent to prison rather than probation, especially for drug offenses. That could mean that persons entering prison have shorter and less serious criminal records than those leaving prison, with correspondingly lower recidivism rates. On the other hand, in light of the growing fraction of prison admissions represented by persons who are returned to prison for violating the technical conditions of their release or for committing a new crime (Blumstein and Beck 1999), we would expect the recidivism rates of persons entering and leaving prison to converge. Both types of error should be kept in mind when considering the results of this policy experiment.

The exercise is straightforward: We apply our sample's rearrest probabilities for the first, second, and third years to the difference between the number of persons leaving and entering prison during 1992, 1993, and 1994 to obtain estimates of the cumulative impact of that difference on state arrest levels for 1994–1995. (This procedure is analogous to our earlier estimate of the proportion of crime in 1994–1995 attributable to prisoners released in 1992, 1993, and 1994.) Roughly 126,000 more persons entered than were released from prison in the 13 states in our sample in 1992, 1993, and 1994. Had they remained on the street, in 1994–1995 they would have been arrested for an estimated 10,900 violent crimes, 17,110 property crimes, and 20,450 drug crimes. Those arrests, in turn, would have increased overall violent, property, and drug arrests in the 13 states by 1 percent to 2 percent.

The gap between prison admissions and releases has been shrinking over time. By 2000, only about 60 more persons entered than were released from prison in our sample. Every 100 persons leaving or entering prison will add or subtract about 25 violent crimes, 39 property crimes, and 47 drug crimes in their community over the next 3 years, based on the 3-year arrest probabilities of the 1994 release cohort. The growth in the U.S. prison population has slowed to a rate not seen since the early 1970s (Harrison and Beck 2002). Absent an abrupt reversal in this trend, the nation will soon see more prisoners returning from than entering its prisons – several

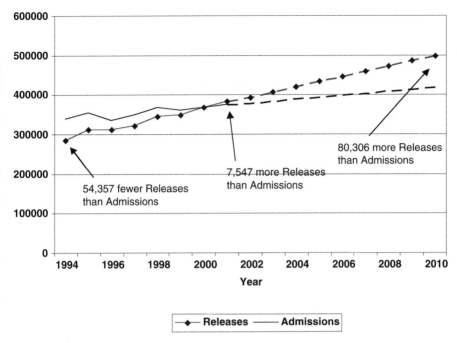

Figure 4.3 Prison Admissions and Releases, 1994–2001, and Estimates to 2010

states already have. All else equal, the net growth in prisoners released to the community will result in higher crime rates.

Figure 4.3 portrays the changing balance of prison admissions and releases in our sample of 13 states from 1994 to 2001, the most recent year for which these data were available. The figure shows a declining ratio of admissions to releases until the year 2000, when the two trend lines converge and after which releases begin to exceed admissions. In 2001, 7,547 more persons were released from than entered prison in the 13 states. Figure 4.3 also shows an extrapolation of the admission and release trends to the year 2010. Assuming no change in those trends after 2001, 80,306 more persons will be leaving prison and returning to the community than entering prison by 2010. At the 3-year rearrest rates of the 1994 release cohort, those persons will add about 20,240 violent, 31,100 property, and 37,610 drug crimes to the 13 states in which they are released. It is important to keep in mind that these projections are "net" estimates; that is, they take into account those crimes that would have been committed by offenders entering prison had they remained free.

101

Conclusion

The message of this chapter should be clear enough. The nation faces a growing threat to public safety not simply from the escalating number of ex-prisoners reentering the community but from the growing ratio of persons exiting to those entering prison. How much the net increase in prisoners coming home will contribute to community crime rates depends on a number of factors, many of which can be influenced by policymakers. Faced with the growing negative balance between admissions and releases, policymakers could reverse the trends by lengthening sentences and time served in prison, thereby reducing the outflow of prisoners to the community, and continuing to toughen mandatory minimum and "three-strikes" sentences, thereby increasing the inflow. Although such policies might well reduce crime rates in the short run, or at any rate ex-prisoners' share of crime, they would also increase the costs of imprisonment to already over-stretched state budgets and probably result in reductions in expenditures for family therapy, life-skills training for adolescents, mentoring, and other programs of proven effectiveness in reducing delinquency and crime (see Rosenfeld 2002; Wilson and Petersilia 2002).

In principle it is possible to both maintain a high and growing incarceration rate and provide needed services and treatments to persons and populations at risk for crime and related problems – including ex-prisoners. But the record of the past decade suggests that the required combination of political will and fiscal largess is exceedingly difficult to achieve in practice. Moreover, given evidence that high levels of "churning" of returning and exiting prisoners may further diminish the social capital of those communities hit hardest by escalating imprisonment, the balancing act of reducing prison releases while increasing admissions could result in higher crime rates in the long run (see Clear, Waring, and Scully, present volume).

Rather, the record shows a new willingness on the part of policymakers confronting massive shortfalls in state budgets to rethink the sentencing practices that have contributed to an escalation in incarceration even during a period of declining crime. Several states have been experimenting with early release for prisoners who have committed lesser felonies (Levitan 2003). If such efforts continue, they will of course add to the flow of prisoners back to streets, but they also will free up resources that could be used to address the needs of ex-prisoners, their families, and their communities. Other chapters in this volume describe those needs and evaluate the costs of meeting them. To reduce the risk to public safety posed by released prisoners, evidence presented in this chapter supports the expanded use of discretionary parole supervision in the community. Even the small relative reductions in crime associated with discretionary release and community supervision will save lives, reduce injury, and protect property.

References

Axtman, K. 2002. "A Flood of Parolees Hits Streets." *Christian Science Monitor* 95: 1.

Beck, Allen J. 2000, April. *State and Federal Prisoners Returning to the Community: Findings from the Bureau of Justice Statistics*. Paper presented at the First Reentry Courts Initiative Cluster Meeting, Washington, DC.

Beck, Allen J., and Bernard E. Shipley. 1989. *Recidivism of Prisoners Released in 1983*. Washington, DC: U.S. Department of Justice.

Blumstein, Alfred, and Allen J. Beck. 1999. "Population Growth in U.S. Prisons: 1980–1996," M. Tonry and J. Petersilia, eds., *Crime and Justice: A Review of Research*, vol. 26, pp. 17–62. Chicago: University of Chicago Press.

Blumstein, Alfred, and Jacqueline Cohen. 1979. "Estimation of Individual Crime Rates from Arrest Records." *Journal of Criminal Law and Criminology* 70: 561–585.

Blumstein, Alfred, and Elizabeth Graddy. 1982. "Prevalence and Recidivism in Index Arrests: A Feedback Model Approach." *Law and Society Review* 16: 265–290.

Blumstein, Alfred, and Joel Wallman, eds. 2000. *The Crime Drop in America*. New York: Cambridge University Press.

Boyum, David A., and Mark A. R. Kleiman. 2002. "Substance Abuse Policy from a Crime-Control Perspective," J. Q. Wilson and J. Petersilia, eds., *Crime: Public Policies for Crime Control*, pp. 331–382. Oakland, CA: ICS Press.

Bureau of Justice Statistics. 2000. *Correctional Populations in the United States, 1997*. Washington, DC: U.S. Department of Justice.

Bureau of Justice Statistics. 2003. *Probation and Parole Statistics*. http://www.ojp.usdoj.gov/bjs/pandp.htm, accessed June 27, 2003.

Harrison, Paige. 2000. *Sentenced Prisoners Released from State or Federal Jurisdiction*. Bureau of Justice Statistics, National Prisoner Statistics (NPS-1). http://www.ojp.usdoj.gov/bjs/dtdata.htm#corrections, accessed May 2, 2003.

Harrison, Paige, and Allen J. Beck. 2002. *Prisoners in 2001*. Washington, DC: U.S. Department of Justice.

Hughes, Timothy A., Doris James Wilson. 2003. Reentry Trends in the United States. http://www.ojp.usdoj.gov/bjs/reentry/reentry.htm, accessed June 23, 2003.

Hughes, Timothy A., Doris James Wilson, and Allen J. Beck. 2001. *Trends in State Parole, 1990–2000*. Washington, DC: U.S. Department of Justice.

Langan, Patrick A., and David J. Levin. 2002. *Recidivism of Prisoners Released in 1994*. Washington, DC: U.S. Department of Justice.

Landsberg, M., and O. Casillas. 2000. "No Simple Explanation for Jump in L. A. Murder Rate." *Los Angeles Times* December 1: A1.

Levitan, Benjamin. 2003. "The Cost of Justice." *Columbia Political Review.* http://www.columbiapoliticalreview.com/article004.shtml, accessed March 14, 2003.

Long, J. Scott. 1997. *Regression Models for Categorical and Limited Dependent Variables.* Thousand Oaks, CA: Sage.

Lynch, James P., and William J. Sabol. 2001. *Prisoner Reentry in Perspective.* Washington, DC: Urban Institute.

Petersilia, Joan. 2002. "Community Corrections," J. Q. Wilson and J. Petersilia, eds., *Crime: Public Policies for Crime Control,* pp. 483–508. Oakland, CA: ICS Press.

Petersilia, Joan, and Susan Turner. 1993. "Intensive Probation and Parole," Michael Tonry, ed., *Crime and Justice: An Annual Review of Research,* pp. 281–335. Chicago: University of Chicago Press.

Rashbaum, W. 2002. "Falling Crime in New York Defies Trend." *New York Times* November 29: B1.

Rice, Coliece, and Paige Harrison. 2000. *Sentenced Prisoners Admitted to State or Federal Jurisdiction.* Washington, DC: Bureau of Justice Statistics, National Prisoner Statistics (NPS-1). http://www.ojp.usdoj.gov/bjs/dtdata.htm#corrections. accessed May 2, 2003.

Ripley, A. 2002. "Outside the Gates." *Time Magazine* January 21: 56–63.

Rosenfeld, Richard. 2002. "The Limits of Crime Control." *Journal of Criminal Law and Criminology* 93: 289–298.

Travis, Jeremy, Amy L. Solomon, and Michelle Waul. 2001. *From Prison to Home: The Dimensions and Consequences of Prisoner Reentry.* Washington, DC: Urban Institute.

Wilson, James Q., and Joan Petersilia. 2002. *Crime: Public Policies for Crime Control.* Oakland, CA: ICS Press.

5

Does Supervision Matter?

Anne Morrison Piehl and Stefan F. LoBuglio

The answer to the question, "Does supervision matter?" is central for designing postincarceration policy for those released from prison. Knowing how much supervision can help and which elements of supervision are efficacious could lead to better outcomes for communities and for recent inmates. The improvement could take the form of reduced criminal offending, the particular emphasis of this book, or other benefits such as reduced substance abuse or better employment outcomes.

Before attempting to answer the question posed by the title of this chapter, it is helpful to be more precise. What do we mean by *supervision*? This term generally refers to the structured monitoring and support by law enforcement following release from prison, such as "parole supervision." Even if the term *parole* has ever been sufficient to describe the various state practices for monitoring ex-inmates in the community, it certainly is not sufficient now.[1] Depending on the state, postincarceration supervision can be provided by parole departments (some of which fall under departments of correction), probation departments, other entities, or some combination of these. The status of being supervised in the community may be the result of a decision by a parole board to offer conditional release for the remainder of the sentence or it may result from the original sentence from the court.

The authors wish to acknowledge the excellent research assistance of Steven Kapsos and Beau Kilmer, the provision of national prisoner data by Timothy Hughes, and the helpful reviews of this chapter by Jeremy Travis and the book's other contributors. Please address correspondence to Anne Piehl, 79 JFK Street, Cambridge MA 02138, *anne_piehl@harvard.edu*.

[1] See Sutherland (1924) for a discussion of how parole operated early in the 20th century, when many states shifted toward indeterminate sentencing.

The latter is generally referred to as "mandatory supervision." Those states that "abolished parole" have by and large replaced it with some other form of community supervision, lending yet another dimension of complexity to the nomenclature. Across the United States, requirements for those under community supervision include a mix of elements, often crafted for individual offenders. The requirements generally include some of the following: curfew, employment or job search, testing for alcohol and other drug use, periodic meetings with a parole (or other name) officer or agent, enrollment in mandated treatment programs, and restrictions on certain types of activities, such as congregating with other felons.

States vary in the way they organize postincarceration supervision, and they also vary in the extent to which they do it. Some states leave many released from prison unsupervised, whereas others require supervision of nearly all of those released. For some ex-inmates, terms under supervision may be decades long; for others, only a few months. Also, what constitutes supervision at any given point is subject to interpretation. Intensive supervision in one state may mean monthly contact between a parolee and an agent in a regional parole office; in another, it may mean 24-hour electronic monitoring with officers in the field checking compliance with daily itineraries. Ideally, a continuum of supervision sanctions exists to account for the different risks and needs presented by released inmates and to allow for progressive sanctioning for offenders in noncompliance with their terms of conditional release, so-called intermediate sanctions. We will discuss the great variety in supervision in more detail below.

Now that we have introduced the meaning of supervision, how will we judge whether it "matters?" In the spirit of this volume, we consider the role of supervision in promoting public safety. Does postincarceration supervision lead to a lower crime rate than no supervision? Does supervision lead to lower rates of recidivism? Supervision might have an advantageous effect on crime through extensive use of incarceration as a punishment to back up the conditions of supervision. Because of this, and the tremendous cost of incarceration, the efficacy of supervision depends on how supervision impacts the prison population. For the purposes of this chapter, the cost of incarceration resulting from supervision is another way that supervision can "matter." This is particularly relevant now that states, facing historic fiscal crises, are being reminded that correctional resources are finite.

How Should Supervision Improve Public Safety?

In theory, postincarceration supervision serves two goals. First, it should help offenders make the very difficult transition from secure confinement to independent living in the community. Second, early detection of noncompliance with the conditional terms of release combined with swift sanctioning may prevent individuals from committing more serious offenses. Supervision can provide the structure and incentives necessary to keep people newly released from prison focused on the activities that will give them the greatest chance of remaining crime free and, as a result, from returning to prison or jail. Parole officers may support those under their supervision by referring them to needed treatment and education programs, and may serve as intermediaries in helping them navigate complicated social service systems and in securing employment.

Over recent decades, the profession has moved from social service to largely surveillance (Lynch and Sabol 2001; Petersilia 2003), although finding the right balance between supervising agents' emphasis on assistance and on control has long been an issue of inquiry (Glaser 1964). People often discuss the support functions for ex-offenders as qualitatively distinct from the surveillance functions. For example, a parole division organized around the goal of providing support may have hiring practices and employment conditions that differ from those in a division organized around surveillance. But it may not be productive to draw a strict dichotomy between support and surveillance.[2] The threat of surveillance can be an aid to compliance with activities to support the transition such as substance-abuse programming and employment assistance. Likewise, the support activities can provide the structure and meaning to day-to-day life that allows people to avoid the situations in which they tend to get in trouble. In one sense, these activities can be "incapacitating." Inmates who choose to waive parole often explain that it is easier for them to do prison time than meet the requirements of parole.

The surveillance function of supervision may directly enhance public safety by deterring and detecting criminal activity. Even by sanctioning technical violations, parole agents may preempt more serious criminal

---

[2] One of the more compelling aspects of the Boston strategy against youth violence in the 1990s was the blurring of support and surveillance functions, both within and across agencies (Kennedy, Braga and Piehl 2001).

offending. The "Broken Windows" philosophy would argue that paying attention to the smaller indicators of disorder in the long run will provide a greater public safety payoff (Wilson and Kelling 1982; Kelling and Coles 1996). In this light, the revocation of the conditional terms of release for a large number of recent inmates, who increasingly comprise a larger percentage of new commitments to prison, may be a desired outcome. It is important to note that this perspective, claiming large gains to enforcement of small infractions, is controversial (Heymann 2000). In fact, as will be outlined and assessed below, there is little detailed, direct evidence on how much crime is averted by enforcement of violations of technical conditions.

If supervision is efficacious, clearly it is possible to have too little of it. Increasing its intensity, expanding its reach to more ex-offenders, or extending the length of terms could be called for. Some argue that funding for supervision relative to the number of inmates being released from incarceration has declined dramatically over the past 30 years, but it is hard to come by expenditure information detailed enough to make precise calculations.[3]

Less frequently discussed is the possibility of providing too much supervision, which could happen in several ways. Some people are very unlikely to reoffend after a term in prison, and supervising them can needlessly use social resources. Another way to oversupervise is to have so many requirements that they get in the way of obtaining or retaining employment, actually impeding successful reentry.[4] Finally, supervision conditions require that noncompliance be sanctioned, but there may not be sufficient availability of intermediate sanctions to allow punishment of modest infractions. In this case, the choice may be between revocation to prison and no punishment, both of which have substantial drawbacks. The impossibility of sanctioning for violations of multiple requirements may engender a disregard for any one of them.

If there is no strict trade-off between treatment and surveillance, then it is hard to set a rigid protocol for a parole officer to follow. Rather, the precise

---

[3] The numbers behind the observation in Petersilia (1999) are dated, and based on an article by Patrick Langan published in 1994 and covering the period 1977 to 1990 (Langan 1994). Calculations from the Justice Employment and Expenditure series collected by the Bureau of Justice Statistics show that noninstitutional spending was 20 percent of all spending on corrections in 1980 and 18 percent in 1999. Excluding capital expenditures, the percentages are 22 and 19, respectively (U.S. Department of Justice 2003, Table 10).

[4] There is anecdotal evidence that meetings with parole officers and drug testing can get in the way of maintaining employment, but no broad-based survey measures how frequently it occurs.

allocation of these elements must be a discretionary choice. Implementing this broadly may require reversing some of the changes made over the past 25 years. Reports of a National Institute of Corrections project to assist jurisdictions in developing more uniform and appropriate polices with regard to parole and probation violations provide some optimism that this can be accomplished (see Burke 1997). The lessons learned from these efforts include the need for collaboration and risk-sharing among correctional agencies; improved and uniform assessment procedures to more accurately determine offender risk and needs; effective, consistent, and timely processes between violations and dispositions; more widespread use of intermediate sanctions; and a greater focus of supervisory resources on the highest risk offender (Burke 1997).

None of this should be taken as suggesting that supervision is easy to provide or that, by itself, it will yield tremendous benefits for public safety. As indicated in the earlier chapter by Joan Petersilia, those released from prison have characteristics that are associated, not surprisingly, with poor success in the broader society. Recidivism rates are very high; nearly 50 percent of those released in 1994 were reconvicted for a new crime within 3 years of release (Langan and Levin 2002). And, as noted by Beck and Blumstein in this volume, the population under supervision is increasingly comprised of those who previously have been released and reincarcerated during the same criminal sentence. These facts represent challenges for any agency or agent providing post-incarceration supervision.

Facts about Supervision in the United States

Most prisoners released from correctional facilities receive some form of postrelease supervision, although the scale of those under supervision, the release decision-making processes, the supervising correctional agencies, and the supervision practices have changed significantly over time and vary widely from state to state. At year-end 2002, the number of adults on parole was 753,141. Although this number is high and represents a 2.8 percent increase from the previous year, it belies the tremendous flow of individuals entering and exiting parole and the 60 percent turnover of the census in the course of a year. The large number of released prisoners on parole reflects the growth of the prison population, but the growth has been smaller than the prison population's: whereas the state prison population increased fourfold between 1980 and 2000, reaching 1.2 million, the parole population little more than doubled during this same period. Furthermore, the share of supervised prison releases reached historically high levels in the last two decades of the 20th century (Travis and Lawrence 2002).

The Release Decision

Historically, discretionary parole served as the principal release mechanism by which prisoners left correctional facilities, accounting for 69 percent of state prison releasees in 1977. In a system that allows discretionary release, a parole board assesses an inmate's likelihood of reoffending by considering their criminal history, institutional conduct, remorse, and motivation to live law-abiding lives postrelease. For those inmates deemed to pose a minimal risk of reoffending, the board may choose to grant a parole date and allow them to leave prison to complete their original sentences under terms of conditional release spelled out by the board and monitored by parole officers in the field. In an era of indeterminate sentencing, the possibility of parole encouraged inmates to participate in prison-based education and treatment programs and also served to balance out disparities in sentences across offenders convicted of similar crimes (Petersilia 1999; Tonry 2000). Parole usually followed after actions by an institutional correctional agency to "step down" inmates to lower security and prerelease programs. Daniel Glaser's influential 1964 study titled "The Effectiveness of a Prison and Parole System" demonstrated the common understanding at the time that these correctional institutions and agencies operated together to form the prisoner reentry system (Glaser 1964).

From the late 1970s to the late 1990s, new "get tough" sentencing and correctional practices were ushered in that, in some states, led to diminished use of indeterminate sentences and institutional prerelease programs. Maine and Indiana abolished discretionary parole in 1975 and 1977 respectively. By the end of 2000, 16 states had abolished discretionary release and, with the exception of Maine and Virginia, introduced mandatory postrelease supervision (Hughes, Wilson, and Beck 2001). Among those states retaining discretionary release, many, including Texas, significantly curtailed its use (Petersilia 1999; Glaze 2002).

Federal legislation in 1994 tied funds for prison construction and expansion to the adoption of state truth-in-sentencing legislation, supporting states that require violent offenders to serve 85 percent of their nominal sentences.[5] It had its desired effect: by 1998, 27 states had such laws. Some

[5] The Violent Crime and Law Enforcement Act of 1994.

other states passed legislation that was similar in spirit but did not meet the federal threshold (because they chose different minimum sentence threshold percentages and/or applied them to a different set of offenses) (Ditton and Wilson 1999).

The shift from discretionary release to mandatory release has been dramatic. Of the 143,543 inmates serving sentences of more than 1 year leaving state prison in 1980, 55 percent left by a decision of a parole board, 19 percent received mandatory parole supervision, 6.5 percent were supervised by probation or another agency, and 14 percent were unconditionally released, almost always after completing the sentence. By 1999, the number of inmates serving sentences of more than 1 year leaving state prison had increased nearly fourfold to 542,950, and the respective percentages of those released on discretionary parole, mandatory parole, or to probation or another agency was 24 percent, 41 percent, and 12 percent, respectively, with 18 percent unconditionally released (Hughes et al. 2001).

Supervising Agencies

In addition to parole, probation now plays a substantial role in supervising adults following release from prison. An estimated 360,000 adults were supervised by probation following incarceration, which constituted 9 percent of the almost 4 million adults on probation at year-end 2002 (Glaze 2002).[6] This use of probation to provide postincarceration supervision represents a historical shift away from using probation chiefly as a sentencing alternative to prison. Increasingly, judges impose sentences to both incarceration and probation (known as a split sentence) to ensure a period of postrelease supervision for a convicted offender. Former prisoners may also face the remainder of a term of probation that was never completed before they were incarcerated on a different set of charges. Individuals within the correctional system have very complex legal issues and often do not follow

---

[6] It is hard to reconcile these figures with others on the use of probation for post-incarceration supervision. For example, among those released from prison, approximately 10 percent are listed as being conditionally released to probation (National Prisoner Statistics, unpublished data provide by the Bureau of Justice Statistics). These figures are starkly different from those calculated from the Annual Probation and Parole Surveys cited in the text. It is likely that the National Prisoner Statistics (NPS) miss some inmates with subsequent probation terms. In Massachusetts, for example, case studies of correctional populations reveal substantial post-incarceration probation (Piehl 2002; Massachusetts Executive Office of Public Safety 2003), yet the NPS reveals no people in this category (see Table 5.1 below).

an orderly and predictable movement from institutional to community correctional statuses, a fact that complicates providing services, describing the criminal justice process, and designing policy (Piehl 2002).

The result is that offenders may receive postrelease supervision from more than one agency. In Massachusetts, in a sample study of over 1,500 inmates released from July 2002 through January 2003 from the state department of corrections, 57 percent had postrelease terms of supervision. Of these, 20 percent were solely on parole, 27 percent were solely on probation, and 10 percent were both on parole and probation (Massachusetts Executive Office of Public Safety 2003). Including releases from county correctional facilities, the Massachusetts probation department supervises a far larger number of recent inmates than parole does, and the parole authority estimates that almost 25 percent of their offenders are also serving a term of probation.

Although it is possible that these offenders are receiving double the postrelease supervision and support,[7] agency practices can conflict and make it difficult for offenders to fully comply with the requirements imposed by both agencies. From a recent inmate's perspective, the conditional terms of release for probation and parole are often similar. The biggest differences between supervising agencies usually involve revocation processes and procedures, which are themselves influenced by whether the agency is organized within the executive agencies, under the control of the governor, or within the judiciary and under the control of judges.[8]

State Policies

Table 5.1 provides some indication of the varying scale and character of supervision across states.[9] Using year-end data from 2001, the first column reveals that five states – California, Texas, Pennsylvania, New York, and

---

[7] In rare cases, federal probation and parole can add yet another layer of supervision to state probation and parole.

[8] The courts have ruled that the processes for probation and parole violations must meet some level of due process and include certain safeguards. Morrisey v. Brewer (408 U.S. 471) in 1972 and Gagnon v. Scarpdi (411 U.S. 778) in 1973 govern violations processes for parolees and probationers, respectively.

[9] There is, of course, a federal jurisdiction for sentencing, incarcerating, and providing postincarceration supervision. In this chapter, we emphasize the 50 state jurisdictions that cover approximately 90 percent of both those on parole and those incarcerated in prisons. We exclude the District of Columbia from direct analysis due to its peculiar and changing relationship to the federal system.

Table 5.1. *Parole and Release Data by State, 2001*

	(1) Number of Parolees	(2) Total Released	(3) % Releases Unconditional	(4) % Releases Conditional	(5) % Releases Discretionary
Alabama	5,484	7,617	47.2%	52.8%	26.7%
Alaska	525	2,029	32.6%	67.4%	1.4%
Arizona	3,474	8,933	22.3%	77.7%	3.1%
Arkansas	8,659	6,515	11.3%	88.7%	74.0%
California	117,647	126,409	2.8%	97.2%	0%
Colorado	5,500	6,439	27.7%	72.3%	34.4%
Connecticut	1,868	6,007	53.8%	46.2%	23.0%
Delaware	579	2,019	74.2%	25.8%	0%
Florida	5,982	23,527	63.0%	37.0%	0.4%
Georgia	21,556	15,658	31.7%	68.3%	45.0%
Hawaii	2,504	1,187	13.7%	86.3%	84.9%
Idaho	1,409	2,521	18.5%	81.5%	37.2%
Illinois	30,196	35,980	18.2%	81.8%	0.1%
Indiana	4,917	11,771	10.7%	89.3%	0%
Iowa	2,763	4,786	19.0%	81.0%	46.7%
Kansas	3,829	4,243	26.5%	73.5%	70.4%
Kentucky	4,614	8,034	48.2%	51.8%	36.1%
Louisiana	22,860	14,851	6.5%	93.5%	8.5%
Maine	28	701	36.2%	63.8%	0.3%
Maryland	13,666	9,969	11.8%	88.2%	27.2%
Massachusetts	3,703	2,453	75.7%	24.3%	24.3%
Michigan	15,753	11,636	14.1%	85.9%	82.4%
Minnesota	3,072	4,237	10.9%	89.1%	0.1%
Mississippi	1,596	5,414	50.0%	50.0%	15.0%
Missouri	12,563	13,782	12.7%	87.3%	40.9%
Montana	621	1,226	21.2%	78.8%	40.9%
Nebraska	476	1,730	59.1%	40.9%	40.4%
Nevada	4,056	4,450	42.6%	57.4%	57.4%
New Hampshire	944	1,026	21.0%	79.0%	64.8%
New Jersey	11,709	15,839	33.8%	66.2%	61.5%
New Mexico	1,670	3,182	41.6%	58.4%	49.9%
New York	57,858	27,771	10.7%	89.3%	60.9%
North Carolina	3,352	8,827	62.8%	37.2%	0%
North Dakota	110	711	42.1%	57.9%	27.4%
Ohio	18,248	24,797	34.9%	65.1%	22.0%
Oklahoma	1,825	8,188	42.2%	57.8%	28.3%
Oregon	17,579	3,409	0.4%	99.6%	98.3%
Pennsylvania	82,345	10,083	30.9%	69.1%	69.1%

(continued)

Table 5.1 (*continued*)

	(1) Number of Parolees	(2) Total Released	(3) % Releases Unconditional	(4) % Releases Conditional	(5) % Releases Discretionary
Rhode Island	331	2,806	84.0%	16.0%	16.0%
South Carolina	4,378	8,335	42.2%	57.8%	36.8%
South Dakota	1,481	1,374	26.6%	73.4%	68.5%
Tennessee	8,093	12,631	32.0%	68.0%	25.6%
Texas	111,719	63,790	19.7%	80.3%	50.2%
Utah	3,231	3,137	18.2%	81.8%	81.8%
Vermont	867	1,065	17.6%	82.3%	36.3%
Virginia	5,148	9,743	71.6%	28.4%	7.4%
Washington	160	6,853	29.5%	70.5%	0.6%
West Virginia	1,112	1,121	55.8%	44.2%	44.2%
Wisconsin	9,923	6,979	9.7%	90.3%	26.8%
Wyoming	514	716	40.1%	59.9%	19.7%
Totals	**647,829**	**566,507**	**23%**	**77%**	**25.7%**

Sources: Column (1) "Probation and Parole in the United States, 2001," *Bureau of Justice Statistics* (2002). Columns (2)–(5): calculations from National Prisoner Statistics 2001, Bureau of Justice Statistics, Washington, DC (unpublished data).

Illinois – supervise over 60 percent of all parolees nationwide. Column (2) reports the number of inmates released from prison in 2001. In some cases the number of people released in a year exceeds the number on parole; in some cases it is far smaller. The discrepancy is accounted for by a combination of factors: the proportion of those released who have a term of parole (versus another form of supervision or none at all) and the speed at which parolees leave parole supervision by returning to prison or completing the term of supervision. Glancing down columns (3) and (4), it is obvious that states vary greatly in the extent to which inmates are released to supervisory authorities (mostly parole, but also probation and other programs). Tremendous state-level variation underlies all general characterizations of prison release in the United States. Column (5) shows the percentage of those released by a discretionary decision of a parole board, with the timing of release for the remainder having been determined by the sentence and any goodtime earned in the institution.[10]

[10] In order to see the potential scope for discretionary release, it would be useful to have a statistic that reflects the proportion of the prison population with the potential to be released by a parole board, not just the proportion that succeeds in obtaining release. We have not found any such numbers for any state.

Table 5.2 attempts to summarize the widely varying postrelease parole and supervision policies by state. This table indicates which states have truth-in-sentencing requirements and which have retained discretionary parole for sentences.[11] The last four columns describe the different ways states have chosen to organize postrelease supervision by branch and level of government. Whereas all of the states save Oregon and Pennsylvania place parole as an executive agency, 16 states have chosen to keep probation as an arm of the judiciary (generally at the local level). In four states, parole is also organized at the local level.

Probationary technical violations processed within the court system often require a judge to make a final dispositional decision. Significant delays can occur between the detection of a violation and the final judicial decision; months can elapse during which the offender may continue to commit violations without significant consequences. This problem has driven most states to place the probationary supervising responsibility under an executive agency. Executive supervising agencies typically can process violations more swiftly.

Finally, one cannot discuss state policies in 2003 without acknowledging the extremely challenging fiscal environment. The past several years have seen spending cuts and tax increases. The National Conference of State Legislatures (2003) reports that 39 states faced budget shortfalls at some point in the last year. Aggregate expenditure on corrections was nearly $50 billion in 1999, having doubled since 1990 (Gifford 2002), making it an obvious category to consider when looking for solutions to the budget problems. Certainly more than in recent memory, discussions about criminal justice policies are taking place in the context of concerns about fiscal responsibility (Campbell 2003). Any policy recommendations must take into account the current fiscal situation if there is to be any hope of adoption in the near term.

Evidence on the Relationship between Supervision and Public Safety

Whether postrelease supervision of recent inmates reduces the probability of criminal reoffending is largely unknown despite numerous studies of probation and parole programs. Ideally, to test this proposition, researchers would randomly assign a pool of soon-to-be released prisoners to either a

---

[11] The extent to which states practice discretionary parole can be seen in Table 5.1, column (5).

Table 5.2. *Parole and Probation Policies and Governing Institutions by State*

	Current Truth in Sentencing Requirement[1]	Year in Which State Abolished All Parole[2]	Whether State Abolished Parole for Violent Offenders[2]	Branch of Government Overseeing Parole Supervision[3]	Branch of Government Overseeing Probation Supervision[3]	State/Local Probation Supervision[3]	State/Local Parole Supervision[3]
Alabama	None			Executive	Executive	State	State
Alaska	Other			Executive	Executive	State	State
Arizona	85%	1994	X	Executive	Judicial	Local	State
Arkansas	Other			Executive	Executive	State	State
California	85%		X	Executive	Judicial	Local	State
Colorado	Other			Executive	Judicial	Local	State
Connecticut	85%			Executive	Judicial	State	State
Delaware	85%	1990	X	Executive	Executive	State	State
Florida	85%	1983	X	Executive	Executive	State	State
Georgia	85%		X	Executive	Executive	State	State
Hawaii	None			Executive	Judicial	State	State
Idaho	100%			Executive	Executive	State	State
Illinois	85%	1978	X	Executive	Judicial	Local	State
Indiana	50%	1977	X	Executive	Executive	Local	State
Iowa	85%		X	Executive	Executive	Local	State
Kansas	85%	1993	X	Executive	Judicial	Local	State
Kentucky	Other			Executive	Executive	State	State
Louisiana	85%			Executive	Executive	State	State
Maine	85%	1975	X	Executive	Executive	State	State
Maryland	50%			Executive	Executive	State	State
Massachusetts	Other			Executive	Judicial	State	State
Michigan	85%			Executive	Executive	State	State

116

State							
Minnesota	85%	1980	X	Executive	Executive	Local	State
Mississippi	85%	1995	X	Executive	Executive	State	State
Missouri	85%			Executive	Executive	State	State
Montana	Other			Executive	Executive	State	State
Nebraska	50%			Executive	Judicial	State	State
Nevada	100%			Executive	Executive	State	State
New Hampshire	100%			Executive	Executive	State	State
New Jersey	85%			Executive	Judicial	Local	State
New Mexico	None			Executive	Executive	State	State
New York	85%		X	Executive	Executive	Local	State
North Carolina	85%	1994	X	Executive	Executive	State	State
North Dakota	85%			Executive	Executive	State	State
Ohio	85%	1996	X	Executive	Judicial/ Executive	Local	State
Oklahoma	85%			Executive	Executive	State	State
Oregon	85%	1989	X	Judicial	Judicial	Local	Local
Pennsylvania	85%			Judicial	Judicial	Local	N/A
Rhode Island	None			Executive	Executive	State	State
South Carolina	85%			Executive	Executive	State	State
South Dakota	None			Executive	Judicial	State	State
Tennessee	85%		X	Executive	Executive	State	State

(*continued*)

Table 5.2 (*continued*)

	Current Truth in Sentencing Requirement[1]	Year in Which State Abolished All Parole[2]	Whether State Abolished Parole for Violent Offenders[2]	Branch of Government Overseeing Parole Supervision[3]	Branch of Government Overseeing Probation Supervision[3]	State/Local Probation Supervision[3]	State/Local Parole Supervision[3]
Texas	50%			Executive	Judicial	Local	Local
Utah	85%			Executive	Executive	State	State
Vermont	None			Executive	Executive	State	State
Virginia	85%		X	Executive	Executive	State	State
Washington	85%	1984	X	Executive	Executive	Local	Local
West Virginia	None			Executive	Judicial	Local	Local
Wisconsin	Other	1999	X	Executive	Executive	State	Local
Wyoming	None			Executive	Executive	State	State
Totals	50% (4) 85% (28) 100% (3) None (8) Other (7)	(14)	(20)	Exec. (48) Judic. (2)	Exec. (33.5) Judic. (16.5)	State (34) Local (16)	

Sources:

[1] "Truth in Sentencing in State Prisons," *Bureau of Justice Statistics (1999).*

[2] Sabol, William J. et al. "The Influence of Truth-in-Sentencing Reforms on Changes in States' Sentencing Practices and Prison Populations." *Travis and Lawrence (2002).* Parole boards still have discretion over inmates who were sentenced prior to the effective date of the various states' parole abolition laws.

[3] Burke, Peggy B. "Policy-Driven Responses to Probation and Parole Violations," *Center for Effective Public Policy (1997).*

treatment group that would provide postrelease supervision or to a control group that would have no supervision, and compare the rates of criminal activity across the two groups. Unfortunately, there is an inherent problem with this design: the outcome – recidivism – is intrinsically linked with supervision. In practice, increased supervision will likely lead to greater detection of rule violations and of new criminal offenses. Furthermore, in nonexperimental studies comparing the postrelease criminal activity of offenders released under discretionary parole with those released under mandatory parole or released without supervision, selection bias proves problematic in drawing reliable inference. Parole boards will generally grant parole to those offenders who pose the least risk of reoffending and would be expected to have fewer arrests, on average, than those offenders who were turned down for parole and those who received mandatory parole. This follows from parole board members doing their jobs as charged.

Another challenge to research in this area comes from difficulty in comparing offenders in prison to those under supervision. No matter how effective supervision services are, the risk to public safety will always be greater if an individual is supervised in the community rather than in prison. Studies of offender supervision typically compare offenders under different intensities and mixes of surveillance and treatment services. Necessarily, some behavior will be sanctioned by additional time behind bars. If there is any difference in the extent to which alternative programs rely on incarceration, then the outcomes are incomparable. Without a way to adjust for the differences in risk of further criminal activity or even violating conditions of supervision, it is impossible to credibly compare alternative supervision schemes over a substantial period of time.

Experimental Evidence on Intensive Supervision

Over the past half-century, periods of prison overcrowding have led some jurisdictions to implement intensive supervision programs both as a solution to divert offenders from prison and to release inmates earlier from confined institutions into transitional programs. The few significant studies of intensive supervision have focused on its effectiveness to reduce prison overcrowding while not significantly increasing the public safety risk. In the 1950s, Richard McGee, noted penologist and then the director of the California Department of Corrections, initiated a number of experimental research studies to determine the effectiveness of early parole as a function of offender risk and parole officer caseloads in California. In a series of randomized experiments involving prisoners eligible for parole, the department found little difference in offense rates between those inmates released 90 days earlier into "special intensive parole units" that carried smaller caseloads than those released at their planned parole dates and supervised by agents carrying standard case loads (Glaser 1964, 1995). Only among offenders classified as "medium-poor risks" did those in the treatment group experience significantly lower rearrest rates than those in the control group, 35 percent versus 45 percent. From a cost–benefit perspective, McGee concluded that intensive supervision was effective for offenders on the margin of choosing between criminal and law-abiding behaviors and not effective for either low-risk offenders who may not have needed additional supervision to succeed or high-risk offenders who probably would have failed regardless of the nature of the supervision (Glaser 1964).

The 1980s saw a resurgence of states' interests in intensive supervision programs (ISP), touted as relatively low-cost intermediate alternatives to vastly overcrowded prisons. From 1986 to 1991, the National Institute of Justice funded RAND to conduct a large randomized experiment of ISPs in 14 sites and nine states to assess their cost-effectiveness. As reported by Petersilia and Turner (1993), who designed and oversaw the implementation of this evaluation, at the end of the 1-year follow-up, 37 percent of the ISP treatment group had been rearrested as compared to 33 percent of the control group. Sixty-five percent of ISP offenders experienced a technical violation compared to 38 percent of the controls. Also, 27 percent of ISP offenders were recommitted to prison compared to 19 percent of the controls.

There are two ways to interpret these findings: either the program led to increased criminal behavior of those under heightened supervision (in the opposite direction of the anticipated effect) or the increased surveillance led to an increased probability of detection. If the latter is true, it is impossible to know whether there was in fact a deterrent effect that was overwhelmed by the surveillance effect. Also, the researchers speculated that the ISP may have sanctioned these infractions more harshly in an effort to shore up the credibility of the program (Petersilia and Turner 1993). This too would obscure any true deterrent effect.

Although the evaluation could not provide any definitive evidence that increased supervision intensity provided public safety benefits, the highly elevated rate of technical violations for those in the treatment group suggests that the surveillance did in fact increase the rate of detection. Then the interesting question becomes whether technical violations are a proxy for criminal behavior. Experience in Washington State in the mid 1980s from a program that decreased the average number of conditions of release for probationers and deemphasized the sanctions for technical violations does not support this hypothesis (Petersilia and Turner 1993).

Despite the experience of hundreds of intensive supervision programs in this country and many studies, albeit few experimental, we still know very little about the effectiveness of these programs to reduce prison overcrowding, and more to the point of this chapter, to reduce crime in detectable ways. The same issues that hinder our learning from many criminal justice practices are at work here. There is no consistency in the design and implementation of ISP programs; their surveillance and monitoring practices, caseloads, and their incorporation of rehabilitative requirements vary significantly both within and between programs. Further, we do not know which offenders are best served by these programs from a public safety standpoint. Some researchers have found that judges use ISPs for lower-risk offenders who are not prison-bound – so-called net-widening – and believe that the investment of additional supervision resources for this population can backfire and lead to increased rates of violations and reincarceration. However, if ISPs serve to enforce release conditions that were not previously being enforced under standard probation, and the detected infractions were directly or indirectly related to criminal activity, there could be a public safety benefit. Similarly, ISPs may serve to ensure the quicker detection and apprehension of violations by higher-risk offenders. Also, as McGee found, it is entirely possible that these programs may deter criminal offending by those offenders who are at the margins of choosing between licit and illicit behaviors. However, the bottom line is that the public safety benefit of these intensive supervision programs relies on two mechanisms that have yet to be proven: the deterrence value of supervision and the value of technical violations to prevent crime. Perhaps the most interesting lesson from ISPs is how widely they have spread across the country with such scant evidence demonstrating their effectiveness.

Parole Success

Several recent reports on parole and prisoner reentry have developed and utilized the concept of parole success rates (Hughes et al. 2001; Travis and Lawrence 2002). This statistic is defined as the number of parolees who completed their terms of supervision without having their parole revoked, being returned to jail or prison, or absconding, divided by the total number of parolees leaving parole in a given year. The basic descriptions are these: for 1999, the success rate for the nation as a whole was around 40 percent; there has been a modest increase in success rates over time; those released for the first time on the current sentence are much more "successful" than rereleases; and discretionary releases are substantially more "successful" than mandatory releases. The nationwide figures mask the tremendous amount of variation across states. Massachusetts was one of two states with the highest success rates (83 percent), and California had the lowest (21 percent).[12]

The BJS report notes that there are many factors affecting measured "success":

When comparing State success rates for parole discharges, differences may be due to variations in parole populations, such as age at prison release, criminal history, and most serious offense. Success rates may also differ based on the intensity of super-vision and the parole agency policies related to revocation of technical violators. (Hughes et al. 2001)

In spite of these qualifications, these success numbers have gained a fair bit of currency in the discussion of prisoner reentry. For example, Travis and Lawrence (2002) utilize the same measure to rank states and Petersilia (2003) uses them to support an argument in favor of discretionary release.

Although these authors note that there are other factors one would like to examine in order to make sense of these numbers, the qualifications have not received the same attention as the raw numbers, though they are arguably more important. Reitz critiques these measures for being more a reflection of state policies than measures of behavior of those supervised:

Simply put, it is a serious error to equate failure rates on postrelease supervision with the actual behavior of prison releasees. The states are far too different in their revocation practices to allow us to consider the data compatible from state to state. In any jurisdiction, the number and rate of revocations depends to some degree on the good or bad conduct of parolees, to be sure, but it also depends at least as much on what might be called the "sensitivity" of the supervision system to violations.

---

[12] Because California is so large and is an outlier, the nationwide figures are very sensitive to the experience of this state. In fact, the BJS reports that "[w]hen California data are excluded, the "success" rate for all parole discharges rises to 53 percent (from 42 percent), and the rate for mandatory parolees increases to 64 percent (from 33 percent) in 1999" (Glaze 2002).

Sensitivity varies with formal definitions of what constitutes a violation, the intensity of surveillance employed by parole field officers, the institutional culture of field services from place to place, and the severity of sanctions typically used upon findings of violations. (Reitz 2004, 215)

If these outcomes largely reflect policy differences, then they cannot be used to evaluate policies, further hindering attempts to research the effects of community supervision.

The Connection between the Release Process and the Extent and Effectiveness of Supervision

Some analysts have used success measures to assess the efficacy of different approaches to prison release, comparing the outcomes of those released by a discretionary release process to the outcomes of those released at the completion of their sentences. In addition to the critiques offered above with regard to the way success is measured, there is a fundamental problem with this inference – it does not account for how individuals are assigned to release status. That is, inmates who are released at the discretion of a parole board are likely to have lower risk of recidivism than inmates whom a parole board chooses not to release. Further complicating matters is the variety of statutes that govern whether inmates with given criminal histories are eligible for discretionary release; differences in these laws across states will affect average success measures by release type.

Given that it is not straightforward to compare the effect of release type on the effectiveness of supervision in controlling the criminal behavior of those released from prison, what can be said about the connection between release policy and supervision? Mandatory release may or may not lead to a period of postincarceration supervision. Discretionary release generally leads to supervision for at least several months or the parole board would not take time to hear the case. When faced with an inmate who appears to pose risk for public safety, a parole board must trade off the benefits and costs of discretionary release and the supervision opportunities that provides against the benefits and costs of keeping the inmate incarcerated until the maximum release date. For better or worse, under a policy of mandatory release, these trade-offs are not considered on a case-by-case basis.

Inherently, discretionary release works against the notion that those least equipped to reintegrate should be subject to a period of postrelease supervision from prison. Mandatory release polices provide a greater certainty that these individuals will receive supervision but then raise a secondary

123

resource allocation question. Certainly, if supervising all prisoners dilutes the intensity of supervision of high-risk offenders and needlessly interferes with the reintegration process of low-risk offenders, it could prove costly and counterproductive to making supervision "matter."

Critics of mandatory release call for a return to discretionary release to increase the incentives to encourage rehabilitative behavior among prisoners and to balance disparities in sentences across offenders and jurisdictions. Anecdotally, they also cite that some parolees involved in high-profile crimes, such as the abduction and murder of Polly Klaas, were released as a consequence of mandatory release policies and would have never been released had the state had a discretionary parole release policy (Petersilia 1999). There are two other types of benefits of discretionary release that should also be considered. When making a release decision, a parole board can know about the inmate's plans: does he or she have a job? Where will he or she live? Is there anyone who can vouch for these plans? Having established supports in place may be the most important determinant of successful reentry, and it is useful to require these before agreeing to release a person from confinement. Finally, the existence of discretionary release provides incentives for correctional institutions to provide rehabilitative opportunities. Particularly in tight fiscal times, it may be socially valuable to provide some pressure to counter the pressure to cut all nonsecurity and basic services.

Those on the other side of the debate, including Reitz and others, argue that the discretionary release process lacks both moral and practical benefits (Reitz 2004). Parole boards can analyze institutional conduct within prison and can observe an individual's penitence and readiness for release, but it is not clear whether the use of this information by parole board members in a less open process should be of any greater value in determining release conditions than the information available at the time of sentencing. It is conceivable that the discretionary process would reward prisoners who can present themselves effectively and who are more adept at hiding conflicting feelings than those prisoners who honestly disclose their fears and concerns about reoffending and reintegration.

One benefit of mandatory release is that the timing of release is known (more or less) from the beginning of the sentence.[13] The advantages of predefined release dates are significant because they eliminate the

---

[13] The precise date of release is often not known with certainty, as earned good time can shift the timing somewhat.

need to repeatedly "retry" cases and reopen the determination of appropriate sanctions.[14] Also, programs to improve the transition to the community can be better timed to coincide with actual release. In addition, critics of discretionary release argue that it is possible to attain some of the benefits of that policy through other means. Practically, correctional agencies have many institutional mechanisms that can promote good behavior in prison such as graduated privileges in housing, visits, programming, and through the award of earned good time subtracted from their sentence, that obviate the need for the use of discretionary release as an incentive.

Finally, the tragic cases cited by proponents of discretionary release seem to raise questions about the type and intensity of supervision more than they criticize mandatory release. If these prisoners had completed their sentences without receiving discretionary release, they would have been released later but with no supervision. Discretionary release per se does not solve the fundamental tensions with regard to very serious offenders.

As this discussion makes clear, the issue of whether discretionary release is preferable to mandatory release has many dimensions in addition to its relationship to successful reentry following release from prison. From the perspective of reentry and public safety, release policy is important both to how parole outcomes are interpreted and to how other aspects of reentry and supervision are designed. Most states have some people released under the discretion of a parole board and others released at the end of their sentences. This fact suggests that the debate about "mandatory" versus "discretionary" should begin to consider the best way to support reentry in a system that contains multiple release types.

The Role and Meaning of Technical Violations

A key question for assessing supervision outcomes is whether jurisdictions respond too harshly to noncriminal violations of the terms of conditional release. The most common of these so-called technical violations occur when parolees fail drug tests, fail to report, fail to notify about address or employment changes or out-of-jurisdiction movements, fail to follow

---

[14] In spite of the fact that victims groups have advocated for a role in parole decisions, as a group victims might be better off not having to readdress the details of a crime. That is, given discretionary release, victims may desire a role. But that does not provide any evidence on whether eliminating the discretionary aspect of release will be better or worse for victims.

a prescribed treatment program, and fail to stay away from known felons (Hughes et al. 2001). Often, supervising officers can exercise significant discretion to respond to these infractions, ranging from informal counseling and increased supervision and testing of offenders to a decision to remand them to prison. Much of the discussion on technical violations concerns the transparency of revocation policies, the consistency with which they are applied by supervising officers, and the fairness of the administrative process. As mentioned before, the federal government technical assistance program (that worked with a number of parole and probation agencies over the past 15 years) found that many agencies had neither a complete understanding of how their revocation polices worked in practice nor simple guidelines that specified ranges of sanctions for certain common infractions (Burke 1997).

How technical violations are punished has a huge impact on prison populations. Because the parole population is of the same order of magnitude as the flow of prison admissions in a year, a modest change in the revocation rate will translate into a meaningful change in prison admissions. Due to the larger size of the probation population, this phenomenon is more dramatic when it comes to revocations of probation, as revealed in an extensive study of responses to probation violations in Texas (Criminal Justice Policy Council 2002).

Parole and probation supervision policies diverge most significantly on the revocation process to remand an offender under supervision back to prison. Whereas probation officers must gain the consent of a judge to revoke the terms of conditional release and remand an individual to prison, parole agents follow an administrative and nonjudicial process and typically have the power to remand an individual to prison immediately. In practice, the trade-off between these two processes comes down to timeliness versus due process. In Massachusetts, field parole officers typically have significant discretion in choosing informal counseling and in applying some intermediate sanctions in response to a technical violation. In response to a positive drug test, they can require a parolee to submit to more frequent drug tests and supervision. They can also require a parolee to seek a residential substance abuse program. To send a parolee to prison, the parole officer must get the consent of a regional parole supervisor, at which point he or she can issue a 15-day detainer. Within that time, a separate hearing officer must meet with the parolee in prison, review the reports on the infraction, and then submit a report to the parole board, which has 60 days to decide on the final sanction for the infraction. Those parolees whose terms of conditional release are formally revoked may serve the remainder of their sentences in prison, although they remain eligible for but are less likely to receive, a subsequent parole release decision. Sanctioning a probation violation with prison requires field officers to schedule a hearing before a judge and to prepare and present the case to surrender the probationer to prison. This additional procedure step leads to delays between the time of the infraction and the punishment, if ordered, and provides for more oversight of the grounds for revocation. In practice, a substantial difference is that parolees are detained behind bars during the review process.

Critics contend that parole agencies overuse prison as the primary sanction for so-called "technical" violations when intermediate sanction programs might prove less costly and more effective from a public safety and rehabilitative perspective. However, this argument does not reflect the extent to which new criminal activity can generate a return to prison. According to a survey of prisoners in 1997, among those who report that their parole was revoked for violation of terms of supervision, 70 percent said the cause was a new arrest or conviction (although this statistic varies by state). Among the states with the largest parole populations, it ranged from 60 percent in California to 87 percent in New York (Hughes et al. 2001). Some researchers, though, believe that technical violations account for the majority of all parole violators returned to prison and that parole returns for criminal activities are proportionately much smaller (Travis and Lawrence 2002 cite the statistic as two thirds). Suffice to say that we do not have definitive administrative data at the national level to precisely sort out this ratio (Burke 1997).

The role and meaning of technical violations is also confused for definitional and data reasons. First, parolees can be sent to prison for a combination of criminal and noncriminal violations, making it difficult to sanction these infractions separately. Second, there is considerable confusion in the data as to whether those parolees returned to prison for a criminal offense are subsequently prosecuted and convicted of that offense. In California, parole data from 1990 to 2000 reveals that the percentage of parole violators classified as administrative criminal returns decreased from 89 percent to 80 percent, whereas those classified as administrative noncriminal returns[15] doubled from 10 percent to 20 percent (Travis 2003).

---

[15] An "administrative criminal return" in California is a return to prison for a technical violation (not a new criminal conviction) where the basis for the violation was a finding of criminal behavior.

Yet researchers found that the average time served on the violations did not differ markedly between criminal and noncriminal violations (5.4 versus 4.3 months), which raises concerns about the proportionality of the sanction and the distinction between the violations.

Without clearer, cleaner definitions, we cannot judge whether the response to technical violations is disproportionate and leads unnecessarily to increasing prison populations. It is of great concern if the system is enforcing conditions that do not matter much in terms of immediate crime control but impose great costs on the ability of a person to put the right structures in place to be law abiding. Studies such as Burke's and those by the Texas Criminal Justice Policy Council should be encouraged. The issue of how particular behavior is being sanctioned (the threshold for action and the magnitude of the punishment, as well as its frequency) should be the top research priority in the field of corrections, as it is the key unknown prohibiting a better understanding of the costs and benefits of supervision.

Technology as an Accelerant of the Surveillance Function

New technologies have transformed the ability of supervising agencies to detect noncompliance but now raise questions about whether we can learn too much and be forced to sanction without a clear benefit to public safety. The most obvious example is drug testing. In the early 1970s, drug testing was relatively costly and unreliable with error rates in the best toxicology laboratories ranging from 20 to 70 percent (West and Ackerman 1993). By the late 1980s and through the 1990s, both measures improved dramatically, and supervising agencies across the country began universally adopting regular drug testing as a condition for release for those offenders convicted of drug-related crimes (U.S. Department of Justice 1999). In the past, supervising agents could choose to turn a blind eye or informally counsel offenders who continued to use drugs but were able to meet all of the other conditions of release including employment, housing, programming, and family relationships. However, accuracy and prevalence of drug testing has changed this dynamic and is more likely to flag such an individual for a violation and require some formal action on the part of the supervising agent. The question about whether an agency wants to even look for noncompliance in a certain area is real, and probably explains why the New York City Probation Department indicates on its website that it does not routinely screen for marijuana unless directed by the court.

Other technological advances in information databases, processing, and networking allow agencies to share criminal history and postrelease data across public safety and law enforcement agencies more easily and at lower cost. Whereas individuals leaving prison may have slipped into a community previously, their returning location may now be mapped and presented to officers in a police district, and even shared with the public. Electronic bracelets tied into telephone systems or GPS location satellites offer correctional agencies vast improvements in enforcing home confinement and daily itineraries. Faced with rising caseloads and few support resources in the community, the shift of supervising officers' roles from providing support to surveillance was probably inevitable, but certainly greatly accelerated by new technologies. Now, agencies could benefit from specific research on which technologies work best with certain types of offenders, and from the development of best practices that would moderate the instinct to overuse technology.

Supervision as One Criminal Sanction

If the prevailing measure of supervision "success" is inadequate, how should we consider the effectiveness of postrelease supervision of ex-prisoners? We must begin by acknowledging that it proves difficult to understand postrelease supervision as a separate program, distinct from the mechanisms that assign and provide it. Rather, any evaluation of supervision must begin with an understanding of the effects of the multiple system factors – laws, agencies, and practices – that govern who receives parole (or its equivalent) and the duration, intensity, and enforcement practices of the postrelease supervision.

Sentencing laws and practices play the most obvious and direct role (Piehl 2002). In some determinate-sentencing states, postrelease supervision is mandated for all released offenders at the point that they have served some specified percentage of their sentence. Laws can also exclude individuals who should be supervised postrelease from receiving it. Statutes sometimes prescribe security classifications for certain types of offenders, precluding correctional agencies from stepping down from prison to prerelease programming or postrelease supervision. When supervision is inadequate, this can have repercussions on the sentence structures and length.

In states with discretionary release policies, parole board decisions are highly sensitive to the political environment, which governs the appointment process for parole board members. Under some sentences, prisoners can self-select out of postrelease supervision by choosing to waive parole or, more indirectly, by exhibiting poor institutional behavior so as to make a positive parole decision unlikely. Even in states with mandatory postrelease supervision policies, rereleasees (prisoners released once who had their terms of conditional release revoked) can leave prison subsequently without any further postrelease supervision if they have served the entirety of their original sentence. To avoid this circumstance, some states add time to an offender's sentence or stop the parole clock to ensure that they complete successfully some minimum period of postrelease supervision before full release.

The enforcement of the terms of conditional release may also be affected by the actions of police and other law enforcement agencies working independently or cooperatively with correctional agencies. Crime sweeps enforcing nuisance laws may (intentionally or not) target recently released offenders and necessitate action by correctional agencies. As will be discussed in the next section, new partnerships between police and corrections can enhance postsupervision surveillance.

Given these factors, it may prove useful to consider postrelease supervision as just one criminal sanction of a set of interrelated punishments rather than simply as a mechanism to provide postrelease prisoner reintegration. Reintegration requires a set of services and supports that may be beyond the organizational and political abilities of supervising agencies. Acknowledging this could shift attention to the effectiveness of the criminal sanctioning process of parole.

As noted by Blumstein and Beck in Chapter 3, those released from prison and entering parole supervision are increasingly likely to have previously exited prison during the same criminal sentence. From 1985 to 2001, the number of rereleases from prison entering parole increased from 48,600 to 196,000 – a 303 percent increase – whereas the number of new releases entering parole increased only 93 percent from 126,100 to 243,100 in the same time period. (See also Lynch and Sabol 2001 for a discussion of "churners.") How should we think about this increasing number of rereleases, this revolving back door? Studies of serious criminal offenders find that offending is highly concentrated. That is, that much of the offending is committed by a minority of the population (Kleiman 1999; Piehl, Useem, and DiIulio, Jr. 1999). One could imagine a well-functioning system, repeatedly offering chances for reintegration into society, with those who do not succeed returning to prison to continue the process. Over time, such a system would produce a prison population more and more comprised of high-rate offenders. Postincarceration supervision, then, would be properly seen as an integral part of this larger sorting process, not as a distinct set of activities. Although it is clear that the current situation does not reflect the idealized "system" described here, it is important to recognize several features shared by both. First, although many of those released from prison recidivate, many do not. Second, as the population becomes more highly concentrated with those who have failed before, those released from prison may require more intensive resources if they are going to be reintegrated.

Note that a system designed to sort high rate offenders is not the same thing as imposing long sentences for those with criminal histories. Rather than having the courts predict those who are likely to recidivate, this system uses tight supervision to observe behavior in order to determine who is a high-rate offender. It requires effective supervision that responds quickly to signs of trouble. Sorting will not be aided if, in practice, low-rate offenders or those who have changed their behavior get tripped up by the supervision and land back in prison. If this does happen, the system is not sorting offenders but in some sense producing them due to its overreaching, which will not only inhibit reintegration but also increase the cost of administering the correctional system.

Reasonable Expectations for Community Supervision

To think through ways that supervision "matters" and ways to make it matter more, it is important that we first adopt reasonable expectations about achievable supervision outcomes. Failure to abide by the terms of conditional release is inevitable. As detailed in Chapter 3, prisoners, as a group, have multiple social, education, mental, and physical needs and have fewer opportunities to find services to address these needs in prison and postrelease. In their chapter, Blumstein and Beck describe the greatly increased percentage of drug offenders in our prisons and on parole. Barbara Ehrenreich's recent book detailing her cross-country experience in trying to make ends meet while working a series of entry-level jobs provides a sober reminder of the difficulties faced by poor and low-skilled individuals even when they are motivated and do not have the added burden of a criminal history (Ehrenreich 2001).

The vastly improved technologies in drug testing and location monitoring (electronic bracelets, GPS, etc.) provide supervising agencies with more efficient and less costly means to detect noncompliance. In comparison, fewer program resources are available to support ex-offenders, and the mechanisms by which they might prevent recidivist behavior operate much less directly and less linearly. Even with additional resources, we have to be realistic about the type of support that government can provide. The realms of possible government intervention – facilitating housing, employment, licensure, identification – still leave prisoners alone to face the arguably more important task of building healthy and supportive social and family networks that will sustain law-abiding and civil behavior. Faced with the certainty of noncompliance detection versus the uncertainty of program "correction," the shift in supervision's focus is understandable and likely to continue.

Further, in past years, sloppy administrative relationships between correctional and law enforcement agencies meant that individuals released from prison could more easily slip into neighborhoods and reestablish themselves without the knowledge of the police or other agencies. Today, technology makes sharing information across agencies simple and less costly. New police and correctional partnerships have been formed to identify returning offenders, particularly those presenting high risks to a community's public safety, and should be applauded. Efforts underway on behalf of homeland security have sparked increased informational exchanges across agencies and are likely to expand substantially.

The challenge, then, is to recognize that the ability to detect violations has vastly outpaced our ability and perhaps willingness to provide support. As a result, we need to better manage the surveillance function. One way to begin to do that is to think carefully about why we collect the information we do. The New York City Probation Department's decision to stop routinely testing for marijuana reflects both fiscal and operational realities. Including marijuana in the "panel" of drug tests in urine screening costs money, and a positive test is likely to necessitate some action by the department. (If a department does not generally act on positive test results, then not only is the cost of the test wasted but the notion of mandatory conditions of supervision is undermined.) Of course, this decision reflects a harm-reduction philosophy that continued marijuana usage poses less risk to public safety than the use of opiates, cocaine, methamphetamines, and the newer designer drugs.

Judicious surveillance requires the development of consistent assessment and enforcement of supervision policies that maximize the efficient use of expensive prison beds. It is surprising how many supervising agencies continue to operate without guidelines that govern the initial intake process or the processes of revocation.[16] Most importantly, on the back end, it seems commonsensical to provide clear delineations of authority to resolve issues of noncompliance in the field or in more formal administrative and judicial processes according to specified guidelines to ensure proportionate and consistent responses to infractions. Common sense would also dictate that these guidelines should reflect a graduated approach toward sanctioning less serious infractions. The codification is important for perceptions of procedural fairness. The graduated response is important to allow for missteps in the process of reintegration and to provide the best use of scarce correctional resources.

Even if supervision is thought of more as a custodial status than as a program, supervision agencies bear a significant political risk of "program failure" on their watch. Parolees who are on the road to successful reintegration continue to bear a risk of tripping up unnecessarily by remaining on parole, for example, if the reporting requirements threaten employment. Both organizations and offenders require incentives to minimize these risks. Several jurisdictions have piloted programs of earned discharge where an offender who successfully completed certain agreed-upon requirements – employment, housing, social services – can move off of parole status. The prospect of earned discharge would encourage supervising agencies to frontload their resources – both support and supervision – to accelerate the movement of clients to full release. Similarly, individuals being supervised would have significant incentives to demonstrate successful community reintegration during the first few months and years of their release, when they are most vulnerable to recidivating (Langan and Levin 2002). Those who are able to comply fully with supervision requirements for 1 to 2 years will have demonstrated an ability to be sufficiently responsible such that further compliance may yield few benefits but continue to impose the same costs on agencies and clients.

If the shift of supervision's function from support to supervision is irreversible, the resulting "support" gap could usefully be filled by nongovernment agencies that can credibly provide these support services. In New York City, La Bodega de la Familia arranges for families to meet with the parole agents of prisoners who have not yet been released to enlist them in

---

[16] This is particularly surprising in light of the substantial benefits of implementing validated assessment instruments at intake that would allow a supervising agency to calibrate the intensity and type of supervision to the risk and needs of the offenders.

developing an overall prisoner reintegration strategy. At the initial meetings, which do not include the individuals who are still incarcerated, the families learn about the terms of conditional release and go through several exercises to help them prepare for the return of their family members. Using simple but effective visual questionnaires, this nonprofit agency helps families map out the strengths and weaknesses of the available support system for the returning prisoner. Case managers work to obtain resources and referrals to avoid drug relapse and therefore to avoid the behavior that would precipitate a parole revocation.

A new form of supervision results when prison authorities develop direct relationships with police and nongovernment agencies. In Boston, a local correctional agency partners with police, the district attorney's office, and the U.S. Attorney for the District of Massachusetts to identify individuals who may pose a substantial public safety risk to communities upon their eventual return. This effort is known as the Boston Reentry Initiative. Through various group and individual meetings, these prisoners are notified of the significant prosecutorial sanctions that face them should they reoffend and are strongly encouraged to avail themselves of a number of community-based resources. In cases where these offenders will leave prison on probation or parole, these supervising agencies are asked to play a critical role in ensuring compliance with a postrelease transition plan formed within the institution. However, in cases where individuals are released without conditional supervision, the faith-based and secular nonprofit organizations that provide case management and mentoring services to these offenders will freely report to police authorities if certain individuals disappear or seem highly resistant to taking the steps necessary for their reintegration.

In the Boston Reentry Initiative, as in other similar programs, the mentors (who are typically ex-cons) perform such functions as meeting the individual at release, sharing a meal or a cup of coffee, participating in a fellowship meeting, helping navigate social service and government bureaucracies, and just being available around the clock to provide an encouraging word. Even for those under criminal justice supervision, neither parole nor probation officers normally have the time, resources, or charge to perform these functions, and the resulting partnership is mutually advantageous.

The correction and police partnerships prove very effective at enhancing postrelease surveillance for those under supervision. Police agencies are typically better funded and staffed than parole, work around the clock in the communities, and have a mission entirely consistent with the surveillance function of parole (Petersilia 2003, p. 202). The ascendancy of community policing strategies in most major police departments to focus on the factors that prevent crime and disorder fully supports these partnerships. Also, parole and probation agencies offer police additional powers of search and seizure that can prove very effective in preempting and detecting criminal behavior. In Massachusetts, Operation Nightlight is a partnership that pairs probation officers and police for unannounced home and community visits to monitor high-risk offenders during evening hours. Similarly, the state parole board has begun aligning parole districts with police districts in Boston. This arrangement forces recently released prisoners to report to the local police district headquarters to meet their parole officers and facilitates the exchange of information between these agencies. Interestingly, this arrangement was initiated in response to cuts to the state parole department's budget, not due to the potential advantages of the partnerships.

These partnerships and special programs have all developed in response to perceived gaps in the organization and practices affecting prison release. As such, they can both teach us about the deficiencies in the current system and offer suggestions for potential solutions.

Concluding Thoughts

Community supervision of those released from prison matters because it is a large program with high stakes for both those supervised and the government. It is likely that supervision will become increasingly important in the near future due to improvements in technology and increasing collaborations among law enforcement. The current challenge for policy is to ensure that the new technology and thinking is utilized to support crime control, not just to increase the reach of law enforcement. It may be that it is better to separate out the law enforcement and social support functions to a degree rather than try to rebalance them within supervisory agencies. One way to do this is to have supervisory agencies focus on crime outcomes and assign responsibility for social integration to other entities.

For any jurisdiction supervising criminal offenders in the community, the punishment of violations of the conditions of supervision requires careful attention. The multifaceted job of parole supervision means that a technical violation may indicate success for the organization if not for the individual under supervision. The most pressing questions are whether technical violations predict criminal behavior and whether the structure of supervision itself makes it more difficult for ex-inmates to reintegrate into society.

Some analysts dismiss technical violations as trivial infractions and interpret evidence as suggesting that these infractions are responsible for a large proportion of the flow into prisons. Others generally assume that the system only uses prison time to punish serious offending. To improve policy in this area, it is essential that this debate be policed with evidence rather than conviction.

The logic of community supervision and its long-standing and widespread practice suggests it has the potential to be effective, but it is quite possible that policies or practices have evolved such that we have exceeded the optimal level of interference and are "oversupervising." As always, how much supervision matters and how much supervision can matter depend on the way the details are implemented. Unfortunately, the research literature does not provide clear lessons about how much and in what ways supervision matters directly to crime control. One reason that it is hard to know how supervision relates to crime is the tremendous variation across states in supervision and other policies. This variation suggests two puzzles: why have we not learned more from these "50 experiments" in supervising those released from prison and why have we not observed convergence across states to a handful of models?

Although one might think that the enormous variation in sentencing laws, discretionary release policies, and supervision practices across and within states would provide natural experiments from which to learn much about the effectiveness of supervision, the inability to cleanly delineate differences in supervision practices from system differences itself makes inference from cross-jurisdictional comparisons difficult. The fact that it is difficult to evaluate the effectiveness of supervision irrespective of system factors that determine who receives supervision and the duration, intensity, and enforcement of the terms of conditional release should lead us to consider alternative research strategies.

There are two research approaches that may prove more promising than analyzing supervision as a single program. One approach is to conduct much more comprehensive evaluations that consider the system variables that affect supervision outcomes. Such a research strategy would examine the effectiveness of sentencing laws and correctional practices in meting out appropriate postrelease supervision resources calibrated to the risks and needs of the offenders. The other research strategy is to focus on basic practices. For prisoners of certain attributes (offenses, age, employment/education history, return destination) what should be the supervision strategy? How many times a month should these type of offenders report to supervising officers and what is the nature of this reporting relationship? For offenders who seem to pose a significant threat to public safety such as sexual predators, what type of technology proves most useful in providing round the clock surveillance and what pharmacological and other treatment remedies are most effective? Does it make sense to front-load supervision services? Some of these studies have been conducted in Washington State and elsewhere, but it seems that these are eminently doable and can have an immediate effect on practice. It is time for a serious discussion about the best way society can learn from our ongoing activities in order to improve the design of prison release and postincarceration supervision; the costs of not doing this are too high.

References

Burke, P. B. 1997. *Policy-Driven Responses to Probation and Parole Violations*. Silver Spring, MD: Center for Effective Public Policy.

Campbell, R. 2003. *Dollars & Sentences: Legislators' Views on Prisons, Punishment, and the Budget Crisis*. New York: Vera Institute.

Criminal Justice Policy Council. 2002. *Trends, Profile, and Policy Issues Related to Felony Probation Revocations in Texas*. Austin, TX: Criminal Justice Policy Council.

Ditton, P. M., and D. J. Wilson. 1999. *Truth in Sentencing in State Prisons*. Washington, DC: Bureau of Justice Statistics.

Ehrenreich, B. 2001. *Nickel and Dimed: On (Not) Getting by in America*. New York: Henry Holt and Co.

Gifford, S. L. 2002. *Justice Expenditure and Employment in the United States*. Washington, DC: U.S. Department of Justice, Bureau of Justice Statistics.

Glaser, D. 1964. *The Effectiveness of a Prison and Parole System*. Indianapolis: Bobbs-Merrill Company.

Glaser, D. 1995. *Preparing Convicts for Law-Abiding Lives*. Albany: State University of New York Press.

Glaze, L. E. 2002. *Probation and Parole in the United States, 2001*. Washington, DC: Bureau of Justice Statistics.

Heymann, P. B. 2000. "The New Policing." *Fordham Urban Law Journal* 28: 407.

Hughes, T. A., D. J. Wilson, and A. J. Beck. 2001. *Trends in State Parole, 1990–2000*. Washington, DC: Bureau of Justice Statistics.

Kelling, G., and C. Coles. 1996. *Fixing Broken Windows: Restoring Order and Reducing Crime in Our Communities*. New York: The Free Press.

Kennedy, D. M., A. A. Braga, and A. M. Piehl. 2001. *Reducing Gun Violence: Developing and Implementing Operation Ceasefire*. Washington, DC: U.S. Department of Justice, National Institute of Justice.

Kleiman, M. 1999. "Community Corrections as the Front Line in Crime Control." *UCLA Law Review* 46(6):1909–1925.

Langan, P. 1994. "Between Prison and Probation: Intermediate Sanctions." *Science* 264: 791–793.

Langan, P. A., and D. J. Levin. 2002. *Recidivism of Prisoners Released in 1994*. Washington, DC: Bureau of Justice Statistics.

Lynch, J. P., and W. J. Sabol. 2001. *Prisoner Reentry in Perspective*. Washington, DC: Urban Institute Justice Policy Center.

Massachusetts Executive Office of Public Safety. 2003. *2002–2003 Annual Report*. Boston, MA: Massachusetts Department of Correction.

National Conference of State Legislatures. 2003. *State Budget & Tax Actions 2003*. Washington, DC: National Conference of State Legislatures.

Petersilia, J. 1999. "Parole and Prisoner Reentry in the United States," M. Tonry and J. Petersilia, eds., *Prisons*, vol. 26, p. 554. Chicago: University of Chicago Press.

Petersilia, J. 2003. *When Prisoners Come Home*. New York: Oxford University Press.

Petersilia, J., and S. Turner. 1993. "Intensive Probation and Parole," M. H. Tonry, ed., *Crime and Justice: A Review of Research*, p. 17. Chicago: University of Chicago Press.

Piehl, A. M. 2002. *From Cell to Street: A Plan to Supervise Inmates After Release*. Boston: Massachusetts Institute for a New Commonwealth.

Piehl, A. M., B. Useem, and J. J. DiIulio Jr. 1999. *Right-Sizing Justice: A Cost-Benefit Analysis of Imprisonment in Three States*. New York: Manhattan Institute for Policy Research Center for Civic Innovation.

Reitz, Kevin R. 2004. "Questioning the Conventional Wisdom of Parole Release Authority," M. Tonry, ed., *The Future of Imprisonment*. New York: Oxford University Press: 199–235.

Sabol, William J., Katherine Rosich, Kamala Mallik Kane, David Kirk, and Glenn Dubin. 2002. *The Influence of Truth-in-Sentencing Reforms on Changes in States' Sentencing Practices and Prison Populations*. Washington, DC: Urban Institute Press. Available at: http://www.urban.org/UploadedPDF/410470_FINALTISrpt.pdf (Accessed January 24, 2005).

Sutherland, E. H. 1924. *Principles of Criminology*. New York: J. B. Lippincott.

Tonry, M. 2000. "Fragmentation of Sentencing and Corrections in America." *Alternatives to Incarceration* 6(2): 9–13.

Travis, J. 2003. *Parole in California 1980–2000: Implications for Reform, Testimony before Little Hoover Commission*. Washington, DC: Urban Institute.

Travis, J., and S. Lawrence. 2002. *Beyond the Prison Gates: The State of Parole in America*. Washington, DC: Urban Institute.

U.S. Department of Justice. 2003. *Expenditure and Employment Statistics, 2003*. Washington, DC: U.S. Department of Justice, Bureau of Justice Statistics.

U.S. Department of Justice. 1999. *Integrating Drug Testing into a Pretrial Services System*. Washington, DC: Bureau of Justice Assistance.

West, L., and D. Ackerman. 1993. "The Drug-Testing Controversy." Journal of Drug Issues 23: 579.

Wilson, J. Q., and G. Kelling. March 1982. "Broken Windows: The Police and Neighborhood Safety." The Atlantic Monthly, Volume 249, No. 3; pages 29–38.

6

The Impact of Imprisonment on the Desistance Process

Shadd Maruna[1] and Hans Toch

Central to the promotion of public safety is an understanding of how and why offenders "go straight" or "desist from crime." The study of desistance from crime has received an increasing amount of attention in recent years (see Giordano, Cernkovich, and Rudolph 2002; Laub and Sampson 2001), yet little of this work has focused on the role of the correctional system in this process. Indeed, something of a passive consensus has been reached in both the basic science on criminal careers and the more applied research on the effects of incarceration that the experience of imprisonment is largely irrelevant to the subsequent offending patterns of individuals. Farrall (1995) writes, "Most of the research suggests that desistance 'occurs' away from the criminal justice system. That is to say that very few people actually desist as a result of intervention on the part of the criminal justice system or its representatives" (p. 56).

Yet, surely an experience as profound as imprisonment has some impact (malignant or benign) on a person's life course trajectory. Most likely, these effects differ across individuals depending on a complicated mix of factors such as age, status, personality, previous life experiences, and the like. Prisons and the people who inhabit them are complicated, multifaceted, and diverse. Presumably, the experience of imprisonment varies across institutions, individuals, time, and place (see, e.g., Walters, 2003). All of the above

[1] Correspondence to Shadd Maruna, Institute of Criminology, University of Cambridge, 7 West Road, Cambridge CB3 9HD, United Kingdom. Email: sm457@cam.ac.uk. The authors wish to thank Alison Liebling and the editors of this volume for their helpful editorial comments. Also, portions of one of the subsections of this chapter have been reprinted with permission from Toch, H. (Nov–Dec 2003), 'Prison Walls do a Prison Make,' Criminal Law Bulletin, published by West, a Thomson business.

make the question we will address in this chapter – how imprisonment affects the likelihood of desistance from crime – more than a little challenging to answer.

Before starting, we should skip to the punch line and state up front that "more research is needed" to make sense of these complicated interactions between life course trajectories and prison experiences. To quote Gendreau, Goggin, and Cullen (1999):

> The sad reality that so little is known about what goes on inside the "black box" of prisons and how this relates to recidivism (Bonta and Gendreau 1990). Only a mere handful of studies have attempted to address this matter (Gendreau et al. 1979; Zamble and Porporino 1990). Analogously, could one imagine so ubiquitous and costly a procedure in the medical or social services fields receiving such cursory research attention?

Indeed, until recent years (see especially Bushway, Brame, and Paternoster 2004; Petersilia 2003), there has been limited overlap between the research on desistance from crime and the research on prison outcomes or so-called recidivism studies. This is more than a little ironic because desistance and recidivism are arguably two sides of the same coin. Longitudinal research designs that combine a focus on institutional experiences with an interest in issues of human development (e.g., Visher 2002) are badly needed to explore some of the hypotheses we present here.

In what follows, we try to synthesize the various theories of desistance from crime with the theoretical accounts of the effects of imprisonment in hopes that this might be a catalyst for such research designs in the future. Our formula here is a fairly standard one. First, we discuss our understanding of the desistance process. Following that, we selectively review the literature on the effects of imprisonment. Finally, we try to merge the two, using our interpretation of the desistance process to illuminate the "black box" of the prison effects research. In the name of "positive thinking," we use this concluding section to describe potentially "desistance-enhancing" features of the prison experience (knowing well, of course, that there are many more aspects of imprisonment that are desistance-degrading factors, at best).

Desistance from Crime

Of course, understanding desistance is not exactly rocket science. The most robust and important finding in this research to date has been that persons who desist from crime seem to be better integrated into prosocial roles and positions of familial, occupational, and community responsibility than persons who continue offending (see Uggen, Wakefield, and Western, this volume). We know, for instance, that older men (over 27) who are employed are more likely to desist than men of the same age who are not (e.g., Uggen 2000). Likewise, a former offender who develops an attachment and commitment to a noncriminal spouse is more likely to desist than one who does not (e.g., Sampson and Laub 1993).

Such findings come as no surprise to the average parole or probation officer. These efforts to "settle down" have always been understood as largely incompatible with criminal behaviors. What remains in question is the *process* through which these variables come to be associated with the avoidance of crime (e.g., Is it the social control of the time clock or of the spouse waiting at home? Or is it instead the prosocial socialization and role-modeling?). In other words, there is still some question as to the theory of desistance that best fits the data we have on the subject (see especially Warr 2002). This theory question is, in many senses of the word, an academic issue. It may matter little in practical terms what it is about being employed or being part of a family that helps to sustain desistance. What matters may be simply that ex-offenders need to be given opportunities to make such attachments.

Nonetheless, there is a role for criminological theory in the applied world of corrections. Most criminal justice programming is not based on a coherent theory of desistance from crime or indeed any real theory (Gendreau 1996). The dominant ethos in corrections has been described as "anything goes" (Cohen 1985) with a little of this and a little of that thrown in to please various camps. Much of what is done in the name of "corrections" can be psychologically counterproductive – provoking defiance or creating dependence rather than strengthening the person's ability to go straight (see Maruna and LeBel 2003). As such, desistance-enhancing efforts to promote employment or change negative thinking patterns can be and often are coupled with desistance-degrading interactions (e.g., stigmatization and social exclusion). Such odd couplings can leave promising efforts looking ineffective in formal evaluations (and in terms of overall effects on public safety) when in fact babies are being thrown out with the bath water. At the very least, then, developing a coherent account of how and why former offenders go straight can help those of us in the research world make sense of our null findings in corrections research. More optimistically (naively?), correctional programming could become "desistance focused" (Farrall 2002)

141

or organized around a coherent theoretical model of desistance (Maruna and LeBel 2003).

What Is Desistance?

The phrase *desistance from crime* gained popularity in the study of criminal careers and was typically used to describe groups of subjects in probabilistic models of offending career trajectories (e.g., Barnett, Blumstein, and Farrington 1987). In this context, the concept was perfectly understandable and a useful tool for dividing up subpopulations within a cohort of known criminal offenders. Yet, outside of this aggregate framework, and in particular in trying to understand the lived experiences of actual individuals, the phrase's meaning becomes less clear. That is, for Joe Schmo, who was caught shoplifting three or four times as a kid, got into a few bar fights as a young adult, and, in later life, assaulted his partner in a drunken row, it is difficult to know when desistance starts, what desistance looks like, and what desistance means.

On the occasions when definitions of desistance are offered, they tend to be something like the "moment that a criminal career ends" (Farrall and Bowling 1999, p. 253) or "the voluntary termination of serious criminal participation" (Shover 1996, p. 121). This understanding has been widely criticized (see Bushway, et al. 2001; Laub and Sampson 2001), perhaps most noisily by Maruna (2001), who argues that the termination of offending occurs all the time in a so-called criminal career. All of the persons we describe as "offenders" go days, months, even years between offenses. As such, it is impossible to know when offending has finally ended until the person is dead. Even if we were interested only in understanding dead people's desistance, however, this definition still seems unhelpful. Maruna (2001, p. 23) gives the example of a purse-snatcher who stops offending:

> Suppose we know conclusively that the purse-snatcher (now deceased) never committed another crime for the rest of his long life. When did his desistance start? Is not the ... concluding moment the very instant when the person completes (or terminates) the act of theft? If so, in the same moment that a person becomes an offender, he also becomes a desister. That cannot be right.

In an inventive response to such criticisms, Laub and Sampson (2001) distinguish between what they call *termination* (the outcome) and *desistance* (the process) in their important reformulation of desistance. They write: "Termination is the time at which criminal activity stops. Desistance, by contrast, is the causal process that supports the termination of offending." Desistance, according to this reformulation, is the process that "maintains the continued state of nonoffending" (p. 11) beginning prior to termination but carrying on long after.

Although this represents a significant improvement over past working definitions of desistance, Laub and Sampson add new confusion by conflating the causes of desistance with desistance itself. The verb *to desist* means to abstain from doing something. As such, in criminology, desistance is almost always used to mean "the continued state of nonoffending" – not the factors that lead to it. Suppose, for instance, that deterrence is identified as a major "causal process" in the "outcome" of termination. The Laub and Sampson definition would seem to suggest that when an individual steals a purse and then is engaged in the process being deterred (i.e., getting busted), he is actively involved in desisting from crime. The definition therefore ends up confusing desistance with its opposite. That is, usually when someone is arrested we think of this as evidence of offending, not the process of abstaining. Moreover, like other efforts to define desistance as a "process" (e.g., Bushway et al. 2001), the Laub and Sampson definition also confounds desistance with the process of *deescalation* or the slowing down of criminal behaviors that sometimes happens over time. Deescalation may (or may not) eventually build into full-fledged desistance, but there is no reason to force the two perfectly understandable processes to share the same name. It seems to us that deescalation should remain deescalation and desistance should remain desistance.

We think some clarification can be found by pilfering from the literature on criminal etiology. A half-century ago, Edwin Lemert (1948, p. 27) introduced considerable clarity into the debate on the origins of deviance by differentiating between two "sharply polarized or even categorical phases" in this developmental process: primary deviation and secondary deviation. Primary deviation involves the initial flirtation and experimentation with deviant behaviors, whereas secondary deviation is deviance that becomes "incorporated as part of the 'me' of the individual" (Lemert 1951, p. 76). Lemert's argument was that "criminal careers are fashioned in the time of personal identity" and that "to deviate over time is to assume a self-understanding consistent with the behavior" (C. C. Lemert 2000, p. 5).

This two-pronged understanding of deviance allowed Lemert (1951, p. 75) to avoid "the fallacy of confusing original causes with effective causes":

Primary deviation can arise from a wide variety of "causes." ... Each theory may be a valid explanation ... Thus, it can be freely admitted that persons come to drink alcoholic liquors excessively for many different reasons: death of loved ones, exposure to death in battle, ... inferiority feelings, nipple fixation, and many others. (Lemert 1948, p. 57)

Freed from what he saw as a "burdensome" debate around initial etiology, Lemert focused on why some primary deviants underwent a symbolic reorganization at the level of their self-identity and others did not.

This same framework might clarify some issues in the study of desistance. Perhaps there are (at least) two, distinguishable phases in the desistance process: primary and secondary desistance. Primary desistance would take the term *desistance* at its most basic and literal level to refer to any lull or crime-free gap in the course of a criminal career[2] (see West 1961, 1963). Because every secondary deviant experiences a countless number of such pauses in the course of a criminal career, primary desistance would not be a matter of much theoretical interest. The focus of desistance research,[3] instead, would be on secondary desistance: the movement from the behavior of nonoffending to the assumption of the role or identity of a "changed person." In secondary desistance, crime not only stops, but "existing roles

---

[2] The term would only apply to the crime-free gaps of secondary deviants. It makes little sense to talk of desisting from a once-off behavior. Although many of us dabble in criminal behaviors, if this activity does not become a routine pattern (i.e. secondary deviation), then it is more the original dabbling (why do people experiment with crime?) rather than the termination from this dabbling that is theoretically interesting.

[3] Like all definitions of desistance, this dichotomy would be difficult to operationalize. Still, for research purposes, periods of desistance can always be differentiated simply by their lengths. Primary desistance, like primary deviation, could be expected to occur only sporadically, for short periods – a week here, two months there. Secondary desistance, on the other hand, involves a more sustained pattern of demonstrable conformity – a measurable break with previous patterns of offending. If researchers had no other access to means of triangulating a measure of secondary desistance (e.g., through self-identification or the views of proximal others), arbitrary lengths of time could be selected to differentiate between the two types of desistance. Indeed, this is how desistance has traditionally been identified in existing research and makes perfect sense on pragmatic grounds. Optimally, the chosen length could be based on a measure of previous experiences of primary desistance. That is, if sample members tended to desist for a week or less between criminal acts, then a six month period of desistance might be enough to qualify as evidence of secondary desistance. Whereas, if a group seems to experience lulls of several months between criminal acts, then a six month cut-off would not be enough evidence that this is a significant change (see Bushway et al. 2001 for an inventive discussion along these lines).

become disrupted" and a "reorganization based upon a new role or roles will occur" (Lemert 1951, p. 76). Indeed, recent research (Giordano et al. 2002; Maruna 2001; Shover 1996) provides compelling evidence that long-term desistance does involve identifiable and measurable changes at the level of personal identity or the "me" of the individual.

Theories of Desistance

So, what processes can account for this move from a lull into secondary desistance? Until recently, criminological theory was largely silent on this issue. As recently as 1990, Gottfredson and Hirschi argued against theorizing desistance at all. They write: "Crime declines with age. Spontaneous desistance is just that, change in behavior that cannot be explained and change that occurs regardless of what else happens" (p. 136). More recently, efforts to "unpack" the age–crime relationship have been dominated by three basic paradigms: informal social control theory, differential association theory, and cognitive/motivational theory. A more comprehensive review of the different theoretical approaches can be found in Laub and Sampson's (2001) recent review, so no attempt is made here to be all inclusive. Additionally, we forgo the standard ritual of discrediting these existing theories, all of which seem to us to be perfectly plausible accounts, and instead use our conclusion to draw out plausible commonalties among all the views.

Informal Social Control   Sampson and Laub's (1993) theory of informal social control is by far the best developed and best known theory of desistance. They argue that desistance is largely the result of social bonds developed in adulthood. Following the control theory axiom that a person who is attached to mainstream institutions will be less likely to risk the consequences of offending, the theory suggests that new opportunities for attachments in young adulthood (especially to a spouse or a career) account for the process of desistance. They provide the individual with "something to lose" by offending. Sampson and Laub further emphasize the "independent" and "exogenous" impact of these bonds. They argue that these triggering events occur, at least in large part, by "chance" (Laub, Nagin, and Sampson 1998, p. 225; see also Horney, Osgood, and Marshall 1995). If these turning points were entirely the result of the reasoned decisions or personal predilections of individual actors, control theorists admit, they could not argue for "the independent role of social bonds in shaping behavior" (Laub et al. 1998,

p. 225). According to Laub and his colleagues (1998, p. 237): "'Good' things sometimes happen to 'bad' actors."

Differential Association   Warr (1998, 2002) has provided the best developed sociological alternative to Sampson and Laub's theory. Warr counters that changes in postadolescent peer relations, rather than the development of adult institutional attachments, are at the heart of the desistance process. In his social learning or differential association-based reinterpretation, Warr argues that changes in social networks (e.g., exposure to offending or delinquent peers, time spent with peers, and loyalty to peers) can account for the decline in crime with age. When a person drifts away from criminal peer networks who promote and rationalize deviant behaviors, they lose both the motivation and the means of committing most types of criminal behavior. Warr does not doubt that adults who are employed and in stable marriages are most likely to desist from crime, but he argues that this is because married and employed individuals have the least amount of time on their hands to associate with their rowdy friends. Therefore, it is the associations, rather than the informal social control factors, that are driving desistance.

Cognitive/Motivational   The other well-known rejoinder to the informal social control theory originates in a critique of the claim that salient life events such as marriage and employment are mainly exogenous occurrences. Gottfredson and Hirschi (1990, p. 188), for instance, scoff at the notion that "jobs somehow attach themselves" to individuals and emphasize that "subjects are not randomly assigned to marital statuses" (p. 188). Similarly, in her review of Sampson and Laub's (1993) *Crime in the Making*, Joan McCord (1994, p. 415) argues that the authors' own qualitative case histories "seem to show that attitude changes precede the attachments which Sampson and Laub emphasize in their theory." In what Uggen and Kruttschnitt (1998) refer to as "motivational models of desistance," desistance theorists have started to focus on what specific changes on the level of personal cognition (Giordano et al. 2002; Zamble and Quinsey 1997) or self-identity (Burnett 2004; Shover 1996) might precede or coincide with changes in social attachments. Often emerging from a symbolic interactionist tradition, these models suggest that "turning point" events may have a different impact depending on the actor's level of motivation, openness to change, or interpretation of the events (Maruna 2001).

The most fully developed theory of this sort is probably Peggy Giordano and colleagues' (2002) four-part "theory of cognitive transformation." They argue that the desistance process involves the following four stages:

1. A "general cognitive openness to change" (p. 1000);
2. Exposure and reaction to "hooks for change" or turning points (p. 1000);
3. The envisioning of "an appealing and conventional 'replacement self'" (p. 1001); and
4. A transformation in way the actor views deviant behavior (p. 1002).

The "replacement self" most often described in the literature is that of the parent, "family man," or provider (Burnett 2004; Shover 1996). Gove (1985, p. 128), for instance, argues that desistance results at least in part from:

a shift from self-absorption to concern for others; increasing acceptance of societal values ... ; increasing comfort with social relations; increasing concern for others in their community; and increasing concern with the issue of the meaning of life.

Following Erikson (1968), Maruna, LeBel, and Lanier (2003) refer to this as the development of generativity or a concern for promoting and nurturing the next generation – a process that is thought to be a normative aspect of adult development as individuals mature.

Prosocial Labeling Finally, some observers have drawn on labeling theory's notion of a "delabeling process" (Trice and Roman 1970) in understanding desistance. Meisenhelder (1977, p. 329), for instance, describes a "certification" stage of desistance in which, "Some recognized member(s) of the conventional community must publicly announce and certify that the offender has changed and that he is now to be considered essentially noncriminal." Maruna (2001) found considerable evidence of what he calls "redemption rituals" in the life stories of successfully desisting ex-convicts. As with the "degradation ceremony" (Garfinkel 1956) through which wrongdoers are stigmatized, these delabeling ceremonies are directed not at specific acts but to the whole character of the person in question (Braithwaite and Braithwaite 2001, p. 16). Delabeling is thought to be most effective when coming from "on high," particularly official sources such as judges or teachers rather than from family members or friends – where such acceptance can be taken for granted (Wexler 2001). Yet, this sort of certification is most likely to occur when an individual has noncriminal others (especially spouses, employers, or work colleagues) who can act as "personal vouchers" to testify to an individual's credentials as a "changed person" (see Maruna and LeBel 2002).

There is scattered evidence in support of this sort of Pygmalion effect in the behavioral reform process. For instance, in a now-famous experiment, Leake and King (1977) informed treatment professionals that they had developed a scientific test to determine who among a group of patients were most likely to be successful in recovering from alcoholism. In reality, no such test had been developed. The patients identified as "most likely to succeed" were picked purely at random. Still, the clients who were assigned this optimistic prophecy were far more likely to give up drinking than members of the control group. Apparently, they believed in their own ability to achieve sobriety because the professionals around them seemed to believe it so well.

Similarly, Miller, Brickman, and Bolen (1975) demonstrated this process in their experimental research on compliance. They found that when untidy students were instructed to keep their classroom neat, the young people complied with these pleadings only as long as they were reinforced with consequences and no longer. Conversely, when, during one such period of compliance, a random group of the students was identified and praised by the teacher for being especially tidy individuals, the improvements lasted for several months (see also Strenta and DeJong 1981). People tend to persist more in the pursuit of behavior that they see as intrinsically determined rather than imposed by external forces (Kelman 1958). Likewise, some research on desistance suggests that secondary desisters avoid crime because they see themselves as fundamentally good (or noncriminal) people and not because they "have to" to avoid sanctions (Maruna 2001).

Key Commonalities: Agency and Communion

These various theoretical positions are not necessarily in competition with one another; indeed they share numerous commonalities. In particular, all these accounts, in some way or another, reflect a need for "agency" and "communion" (Bakan 1966)[4] in the desistance process. That is, each

---

[4] Bakan may owe this dichotomy to the pre-Socratic philosopher, Empedocles. Dan McAdams and his colleagues (1996: 340) write, "That human lives are animated by two broad and contrasting tendencies resembling Bakan's concepts of agency and communion is an idea that is at least 2,000 years old." Agency and communion themes have also been a central feature of almost every scientific effort to quantify significant aspects of interpersonal behavior for at least the last 45 years (see the review in Wiggins, 1991).

theory predicts that desistance should be associated with the achievement of success and autonomy in the prosocial world (usually in the form of a career) and the development of intimate interpersonal bonds (usually in the form of a family) (see Uggen, Wakefield, and Western, this volume). That such things are important to one's ability to go straight is not surprising. Sigmund Freud nominated these two aspects of life – work and love – as the two essential ingredients of a happy and well-adjusted personality. More recently, Deci and Ryan (2000, p. 229) have included the polarities of agency and communion as among the basic human "needs" or "innate psychological nutriments that are essential for ongoing psychological growth, integrity, and well-being."

If it is true that human beings have a natural predisposition "to experience themselves as causal agents in their environment" and to earn the esteem and affection of valued others (Gecas and Schwalbe 1983), then crime might be associated with constraints on these human needs. For instance, Moffitt (1993, p. 686–687) describes the 5- to 10-year role vacuum that teenagers and young adults face during which "they want desperately to establish intimate bonds with the opposite sex, to accrue material belongings, to make their own decisions, and to be regarded as consequential by adults" only to find they are "asked to delay most of the positive aspects of adult life." When social structures constrain one's ability to achieve agency and autonomy (or, in Marxist terms, when the individual is alienated from his or her labors), an individual might turn to criminal or delinquent behaviors to "experience one's self as a cause" rather than an "effect" (Matza 1964, p. 88; see also Messner and Rosenfeld 2001). This deviant behavior itself can become a kind of "chimera" (Patterson 1993), "mortgaging one's future" (Nagin and Paternoster 1991) by cutting off opportunities for achieving success in employment, education, and even in marriage (on incarceration and "marriageability," see Wilson and Neckerman 1987). Such persons are often left with limited opportunity for achieving self-respect and affiliation in the mainstream – but are welcomed among subcultural groups of similarly stigmatized outcasts (Braithwaite and Braithwaite 2001; Sampson and Laub 1997).

Within this vicious cycle, however, there are numerous lulls in offending. By most accounts, a lull can turn into secondary desistance if the person finds a source of agency and communion in noncriminal activities. That is, he or she finds some sort of "calling" – be it parenthood, painting, coaching, or what Richard Sennett (2003) calls "craft-love" – through which they find meaning and purpose outside of crime. The discovery of alternative, intrinsically rewarding sources of achievement and affiliation seems to be an essential component in the successful abstinence from such highs.

The Impact of Imprisonment

Imprisonment can provide one well-known "lull" in an offending career. Of course, there are opportunities for violence, theft, drug sales, and the like inside every prison system. Yet the process of arrest, conviction, and incarceration is a notable disruption in the lives of individuals and conceivably could be a window of opportunity for making a change in one's behavior.

Nonetheless, the major theories of desistance reviewed above do not tend to include an explicit role for the impact of imprisonment. There is a good reason for this. From the best available research, it still remains unclear what impact, if any, prison might have on the desistance process (and, for that matter, on public safety). Although inconclusive, research suggests that imprisonment has little if any predictable impact on offending careers, good or bad (Gendreau, Goggin, and Cullen 1999; MacKenzie and Goodstein, 1985). Of course, as Wormith and Porporino (1984, p. 427) argue: "The prison itself does not do anything.... It just sits there. What really matters are the 'subtle specifics of each prisoner's participation in prison life.'" As such, untangling how this process works for different persons in different circumstances is rightly described as a "methodological nightmare" (Wormith 1984). Donald Cressey (1973) famously argued that "Prison life is made up of social interactions that are confused, entangled, complicated, and so subtle in their effects that any detailed attempts to tell what happens in them sounds like the ravings of a crazy man."

Theories of Prison Effects

There are three paradigmatic accounts of how prison experiences affect most prisoners most of the time. Each has had its day and all three continue to be tested and modified in prisons research. The "specific deterrence" hypothesis suggests that the experience of prison scares crooked people straight, convincing them to behave or face the same consequences later. Most other arguments posit the opposite effect: that prison is, in the words of a British Home Secretary, "an expensive way of making bad people worse." The most common version of this story is the "schools of crime" idea that differential association with a group of seasoned offenders will promote further and greater criminal behavior among graduates. Others have argued that the experience of confinement, specifically severe forms of solitary confinement, can produce negative mental health effects that could exasperate future criminality. Finally, sociologists have argued that the pains or deprivations of prison life require the development of social adaptations that may themselves have a lasting impact on the ability of an individual to desist from crime.

Prison as a Specific Deterrence Although the idea that "prison works" as a specific deterrent is favored by vote-seeking politicians (see Austin and Irwin 2000), the idea that the prison experience should reduce offending among ex-prisoners (Andeanaes 1968) has almost no support in the criminological literature. In fact, not only has specific deterrence theory been long pronounced dead (see especially McGuire's 1995 essay, "The Death of Deterrence"), criminologists refuse to offer any respect for the deceased (see, for example, Lynch's 1999 article titled, "Beating a Dead Horse: Is There Any Basic Empirical Evidence for the Deterrent Effect of Imprisonment?").

The most conclusive evidence to date of the futility of the "prisons as deterrence" thesis is Paul Gendreau and colleagues' (1999) meta-analysis synthesizing the findings from 50 prison effects studies dating from 1958 involving over 300,000 prisoner subjects. Combining the data across studies that either compared prison sentences to community sentences or correlated length of time in prison with recidivism outcomes, the authors concluded there was no evidence that prison sentences could reduce recidivism and substantial evidence shows that the relationship works the other way around. Indeed, they found the higher the quality of the study (including two randomized designs), the more likely it was to find a strong positive correlation between time spent in prison and recidivism.

Contemporary research on specific deterrence tends to focus on explaining this "positive punishment effect" (e.g., Paternoster and Piquero 1995; Pogarsky and Piquero 2003). Yet, it is not hard to imagine why the rational-sounding deterrence hypothesis seems to fail in the case of prisons. The use of incarceration as a sanction meets none of the suggested conditions for success (e.g., certainty, severity, and celerity) in the basic psychology of punishment (McGuire 2002; Moffitt 1983). Moreover, the average prison regime meets none of the criteria that various observers have suggested for promoting long-term compliance and conformity (e.g., Bottoms 2000; Kelman 1958; Tyler 1990).

151

Still, dead though this horse certainly is, the idea of the prison as a specific deterrence has some hope for a more modest afterlife. Emerging research, for instance, has focused on identifying individuals who might be more receptive to deterrent effects based on their level of attachment to mainstream institutions (e.g., DeJong 1997), their level of "risk" or immersion in criminal activities (Zamble and Porporino 1990), or cognitive factors (e.g., Pogarsky and Piquero 2003).

Prisons as Schools of Crime   The most enduring assumption used to explain the criminogenic effects of confinement is that prison functions as a "school of crime." On the strength of this assumption, 19th-century penitentiaries carefully restricted communication among prisoners to the extent of hooding newly arrived inmates so that they could not see any of their peers, who were safely locked behind the massively impermeable doors of segregation cells. In subsequent periods of early prison history, permutations of silence rules and solitary confinement were instituted, variously subsumed under rival and fiercely competing schools of penology. Despite warmly debated differences in cherished prescriptions focused on issues such as the virtues of congregate versus solitary labor, the penological experts of the time unanimously converged on the premise that if their prisoners were allowed to associate and to converse with each other, they would be inevitably reinforcing criminal propensities and honing their felonious expertise.

Though prison inmates were ultimately allowed to freely congregate and associate in general prison populations, the "school of crime" assumption was never completely abandoned. It survived among prison administrators as a standard rationale for administrative confinement, and it earned popularity among social scientists as a subject for prison research studies. Typically, these studies consisted of thoughtfully worded opinion inventories administered to prisoners over the course of their sentences. The expectation of the researchers who conducted the studies was that they would be able to document a process (called "prisonization")[5] whereby inmates would be "taking on in greater or lesser degree the folkways, mores, customs, and general culture of the penitentiary," including "the criminalistic ideology in the prison community" (Clemmer, 1970, p. 299). The survey results showed apparent increases in antiauthoritarian and deviant attitudes,

---

[5] The concept of prisonization, although often attributed to Clemmer, probably originated in 1898, under the diagnosis of "Ganser Syndrome" (Shorer 1965).

which, however, usually dissipated as prisoners approached the end of their terms (Garabedian, 1963; Wheeler, 1961). This "inverted U curve" usually described in early studies was eventually proved to be a misleading composite, covering subgroups of inmates who held divergent attitudes and experienced varying patterns of attitude change over time.

The idea of "schools of crime" implicitly raised the presumption that older, seasoned, recidivistic offenders would exercise formative criminogenic influences over young, incipient delinquents at the threshold of their inauspicious careers. This hypothetical scenario contrasts sharply with the interaction patterns generally observed in non-age-graded prison yards, which include frantic efforts by older prisoners to insulate themselves and avoid contact with youthful fellow inmates, who in turn tend to congregate and associate with each other.

This does not mean that some prisoners are not exposed to pressures and influences from other prisoners. Such influences can be criminogenic if they sustain or reinforce an offender's interest in offending, such as through nostalgic war stories involving inflated accounts of criminal accomplishments. Fellow inmates can also interfere with other prisoners' self-improvement efforts by distracting them or belittling their accomplishments or promulgating antiadministration subcultural norms.

The main criminogenic effect may therefore consist of opportunities for the peer reinforcement of antisocial norms and behavior patterns among younger offenders. This interaction pattern became of particularly pressing concern to prison administrators in relation to gang activity, which was said to include participation in intramural drug trading and in violent incidents resulting from intergroup rivalries.

The perceptions of the refractory nature of gang behavior recently contributed to the proliferation, in American prisons, of administrative segregation (or "supermax") settings, reminiscent of early solitary confinement regimes. Given historical experiences with isolation or segregation settings, one would expect that their sensory-depriving regimes will prove multifariously criminogenic, reducing the coping capacity of long-term confinees, cementing their alienation and resentment, impairing their mental health, and disqualifying the ex-prisoners for effective communal existence.

The hypothesis at issue is that "when finally released to the 'free world,' the [supermax] prisoners' rage or damaged mental health, or both will result in continuing criminal, especially violent, conduct" (Ward and Werlich 2003, p. 62). A persuasive case to this effect is made by Craig Haney (2003), who described "social pathologies" that have been reported or observed in

153

segregation settings. The most common include problems with self-control and self-initiation of behavior, apathy, lethargy and despair, bursts of acting out, uncontrollable anger and rage, persecutory delusions, and fantasy lives centered on prospects of revenge. Haney points out that "there is good reason to believe that some prisoners . . . cannot and will not overcome these pathologies; their extreme adaptations to supermax confinement become too engrained to relinquish" (p. 141). Prisoners who break down under stress have diminished prospects for postrelease adjustment. By the same token, "those who have adapted all too well to the deprivation, restriction, and pervasive control are prime candidates for release to a social world to which they may be incapable of ever fully readjusting" (ibid.).

Supermax settings are designed to benefit the prisons from which candidates for supermax placement are drawn but may accomplish this at the expense of public safety in the community. Results of a recent study (Lovell and Johnson, 2003) confirm that supermax graduates may record higher-than-expected recidivism rates. Increments in serious offending were particularly noteworthy among the segregated inmates who were released into the streets directly from confinement. The authors write:

A major concern . . . was that offenders released from [segregation] into the community would be too disoriented, jumpy or hostile to cope with the challenges of society. . . . We found that the time between subjects' release from [supermax] and their release into the community (Time to Release) was correlated with felony recidivism, new person offenses, and length of survival in the community before committing new offenses . . . When entered into logistic regression equations, Immediate Prison Release showed more robust associations with outcomes than Time to Release did. (p. 13)

Prison Adaptation as Criminogenic According to some observers, prisons in general may leave a lasting impact on the prisoner's sense of self and personal identity because of the adaptive challenges that prison environments present (see Petersilia, this volume). Liebling (1999, p. 341) writes:

Fear, anxiety, loneliness, trauma, depression, injustice, powerlessness, violence, rejection, and uncertainty are all part of the experience of prison. It is this 'hidden,' but everywhere apparent, feature of prison life that medical officers, psychologists, and others have failed to measure or take seriously. Sociologists of prison life knew it was there, but have to date largely failed to convince others in a sufficiently methodologically convincing way that pain is a harm.

This concern originated with functionalist sociologists, notably with Gresham Sykes (1965), who saw much of prison behavior reflecting an

154

effort by inmates to retain their self-esteem in the face of custodial assaults. Sykes discussed five "pains of imprisonment," which he defined as "deprivations and frustrations [that] pose profound threats to the inmate's personality or sense of personal worth" (p. 64). The first deprivation discussed by Sykes was the deprivation of liberty, including long-term separation from loved ones and a sense of "rejection or degradation by the free community [which] must be warded off, turned aside, rendered harmless" (p. 67). Sykes highlighted the spartan nature of prison life "in a world where control and possession of the material environment are commonly taken as sure indicators of a man's worth" (p. 69) and discussed the liabilities of a single-sex world in which "an essential component of man's self conception – his status of male – is called into question" (p. 71).

The most obvious problems for the prisoner that is described by Sykes was the deprivation of autonomy, which results from the proliferation of rules and constraints that pose "a profound threat to the prisoner's self image because they reduce the prisoner to the weak, helpless, dependent status of childhood" (p. 75). Sykes wrote that "of the many threats which may confront the individual, either in or out of prison, there are few better calculated to arouse acute anxieties than the attempt to reimpose the subservience of youth" (p. 76). Finally, Sykes dealt with assaultive or threatening behavior by other inmates that "constantly calls into question the individual's ability to cope with it, in terms of his inner resources, his courage, his 'nerve'" (p. 78).

The point made by Sykes and other deprivation theorists was that prisoners are constrained to engage in adaptive behavior that promotes survival in institutional settings. The corollary presumption was that the behavior could be discontinued upon release. Goffman thus wrote that "it seems that shortly after release the ex-inmate forgets a great deal of what life was like on the inside and once again begins to take for granted the privileges around which life in the institution was organized" (Goffman 1961, p. 72). However, there remains the question of whether deprivation-induced adjustments may in fact persist and prove dysfunctional for some offenders following release from confinement. (As cases in point, prison tattoos foreclose employment options, and ex-offenders may carry weapons to counter no-longer-existing threats.)

More to the point is that prison adaptations such as those described by Sykes and others may replicate some of the crime-related subcultural behavior imported from the streets and may help to perpetuate it (Wacquant 2000). The criminogenic carryover patterns, which are accentuated by deprivation, include prison gang behavior, as well as hypermasculine behavioral norms and codes that are prevalent in male maximum security prisons (Toch 1997). These norms include subcultural assumptions that legitimize the use of force and the exploitation of weak or vulnerable peers. To the extent to which the assumptions of deprivation theory hold, the perpetuation of criminogenic norms in prison is a product of harsh custodial regimes. If this is the case, it follows that crime-related dispositions can be reduced where prison deprivations are ameliorated.

Assessing Prison Impact

In a recent issue of the *California Law Review*, J. C. Oleson (2002) advanced the ingenious Swiftian prescription he entitled "The Punitive Coma." Under this tongue-in check proposal judges would not sentence any offender to a conventional prison term but would instead substitute a commensurate period of chemically induced sleep. Among the advantages of this innovation is that it would save a great deal of money, because the prisoners could be stacked in rows of bunk beds, with minimal servicing required. The system would also make the present chapter very short, because the probabilities of reoffending at discharge from the prison could not have been affected by the prison experience. In other words, the impact of the prison would be zero.

A less drastic variation on this same scenario is the contention (by Zamble and Porporino 1988 and others) that adaptational styles and capacities of offenders are basically invariant and largely impervious to effects of imprisonment. According to this view, incarceration is a "behavioral deep freeze" that puts a person's self-destructive propensities on hold until renewed opportunities are presented for these propensities to be freely exercised. Indeed, ethnographic work in prison that indicates that prisoners construct prison time as a sort of "limbo" (Sapsford 1978) or "suspension" of reality (Schmid and Jones 1991), separating their inside selves from their real life (or outside selves).

An argument against this position would be based on the fact that there are well-established maturation effects on criminal behavior in the community, which are manifest in dramatic negative correlations between age and offending (Glueck and Glueck 1937; Gottfredson and Hirschi 1990). Such maturation effects need not be discontinued during confinement. Maturation explains the fact that prison rule violation rates decrease over time (Toch and Adams 2002) and that the key concerns of prisoners and their interests can evolve, especially with long-term confinement. Such changes are often accommodated by prison administrations with differences in the setting in which younger and older prisoners are placed.

Of course, measuring the effects of imprisonment is no easy task. At present, the prison effects literature is redolent with descriptive accounts, vignettes, and imperfect research studies, which can be easily dismissed by discerning critics as invalid documentation of prison impact (see Bukstel and Kilmann 1980). There are also difficulties about attributing increments (or decrements) in postprison adjustment to experiences in the prison. On the one hand, observed changes in attitudes or behavior may not endure once the inmate leaves the prison. Beyond the first hours after release, for example, powerful environmental impingements may supercede any salutary or destructive residues of the prison experience itself. On the other hand, there is also the risk of our crediting the prison with transformations the prisoner may have undergone independently of experiences for which the institution is responsible. The offender may improve on his or her own while incarcerated or may be positively or negatively affected by developments outside the walls. Moreover, institutional influences can reinforce or neutralize each other. As the criminological psychoanalyst Fritz Redl was fond of pointing out, "If I mend a delinquent's arm, I am not to be blamed if he goes out and breaks his leg."

To assess the impact of a program we need to know how much recidivism we can expect from its graduates. With this information at hand, we can take credit for differences between expected and attained recidivism scores. In conventional designs, the source of information about expected recidivism is the success rate of a comparison group, which presupposes strict comparability of expected scores for the groups and a "deep freeze" assumption about the comparison group. Of course, the design does not help us with regard to individual offenders, which is important because program impact is apt to differ for members of any group.

In assessing the effects of imprisonment on an offender's chances of recidivating one would need to know how much recidivism could have been expected under deep-freeze or punitive-coma conditions. A measure that Leslie T. Wilkins called the "Base Expectancy Score" could summarize the predictive indices available at prison intake (very much including anticipated age at release) and could provide the tool for systematic comparisons of prison effects. Discrepancies between expected and observed recidivism in either direction would point to benefits or harms accrued during confinement. Researchers can explore differential effects of various prison programs by grouping prisoners who have higher and lower expectancy scores to assess the impact of the program on inmates varying in criminogenic potential and to compare these effects to the differential impact of various interventions. However, it is important to emphasize in this connection – as did Wilkins (1969, p. 130) – that:

The attractiveness of base-expectancy methods in evaluation lies in its independence of administrative or operational processes. The program may be designed in any way, offenders allocated by any procedure believed to be good, and yet some form of evaluation may still be possible.

Wilkins (1969, p. 106) emphasizes that "if we wish to consider the outcome of treatment on offenders, we should be concerned both with the type of treatment and with the type of offender, because the postulated outcome can be seen only in terms of an interaction." An excellent illustration is provided by one of the principal findings of the original Borstal prediction study (Mannheim and Wilkins, 1955). The authors reported the following:

The 'open' Borstals do get 'better material' upon which to work their reforming influence, so far as the experience tables enable us to classify new entrants into risk groups. But, over and above this, the results show that there is a fair amount of the variance which may be accredited to the type of treatment – or, in other words, those who are sent to 'open' Borstals do better than the prognoses suggest, whilst those who are sent to 'closed' do worse . . . This is, perhaps, not absolute proof that 'open' treatment is better than 'closed,' but it is extremely near complete proof. (p. 112)

The point being that although person-setting interactions are inextricable, we can sometimes parcel out the relative contributions of environments and of personal predispositions to positive or negative outcomes.

Desistance-Supportive Prison Experiences

On the average, one of two paroled inmates return to prison within 3 years (Langan and Levin 2002). Innovative efforts to reduce this average figure through rehabilitative programming come and go occasionally. Of course, these days, such programs in the U.S. prison system tend to be "going" more than "coming," as states cut back on "perks" such as education and treatment inside their prison systems. In some ways, then, it is remarkable that the reconviction rate is not higher than it is, considering what we know about desistance and the experience of imprisonment. In this section, we review the elements of the prison experience that might contribute to the

158

remarkable resiliency of so many of the individuals who pass through the prison system.

Building on Success

Interventions that demonstrate unusually low recidivism of necessity must combine features or attributes that uniquely contribute to promoting personal reform and to enhancing its staying power. An example of an unusually successful enterprise some of whose components have been emulated elsewhere is a small prison located in the state of Sao Paulo, Brazil. This prison – formerly administered by the local police – was adopted in 1973 by a Catholic lay organization (APAC), after which it was named. The prison claims to be nonsectarian, but religiosity and commitment to change are among its admissions criteria. According to Anderson (1991), "Inmates transfer to APAC Prison from government-run prisons throughout Brazil. They must fill out a 12-page written application and undergo an interview process in which APAC Prison staff evaluate the sincerity of their interest in rehabilitation" (p. 100). Serious offense history is no bar to admission into the prison, half of whose inmates are violent offenders, including men convicted of homicide, robbery, and sexual assault. A total of 520 of these inmates were released or paroled from the prison during its first 18 years of existence, and 20 were reconvicted – a recidivism rate of 4 percent, as compared with the Brazilian national reconviction rate of 84 percent. A more recent cohort, comprising 148 APAC prisoners released in 1996, yielded a reconviction rate of 16 percent over a 3-year period. The author of this study acknowledged that the figure was higher than the previously recorded 4 percent, but pointed out that "the recidivism rate . . . is remarkably low by any standard" (Johnson 2002, p. 9).

Among the salient attributes of the APAC Prison is that it has no correctional officers. Three civilians serve as warden-equivalents – with support from a democratically elected inmate council – and other custodial functions are exercised by the inmates themselves. The prisoners' institutional career is divided into three phases of increasing freedom and escalating contributions to the community, culminating in a phase of work release. The prison is unprecedentedly permeable, with continuous involvement by the relatives of the prisoners, who attend many communal functions and religiously tinged educational experiences. Each prisoner is also assigned a citizen-sponsor, who acts as "godparent" during his confinement and following release. An army of religiously motivated citizen volunteers – including

159

mental health professionals – lead prison seminars and weekend retreats that are concerned with issues of ethical behavior and human relatedness. All religiously oriented experiences in the prison, ranging from the didactic sessions to more formal occasions such as mass, are participatory in nature. The prison thus has many of the earmarks of a communitarian social movement.

Correctional officials from various parts of the world have made professional field trips or pilgrimages to the APAC prison. The experience is invariably described as illuminating. A Scottish prison official returned home to report that "there is little doubt that this regime works." He recalled that "during the final week of my visit a five-man Russian delegation arrived at the prison. General Saraikin, Deputy Director of the Russian Prison system, said that 'seeing is believing' what he had already heard and read about the APAC prison" (Creighton 1993, p 11). APAC's own newsletter provides a continuing record of concurrent visits by foreign dignitaries who are cited as voicing their determination to replicate the model in their own countries. One of the visitors who expressed the resolve was Chuck Colson, the founder of Prison Fellowship. In a foreword to a book about APAC, he wrote that:

I first visited Humaita [a preexisting name for the prison] in the spring of 1990: I was overwhelmed. It seemed more of a spiritual retreat center than a prison.... If anything, my second visit to Humaita was more exciting than my first. I didn't see a single inmate who was not smiling. Almost all of the men were wearing crosses around their neck or T-shirts with biblical quotes.... I told them I was glad to be there because the Spirit of God was so evident in the place. The inmates immediately burst into sustained applause.... This is a prison you'd like to stay in.... I couldn't help but think what would happen if we could apply some of these basic concepts to our criminal justice system in America. (Ottobani 2000, 1–2)

The United Kingdom has instituted several prison units modeled after APAC. The first such unit was opened in 1997 at HMP The Verne under the auspices of Geoff Hebbern, a Principal Officer employed by the prison. Three years after its inception, the Verne unit reported that it had released 120 prisoners, but that only 5 had reoffended (Bowers 2000; but see the later evaluation by Burnside, Adler, Loucks, and Rose 2001). In a retrospective letter, Officer Hebbern (1998) wrote that "the success is due to many different elements in the programme," but that these included "the strong Christian component," "the large number of volunteers," "the fact that participants are allowed to make many of the decisions... through their democratically elected councils," an inclusive or "open" admissions policy, and "prison system permission to allow ex-offenders to work on the project." Hebbern also alluded to the unit's morale and social climate, indicating that "this is, without a doubt, the most dynamic and exciting program I have ever been involved in."

In the United States, the Prison Fellowship Ministries opened a religiously oriented prison (Innerchange, in Jester-II in Texas), said to comprise key elements of the APAC model, including the participation of relatives of inmates and the heavy involvement of civilian volunteers. The prison's regime, however, is relatively traditional and does not prominently include the democratic and communitarian elements of the Brazilian and the English prison units. Theologically, as pointed out by Creighton (1998), "the difference between the two models might be described in terms of their Roman Catholic and Protestant/Evangelical perspectives, and different cultural backgrounds" (p. 7). The import of these differences in regime, religious orientation, and culture between the Brazilian model and the Texas adaptation awaits exploration through recidivism research. Such research will be facilitated by the fact that eligible inmates are randomly allocated to Jester or a comparison group of Texas prisoners. Additional comparisons become possible by virtue of the fact that InnerChange programs have been established in prisons in Minnesota, Kansas, and Iowa as well as Texas, so that contextual variations can be explored.

Regenerative Continuity

Among the difficulties that have plagued otherwise potent and effective programs is that of discontinuity between their rarified and specialized environments and the mundane attributes of settings in which their graduates must function. The problem of nontransferability of gains is not confined to specific treatment modalities. Learning-based or behavior-modifying programs have found themselves unable to compete with real-world reinforcement schedules, and the clients of insight-promotive or group-therapeutic programs have encountered outsiders less than hospitable to their disarming displays of openness and honesty.

More generic prison programs have also had to deal with discontinuity issues. Programs that were assiduously engaged in shaping prosocial attitudes and reinforcing beneficent personality traits, for example, had good reason to suspect that on the streets some desirable personal dispositions are more deployable than others. Likewise, vocational trainers discovered that they could expect no impact (other than boomerang effects) from the

161

successful inculcation of skills for which there was no free-world demand or for which they would not be able to practice because of legal restrictions. The *New York Times* (Haberman 2003) recently recounted the story of an ex-prisoner, successfully trained in the barbering trade inside the New York State prison system, who learned upon his release that he could not gain a license to actually cut hair from the state that had taught him barbering.

Some discontinuity problems are insoluble because the disjunctures involved are unbridgeable or the variables that need to be addressed lie beyond one's jurisdiction. Prison administrators, for example, cannot select salubrious associates for ex-offenders or engender employment opportunities for graduates of their vocational training programs. On occasion, however, bridging experiences can be devised that transfer enough elements of rehabilitative interventions into the community to keep the regenerative process alive. In some innovative bridging experiences, supportive arrange-ments can be introduced that allow the offender to practice newly acquired skills or to deploy some of the fruits of recent learning experiences. These protective experiences are designed to preserve some of the rehabilitative gains achieved by the offender in the prison, ensuring their carryover into the community.

Historical precedents for aftercare components are provided by the men-tal health movement in the period preceding deinstitutionalization, when hospital administrators were assigned responsibility for making release arrangements for their patients (Rothman 1980). Continuity was presump-tively ensured (much to the dismay of some hospital administrators con-cerned about their budgets) by specifying that patients would be served by staff members who had worked with them in the institution. Where com-partmentalization of agencies came to preclude continued assignment of the same service providers before and after release, approximations were attained by promoting close links between institutional program staff and staff charged with running (philosophically congruent) aftercare programs, such as trained, specialized parole officers. Conversely, prison programs were sometimes run by the staff of their community components, or by some of their own graduates, on a contractual basis.

In connection with the APAC program, we have already seen continu-ity in religious or faith-based prison units that operate with the support and participation of outside religious groups. Church members who are involved in such programs offer all manner of social and material assis-tance (very much including jobs) to program participants after they leave the prison. This makes it very difficult to attribute an offender's successful

162

adjustment in the community to the (religious) content of the program, as opposed to the material and interpersonal assistance he has received or some combination of these elements.

Bridging Experiences

It has become increasingly obvious that the process of readjustment to the community may be initiated while the offender is still in prison, though this principle is resoundingly violated where shackled prisoners are discharged from segregation units or where jail inmates are released with bus tickets and change. By contrast, intramural transition management can take a variety of forms, ranging from preparole counseling and courses in parenting, job hunting or life skills, to halfway house or work-release settings that provide graduated experiences of community living.

The overwhelming concern when any offender leaves the prison is the prospect of his or her reoffending, but a closely related concern is that the offender may not be able to secure employment so as to keep from reoffending. Programs have consequently been set up to try to initiate the job-hunting sequence while the offender is still confined. The state of Ohio, for example, "invites local business leaders to job fairs at Ohio prisons... inmates must be within 45 days of release and are required to develop a current resume." Preliminary data suggest that "about 26 percent of participating inmates are offered employment... another 73 percent are encouraged to report after their release for additional interviewing and consideration" (Unwin, Mayers, and Wilt 1999, p. 114–115). Ohio prisons also uses teleconferencing facilities for employment interviews. Other technology is deployed by the Washington State prison system, which operates a computerized clearinghouse, called CCH. According to Finn (1999):

At five prisons, CCH instructors register their students with the Employment Security Department, enabling them to access the department's JobNet computerized job data bank so that they can discover job leads while still in the prison. CCH contracts with.... the "Ex-O" program, which provides job search assistance to adult and juvenile ex-offenders, including ongoing post placement services. (p. 8)

The Washington program has instituted a community resource directory, which is staffed by prisoners with computer expertise. Finn (1999) notes that there were "six inmates who designed and wrote the computer software for the disk version of the directory, update the entries quarterly, and staff toll-free telephone and fax lines for ordering copies, receiving

163

updates, and adding resources" (p. 9). The directory represents a twist in transitional programming in that prisoners assist ex-prisoners with problems of community reintegration.

The Washington program showed reduced recidivism, but "the study did not control for the possibility that the Ex-O clients might have been lower risk or more highly motivated than other releases" (ibid.). No such caveat attached to a bridging program in Texas (Project RIO) in which the participants and nonparticipants "had similar demographic characteristics and risk of reoffending." Moreover, participants from minority groups showed disproportionate benefits, and the program proved "of greatest benefit to ex-offenders who were considered the most likely to reoffend" (p. 7). This outcome is particularly telling because it suggests that some bridging experiences might be most profitably deployed with prisoners whose base-expectancy scores are the least promising.

Sequencing of Prison Experiences

If prison terms were to be designed for impact, the average prisoner's experiences would be arranged in chronological order to achieve cumulative effects. A module that inculcates basic skills, for example, could be followed by an opportunity to acquire advanced skills and a set of work assignments in which these skills could be exercised. Treatment and educational experiences might similarly lead to paraprofessional assignments as peer counselors, teacher's aides, and so forth.

Advancement and progression would not only make prison existence more "normal" but also multiply incentives for prisoners to engage in constructive activities. Long prison terms, in particular, have to be reviewed from time to time to ensure that the prisoners do not vegetate or drift along haphazardly. Sentence planning must start with some attempt at an orientation, to ameliorate predictable adjustment problems. Conversely, any programs designed to facilitate reintegration are best deployed close to release. Midsentence planning for the prisoners remains an inordinately difficult challenge, because sequences of constructive experiences are hard to come by in prisons, especially experiences with beneficent carryover potential.

Short sentences promise less chance of impact than long sentences because brief prison terms can be regarded by an offender as intermissions, as substandard vacations, or as routine costs of doing business. However, a revolving door of short-term incarcerations may at some juncture offer a window of opportunity if the offender realizes that he is embarked on a distressingly redundant self-destructive career with no end in sight.

Short prison terms can also be designed (as in shock incarceration experiences) to promote desistance through intensive programming. Typically, the prisoner discovers that he is being concurrently exposed to different interventions, such as substance-abuse treatment, education, and military-style basic training. If the results include low (or nonhigh) recidivism rates, program staff will argue that the effect must be due to the combination of modalities in their program. Such, however, is not necessarily the case, and it has thus been argued that military drills in shock incarceration do not contribute to the outcome of the intervention (MacKenzie, Brame, McDowell, and Souryal 1995). Literacy-based or educational "boot camps," involving intensive educational drills or service learning may be just as likely to promote desistance as is marching about and doing push-ups. Indeed this was empirically documented in Farrington et al.'s (2002) of two qualitatively different boot camp regimes (one militaristic and the other treatment based) in the United Kingdom.

Prison Milieus

In considering the impact of prisons one must not only focus on rehabilitative programs but on differences in the prison environments in which the programs must function (Liebling 2002; Lin 2000). Such differences have been characterized as systematically divergent social climates (Moos 1975; Toch 1992). These are psychometrically describable, but they may also be readily discernible to informed observers.

A prison visiting committee fielded by the Corrections Association of New York thus observed in a recent report (2002) that "it is notable to us that each prison we visit tends to have its own distinct culture, and that traditions and practices are reinforced over time which lend to the facility a certain status or reputation" (p. 10). As cases in point, the committee alluded to "two prisons across the road from each other, [whose] cultures are worlds apart." In the first of the prisons, "inmates and staff refer to the prison as a 'campus.' The atmosphere is markedly peaceful; prisoners and staff report few complaints when we visited. Everyone seemed invested in keeping the prison safe and calm." The second prison proved to be a source of "numerous reports from inmates, attorneys and family members ... about serious correction officer misconduct" pointing to "an unspoken policy of might makes right which appeared largely ignored by a detached administration."

165

Divergences in institutional climate were reinforced by a reputed tendency of security staff to "seek positions at prisons where the culture supports their style of management" (ibid.).

Differences in climate may be unrelated to security level that is associated with offender attributes. One New York prison contains a population, 87 percent of which is under sentence for violent felonies, and is described in an official publication as having "a relaxed low-key feel" resulting from "an attitude created and nurtured by the staff and felt and shared by the inmates." The "spirit of mutual respect" is described as carrying over into "sustained operation of programs for several groups of men with special problems." Clients of the programs "are not victimized. On the contrary, many general population inmates watch out for them, informally or formally as interpreters and mobility guides" (*DOCS Today* 2002, p. 14).

The portrait is noteworthy, in that special populations in the prison include individuals lacking in life skills, whose adjustment to the community could be problematic. Under an inflexible custodial regime, or in a dog-eat-dog inmate environment, any benefits accrued through social skills training could be neutralized by the institutional climate. Given the cooperative, nurturing culture in this prison, however, programmatic benefits can be reinforced, enhancing the potency of treatment modalities.

Prison Visitation and the Limits of the Deprivation of Freedom

Family visits are widely recognized as an important tool in prison management. The idea is that visitation can contribute to correctional goals by modulating the average prisoner's disposition, improving his deportment, and enhancing the prospect of his rehabilitation by cementing tenuous family links. The Code of Federal Regulations, for example, proclaims that "the Bureau of Prisons encourages visiting by family, friends, or community groups to maintain the morale of the inmate and to develop closer relationships between the inmate and family members or others in the community" (cited in Bosworth 2002, p. 133). A sample legislative provision, signed by the governor of California in August 2002, verbalizes this perspective more eloquently than most:

THE PEOPLE OF THE STATE OF CALIFORNIA DO ENACT AS FOLLOWS: SECTION 1. Chapter 10.7. PRISON VISITATION 6400. Any amendments to existing regulations and any future regulations adopted by the

Department of Corrections which may impact the visitation of inmates shall do all of the following:

   a. Recognize and consider the value of visiting as a means to improve the safety of prisons for both staff and inmates.
   b. Recognize and consider the important role of inmate visitation in establishing and maintaining a meaningful connection with family and community.
   c. Recognize and consider the important role of inmate visitation in preparing an inmate for successful release and rehabilitation.

Of the three postulated impacts, the second and third are intimately related to each other, and congruent with several of the key desistance theories we have reviewed.

The achievement of such objectives is furthered if arrangements and conditions for visitation are appropriately supportive, allowing visits to be meaningful experiences for prisoners and their visitors. Visitation generally reduces what has been called the collateral damage of imprisonment. Put another way, visitation reduces the collateral damage inherent in the deprivation of freedom. Importantly, though, visitation accomplishes these ends thanks to the hard work and sacrifice of visitors and at the expense of emotional strain for the inmate. The process of visitation at its best is a far cry from the stereotypical concept of an unfettered "privilege," which connotes enjoyment made available by the prison as a reward for exemplary behavior. Though prisoners who expect to be visited may look forward to their visits with eager anticipation, that does not mean that the visitation experience as it unfolds will be anywhere near pleasurable. Through visits, inmates gain the prized opportunity to play a role other than that of inmate, but few manage to play such roles effectively and convincingly. After all, a great many feelings that are evoked by visitation experiences cannot be easily faced or cannot be freely expressed in the public arena of a visiting room.

Despite the obvious barriers and limitations to the free expression of feelings, visitations offer inmates the only face-to-face opportunities they have to preserve or restore relationships that have been severed by imprisonment. Johnston (1995, p. 138) points out, for example, that parent–child visitation can serve to allow children to express their reactions to separation, and "the more disturbed children are by parent-child separation and the poorer their adjustment, the more important it is that visitation occurs." Very young children are bound to harbor all sorts of irrational feelings and ideas about their incarcerated parents, and "visits allow [the] children to release these feelings, fears and fantasies and to replace them with a more realistic understanding of their parents' characteristics and circumstances."

Yet, for these and other constructive ends to be attained the prison must provide an ambience that makes restorative encounters possible. Not surprisingly, "many incarcerated parents [have raised] concerns about inappropriate and oppressive visiting conditions" (Barry 1995, p. 151). It boggles the mind, for instance, to conceive of what meaningful reassurance one could provide to apprehensive children behind bulletproof glass. A visit under such conditions may in fact impair rather than restore a parental relationship. It is easy to see how a vulnerable child facing her father under scary, noncontact visitation conditions can have her worst unconscious preconceptions confirmed, no matter how the father may act, and how visits under inhospitable conditions may be taxing or onerous for children. Any such practices that appear to further disrupt the lives of families that have already been severed by imprisonment stand as powerful obstacles to future desistance, as it has been explained in this chapter.

Ameliorating Prison Impact

Though we know very little about the beneficial or harmful effects of prison experiences, new types of experiences can be introduced into prisons to ascertain how they work and to determine what impact – if any – they have on recidivism rates. Such an experiment was initiated by the Bureau of Prisons on May 13, 1976. Norman Carlson, the Director of the Bureau, presided over the opening of the experimental facility, which he described as "an institution dedicated to change and innovation." Carlson noted that:

The Federal Correctional Institution at Butner, North Carolina represents an attempt by the Bureau of Prisons to develop an institution where new ideas, concepts and theories can be tested and evaluated. In designing the institution and its programs, we sought to create a safe and humane environment which was conducive to change and to finding new and more effective ways of providing correctional programs for offenders. (Carlson 1981, p. 2)

Butner was a composite prison comprising three subpopulations. The prisoners involved in the most explicitly innovative program were a group of 150 recidivistic and/or violent offenders who had been selected by a computer in Washington, DC. The computer also selected a comparison group of inmates elsewhere in the system. By the time a solid evaluation study of the program could be completed, data had been collected about 345 experimental and 245 control inmates, and 95 prisoners who had sampled the program and decided to "opt out" – mostly, to be closer to their families.

No differences were found in postrelease performance measures between the groups, which meant that desistancewise the experiment was arguably a flop. In other words, one could conclude that "the Butner program probably doesn't affect the likelihood of post-release criminal activity" (Love and Allgood 1987, p. 4).

Given the availability of other measures, however, a second conclusion followed, which was that:

it can be clearly demonstrated that a group of sophisticated, dangerous and experienced criminals can be housed in prisons where a central management philosophy emphasizes individual rights. This difficult to manage population functions very well under these circumstances. When inmates were allowed to volunteer for programs, they not only participated in more programs, but they also completed more programs. There were fewer disciplinary problems and fewer assaults. (p. 5)

Under current trends in correctional management, the second conclusion may be as important as the first. Norval Morris, who originated the reform model implemented at Butner, designed a "deep end" approach, to counter prescriptions that he felt "read like the design of the inner circles of hell" (Morris 1974, p. 88). He also noted that "if a humane and reformative program can be accorded to this category of offenders, then it should have as a direct and inescapable consequence the application of better programs throughout the prison system to less threatening groups" (ibid.). Morris would not have been overjoyed by the results of the evaluation study. He did, however, write in anticipation that:

Of course, reducing recidivism is by no means the only goal of the proposed institution. It is likely, for example, that it will have a beneficial effect on other aspects of the inmate's life upon release, such as job stability and personal relationships; that the inmate's time in the institution will be less damaging; and that the attitudes and career patterns of staff will be improved. Measurement of the achievement of these and other legitimate goals of the institution must be included in the evaluation design. Nevertheless, unless the later violent crime of the test group is less than (*or at least no greater than*) that of the control group, the institution must be determined a failure and its design abandoned for other approaches to dealing with repetitively violent offenders. (p. 119, emphasis added)

The warden of Butner, in a dialogue at a conference 2 years after the prison had been opened, made a comparable point. He said that:

The unique thing about Butner is the atmosphere – the mix of several types of inmates in open, relaxed surroundings, with all kinds of community people inside. The inmates wear private clothing, they have keys to their own room, the come and go as they please, and there are women all over the place. Butner does not have a perfect alignment of programs, but I think it has a good variety...

The only thing that we can now say is being studied is if you take two men who are the same type of violent offender and the one man is in Leavenworth and the other man is in Butner, who participates more in programs? Who does better? Who stays out of trouble? Can you manage the man in the relaxed, open atmosphere just as well as you can manage the man who is locked in? And, finally, how do the two men do when they go onto the street?...

There very well may not be a difference in terms of recidivism rates. All of these men have been locked up under pretty tight security for a long time. Now they are walking around, and they have not gone on a rampage, nothing terribly wrong has happened, and the atmosphere in the prison is good. This is a test of how well inmates can live in the Butner type of prison environment. (Ingram 1981, pp. 106–107)

The prescription by Norval Morris had assumed that inmates in the experimental population would have an assigned parole date and would be released in graduated fashion. But no one had consulted the parole board nor the agency running the halfway houses. As a result, differences relating to release arrangement did not eventuate as planned.

The Morris design had also called for officer-run counselling or "living/ learning" groups in the inmate living units. Staff were not in fact trained for the exercise, however, and thus "many of the meetings degenerated into little more than prisoner 'ventilating' against staff and prison conditions" (Federal Prison System 1981, p. 8). This meant that at best, the only functional consequence of the small living groups appeared to be the release of tension by prisoners during a meeting" (ibid.).

The remaining core of the Butner model was cafeteria-style programming. Prisoners arriving at the facility were invited to sample available programs, on the assumption that informed decisions could be made based on first-hand experience. The model also had other climate-related elements. It called for a diversified staff and freedom of movement within the prison. The evaluation showed that "staff were nearly unanimous in their approval of the degree of open communication between inmates and staff" (Love and Allgood 1987, p. 4).

The liberalized regime passed a subsequent test involving the doubling of the prison's population. According to local research staff (Pelissier 1989), "there may be a natural tendency for custody practices to become tighter with increased population sizes" but Butner's warden held the line with no adverse results, "suggest[ing] that institutions experiencing population increases may wish to use caution in limiting changes in security practices and avoid unnecessary tightening of security" (p. 5).

Conclusions

As evidenced by our review in the opening section of this chapter, desistance theories may differ in detail, but they converge in lamenting the attenuation of links between offenders and society, which include stable employment and membership in stable family constellations. To the extent to which prisons further disrupt and attenuate such links, they can be seen to cement the alienation of offenders; to the extent to which prisons encourage and support visitation and opportunities for success outside the prison walls, they can be credited with supporting desistance. Hence, longer sentences and harsher conditions are hypothetically more damaging than shorter sentences and ameliorated conditions. Likewise, facilitating "new careers" for prisoners, opening up free-world support systems through the involvement of community volunteers, and encouraging visitation and civic participation should all be associated with greater chances for success.

Importantly, though, these proactive efforts toward reintegration are nothing like panaceas for reform. Desistance does not come in the shape of a "prison program," and the best research to date seems to indicate that most prison practices make little difference on offending outcomes, regardless of whether the intent is to scare straight or rehabilitate. Likewise, the promotion of public safety seems largely unrelated to the construction of additional fortress prisons. As such, those hoping to facilitate radical changes in the lives of offenders, let alone in public safety, might be better directed to focus their attention outside the prison walls.

Perhaps the best the prison can do, in the end, is to "do no harm." Keve (1996, p. 1) begins a history of correctional standards by quoting Florence Nightingale, who first wrote that, "It may seem a strange principle to enunciate as the very first requirement in a hospital that it should do the sick no harm." Keve observes that Nightingale "undoubtedly would have expressed a similar principle for prisons." Most likely, Nightingale did precisely that, as keynote speaker to the 1870 Congress on Penitentiary and Reformatory Discipline. The fourteenth principle annunciated by the Congress asserts:

There is no greater mistake in the whole compass of penal discipline, than its studied imposition of degradation as part of punishment. Such imposition . . . crushes the weak, irritates the strong, and indisposes all to submission and reform. It is trampling where we ought to raise, and is therefore . . . unwise in policy. (Wines, 1871)

References

Andenaes, J. 1968. "Does Punishment Deter Crime?" *Criminal Law Quarterly* 11: 76–93.

Anderson, M. 1991. "Brazil Facility Operates on Basis of Inmate Trust." *Corrections Today* December: 96–103.

Austin, J., and Irwin, J. 2000. *It's About Time: America's Imprisonment Binge*, 3rd ed. Belmont, CA. Wadsworth.

Bakan, D. 1966. *The Duality of Human Existence: Isolation and Communion in Western Man.* Boston: Beacon Press.

Barnett, A., Blumstein, A., and Farrington, D. 1987. "Probabilistic Models of Youthful Criminal Careers." *Criminology* 25: 83–108.

Barry, E. 1995. "Legal Issues for Prisoners with Children," K. Gabel and D. Johnston, eds., *Children of Incarcerated Parents.* New York: Lexington.

Bosworth, M. 2002. *The U.S. Federal Prison System.* Thousand Oaks, CA: Sage.

Bottoms, A. 2000. "Compliance and Community Penalties," A. Bottoms, L. Gelsthorpe, and S. Rex, eds., *Community Penalties: Change and Challenges.* Cullompton, United Kingdom: Willan.

Bowers, J. 2000. "No Hiding Place." *Inside Time* Spring: 14.

Braithwaite, J., and Braithwaite, V. 2001. "Part One," E. Ahmed, N. Harris, J. Braithwaite, and V. Braithwaite, eEds., *Shame Management through Reintegration*, pp. 3–69. Cambridge: University of Cambridge Press.

Bukstel, L. H., and Kilmann, P. R. 1980. "Psychological Effects of Imprisonment on Confined Individuals." *Psychological Bulletin* 88: 469–493.

Burnett, R. 2004. "To Re-Offend or Not to Re-Offend? The Ambivalence of Convicted Property Offenders," S. Maruna and R. Immarigeon, eds., *After Crime and Punishment: Pathways to Desistance from Crime.* Cullompton, United Kingdom: Willan.

Burnside, J., Adler, J., Loucks, N., and Rose, G. 2001. *Kainos Community in Prisons: Report of an Evaluation.* London: Home Office.

Bushway, S. D., Brame, R., and Paternoster, R. 2004. "Connecting Desistance and Recidivism: Measuring Changes in Criminality Over the Lifespan," S. Maruna and R. Immarigeon, eds., *After Crime and Punishment: Pathways to Desistance from Crime.* Cullompton, UK: Willan.

Bushway, S. D., Piquero, A., Broidy, L., Cauffman, E., and Mazerolle, P. 2001. "An Empirical Framework for Studying Desistance As A Process." *Criminology* 39(2): 491–515.

Carlson, N. A. 1981. "Foreword," *Federal Prison System, Federal Correctional Institution, Butner, North Carolina*, p. 2. Washington, DC: U.S. Department of Justice.

Clemmer, D. 1970. "Prisonization," N. Johnson et al., eds., *The Sociology of Punishment and Correction*. New York: Wiley.

Cohen, S. 1985. *Visions of Social Control*. Cambridge, UK: Polity Press.

Corrections Association of New York. 2002. *State of the Prisons: Conditions of Confinement in 25 New York Correctional Facilities*. New York: Correctional Association of New York

Creighton, A. 1993. "Seeing Is Believing." *The Scottish Prison Service Newspaper* Autumn: 11.

Creighton, A. 1998. *APAC Case Study: Standards and Norms Replication Project*. Washington, DC: Prison Fellowship International, September.

Cressey, D. R. 1973. "Adult Felons in Prisons," L. E. Ohlin, ed., *Prisons in America*. Englewood Cliffs, NJ: Prentice Hall.

Deci, E. L., and Ryan, R. M. 2000. "The 'What' and 'Why' of Goal Pursuits: Human Needs and the Self-Determination of Behavior." *Psychological Inquiry* 11: 227–268.

DeJong, C. 1997. "Survival Analysis and Specific Deterrence: Integrating Theoretical and Empirical Models of Recidivism." *Criminology* 35: 561–575.

DOCS Today. 2002. "Sullivan." *DOCS Today* January: 14–23.

Erikson, E. 1968. *Identity: Youth and Crisis*. New York: Norton.

Farrall, S. 1995. "Why Do People Stop Offending?" *Scottish Journal of Criminal Justice Studies* 1: 51–59.

Farrall, S. 2002. *Rethinking What Works with Offenders*. Cullompton, UK: Willan.

Farrall, S., and Bowling, B. 1999. "Structuration, Human Development and Desistance from Crime." *British Journal of Criminology* 39: 253–268.

Farrington, D. F., Ditchfield, J., Hancock, G., Howard, P., Jolliffe, D., Livingston, M. S., and Painter, K. A. 2002. "Evaluation of Two Intensive Regimes for Young Offenders." *Home Office Research Study* 239. London: Home Office.

Federal Prison System. 1981. *Federal Correctional Institution, Butner, North Carolina*. Washington, DC: U.S. Department of Justice.

Finn, P. 1999. "Job Placement for Offenders: A Promising Approach to Reducing Recidivism and Correctional Costs." *National Institute of Corrections Journal* July: 2–11.

Garabedian, P. 1963. "Social Role and Processes of Socialization in the Prison Community." *Social Problems* 11: 140–152.

Garfinkel, H. 1956. "Conditions of Successful Degradation Ceremonies." *American Journal of Sociology* 61: 420–424.

Gecas, V., and Schwalbe, M. L. 1983. "Beyond the Looking-Glass Self: Social Structure and Efficacy-Based Self-Esteem." *Social Psychology Quarterly* 46(2): 77–88.

Gendreau, P. 1996. "Offender Rehabilitation: What We Know and What Needs to Be Done." *Criminal Justice and Behavior* 23: 144–161.

Gendreau, P., Goggin, C., and Cullen, F. 1999. *The Effects of Prison Sentences on Recidivism*. A report to the Corrections Research and Development and Aboriginal Policy Branch, Solicitor General of Canada, Ottawa.

173

Giordano, Peggy C., Stephen A. Cernkovich, and Jennifer L. Rudolph. 2002. "Gender, Crime and Desistance: Toward a Theory of Cognitive Transformation." *American Journal of Sociology* 107, 990–1064.

Glueck, S., and Glueck, E. T. 1937. *Later Criminal Careers*. New York: Commonwealth Fund.

Goffman, E. 1961. *Asylums*. New York: Anchor.

Gottfredson, M., and Hirschi, T. 1990. *A General Theory of Crime*. Stanford, CA: Stanford University Press.

Gove, W. 1985. "The Effect of Age and Gender on Deviant Behavior: A Biopsychosocial Perspective," A. S. Rossi, ed., *Gender and the Life Course*, pp. 115–144. New York: Aldine.

Haberman, C. 2003. "Ex-Inmate Denied Chair (and Clippers)." *New York Times*, February 25, p. B1.

Haney, C. 2003. "Mental Health Issues in Long-Term Solitary and "Supermax" Confinement." *Crime & Delinquency* 49: 124–156.

Hebbern, G. 1998. Personal communication, 28 July.

Horney, J., Osgood, D. W., and Marshall, I. H. 1995. "Criminal Careers in the Short-Term: Intra-Individual Variability in Crime and Its Relation to Local Life Circumstances." *American Sociological Review* 60: 655–673.

Ingram, G. L. 1981. "The Federal Correctional Institution, Butner, North Carolina: An Experimental Prison for Repetitively Violent Offenders," D. N. Ward and K. F. Schoen, eds., *Confinement in Maximum Custody: New Last-Resort Prisons in the United States and Western Europe*, pp. 99–108. Lexington, MA: DC Heath.

Johnson, B. R. 2002. "Assessing the Impact of Religious Programs and Prison Industry on Recidivism: An Exploratory Study." *Texas Journal of Corrections* February: 7–11.

Kelman, H. C. 1958. "Compliance, Identification and Internalization: Three Processes of Opinion Change." *Journal of Conflict Resolution* 2: 51–60.

Keve, P. W. 1996. *Measuring Excellence: The History of Correctional Standards and Accreditation*. Lanham, MD: American Correctional Association.

Langan, P. A., and Levin, D. J. 2002. *Recidivism of Prisoners Released in 1994* (NCJ 193427). Washington, DC: U.S. Department of Justice, Bureau of Justice Statistics.

Laub, J. H., Nagin, D. S., and Sampson, R. J. 1998. "Trajectories of Change in Criminal Offending: Good Marriages and the Desistance Process." *American Sociological Review* 63: 225–238.

Laub, J., and Sampson, R. 2001. "Understanding Desistance from Crime." *Crime and Justice: A Review of Research* 28: 1–70.

Leake, G. J., and King, A. S. 1977. "Effect of Counselor Expectations on Alcoholic Recovery." *Alcohol Health and Research World* 1(3): 16–22.

Lemert, C. C. 2000. "Whatever Happened to the Criminal? Edwin Lemert's Societal Reaction," C. C. Lemert and M. F. Winter, eds., *Crime and Deviance: Essays and Innovations of Edwin M. Lemert*. Lanham, MD: Rowman and Littlefield.

Lemert, E. M. 1948. "Some Aspects of a General Theory of Sociopathic Behavior." *Proceedings of the Pacific Sociological Society. Research Studies, State College of Washington* 16: 23–29.

Lemert, E. M. 1951. *Social Pathology: Systematic Approaches to the Study of Sociopathic Behavior*. New York: McGraw-Hill.

Liebling, A. 1999. "Prisoner Suicide and Prisoner Coping." *Crime and Justice: A Review of Research* 26: 283–359.

Liebling, A. 2002. *Measuring the Quality of Prison Life*. London: Home Office Research.

Lin, A. C. 2000. *Reform in the Making: The Implementation of Social Policy in Prison*. Princeton, NJ: Princeton University Press.

Love, C., and Allgood, J. 1987. *Butner Study: The Final Analysis (Research Review)*. Washington, DC: Federal Bureau of Prisons.

Lovell, D., and Johnson, C. 2003. *Felony and Violent Recidivism Among Supermax Prisoners in Washington State: A Pilot Study*. Unpublished report, Department of Psychosocial and Community Health, University of Washington.

Lynch, M. J. 1999. "Beating a Dead Horse: Is There Any Basic Empirical Evidence for the Deterrent Effect of Imprisonment?" *Crime, Law and Social Change* 31: 347–362.

MacKenzie, D. L., and Goodstein, L. 1985. "Long-Term Incarceration Impacts and Characteristics of Long-Term Offenders: An Empirical Analysis." *Criminal Justice and Behavior* 12: 395–414.

MacKenzie, D. L., Brame, R., McDowall, D.C., and Souryal, C. 1995. "Boot Camp Prisons and Recidivism in Eight States." *Criminology* 33: 327–357.

Mannheim, H., and Wilkins, L. T. 1955. *Prediction Methods in Relation to Borstal Training*. London: Her Majesty's Stationary Office.

Maruna, S., 2001. *Making Good: How Ex-Convicts Reform and Rebuild Their Lives*. Washington, DC: American Psychological Association Books.

Maruna, S., and LeBel, T. P. 2003. "Welcome Home?: Examining the Reentry Court Concept from a Strengths-based Perspective." *Western Criminology Review* 3(3): 1–37.

Maruna, S., LeBel, T., and Lanier, C. 2003. "Generativity Behind Bars: Some 'Redemptive Truth' about Prison Society," E. de St. Aubin, D. McAdams, and T. Kim, eds., *The Generative Society*. Washington, DC: American Psychological Association.

Matza, D. 1964. *Delinquency and Drift*. New York: Wiley.

McAdams, D. P., Hoffman, B. J., Mansfield, E. D., and Day, R. 1996. "Themes of Agency and Communion in Significant Autobiographical Scenes." *Journal of Personality* 64: 339–377.

McCord, J. 1994. "Crimes through Time: Review of R. J. Samson & J. H. Laub Crime in the Making: Pathways and Turning Points through Life." *Contemporary Sociology* 23: 414–415.

McGuire, J. 1995. "The Death of Deterrence," J. McGuire and B. Rowson, eds., *Does Punishment Work?* Proceedings of a conference held at Westminster Central Hall, London, UK. London: ISTD.

McGuire, J. 2002. "Criminal Sanctions versus Psychologically-Based Interventions with Offenders: A Comparative Empirical Analysis." *Psychology, Crime and Law* 8: 183–208.

Meisenhelder, T. 1977. "An Exploratory Study of Exiting from Criminal Careers." *Criminology* 15: 319–334.

Messner, S. F., and R. Rosenfeld. 2001. *Crime and the American Dream*, 3rd edition. Belmont, CA: Wadsworth.

Miller, R. L., Brickman, P., and Bolen, D. 1975. "Attribution versus Persuasion as a Means of Modifying Behavior." *Journal of Personality and Social Psychology* 31: 430–441.

Moffitt, T. E. 1983. "The Learning Theory Model of Punishment." *Criminal Justice and Behavior* 10: 131–158.

Moffitt, T. E. 1993. "Adolescence-Limited and Life-Course-Persistent Antisocial Behavior: A Developmental Taxonomy." *Psychological Review* 100(4): 674–701.

Moos, R. H. 1975. *Correctional Institutions Environment Scale*. Palo Alto, CA: Consulting Psychologists Press.

Morris, N. 1974. *The Future of Imprisonment*. Chicago: University of Chicago Press.

Nagin, D. S., and Paternoster, R. 1991. "On the Relationship of Past and Future Participation in Delinquency." *Criminology* 29: 163–190.

Oleson, J. C. 2002. "The Punitive Coma." *California Law Review* 90: 829–901.

Ottobani, M. 2000. *Kill the Criminal, Save the Person: The APAC Methodology*. Washington, DC: Prison Fellowship, International.

Paternoster, R., and Piquero, A. R. 1995. "Reconceptualizing Deterrence: An Empirical Test of Personal and Vicarious Experiences." *Journal of Research in Crime and Delinquency* 32(3): 251–286.

Patterson, G. R. 1993. "Orderly Change in a Stable World: The Antisocial Trait as Chimera." *Journal of Consulting and Clinical Psychology* 61: 911–919.

Pelissier, B. 1989. *The Effects of a Rapid Increase in a Prison Population (Research Review)*. Washington, DC: Federal Bureau of Prisons.

Petersilia, J. 2003. *When Prisoners Come Home: Parole and Prisoner Reentry*. Oxford: Oxford University Press.

Pogarsky, G., and Piquero, A. R. 2003. "Can Punishment Encourage Offending? Investigating the 'Resetting' Effect." *Journal of Research in Crime and Delinquency* 40(1): 95–120.

Rothman, D. 1980. *Conscience and Convenience*. New York: HarperCollins.

Sampson, R. J., and Laub, J. 1993. *Crime in the Making*. Cambridge, MA: Harvard University Press.

Sampson, R. J., and Laub, J. 1997. "A Life-Course Theory of Cumulative Disadvantage and the Stability of Delinquency," T. Thornberry, ed., *Developmental Theories of Crime And Delinquency*. New Brunswick, NJ: Transaction Press,.

Sapsford, R. J. 1978. "Life Sentence Prisoners: Psychological Changes During Sentence." *British Journal of Criminology* 18(2):128–145.

Schmid, T. J., and Jones, R. S. 1991. "Suspended Identity: Identity Transformation in a Maximum Security Prison." *Symbolic Interaction* 14(4): 415–432.

Sennett, R. 2003. *Respect in a World of Inequality*. New York: Norton.

Shorer, C. E. 1965. "The Ganser Syndrome." *British Journal of Criminology* 5: 120–131.

Shover, N. 1996. *Great Pretenders: Pursuits and Careers of Persistent Thieves.* Boulder, CO: Westview Press.

Strenta, A., and DeJong, W. 1981. "The Effect of a Prosocial Label on Helping Behavior." *Social Psychology Quarterly* 44(2): 142–147.

Sykes, G. 1965. *Society of Captives.* New York: Atheneum.

Toch, H. 1992. *Mosaic of Despair: Human Breakdowns in Prison.* Washington, DC: American Psychological Association.

Toch, H. 1997. *Corrections: A Humanistic Approach.* Guilderland, NY: Harrow and Heston.

Toch, H., and Adams, K. 2002. *Acting Out: Maladaptive Behavior in Confinement.* Washington, DC: American Psychological Association.

Trice, H. M., and Roman, P. M. 1970. "Delabeling, Relabeling and Alcoholics Anonymous." *Social Problems* 17: 538–546.

Tyler, T. 1990. *Why People Obey the Law.* New Haven: Yale.

Uggen, C. 2000. "Work as a Turning Point in the Life Course of Criminals: A Duration Model of Age, Employment, and Recidivism." *American Sociological Review* 65: 529–546.

Uggen, C., and Kruttschnitt, C. 1998. "Crime in the Breaking: Gender Differences in Desistance." *Law and Society Review* 32: 339–366.

Visher, C. 2002. *Returning Home: Understanding the Challenges of Prisoner Reentry.* Poster presentation at the American Society of Criminology annual meeting. Chicago.

Wacquant, L. 2000. "Deadly Symbiosis: When Ghetto and Prison Meet and Mesh." *Punishment and Society* 3: 95–134.

Walters, Glenn D. 2003. "Changes in Criminal Thinking and Identity Change in Novice and Experienced Inmates: Prisonization Revisited." *Criminal Justice and Behavior* 30: 399–421.

Ward, D. A., and Werlich, T. G. 2003. "Alcatraz and Marion: Evaluating Super-Maximum Custody." *Punishment and Society* 5: 53–76.

Warr, M. 1998. "Life-Course Transitions and Desistance from Crime." *Criminology* 34: 11–37.

Warr, M. 2002. *Companions in Crime.* Cambridge, UK: Cambridge University Press.

West, D. J. 1961. *Interludes of Honesty in the Careers of Persistent Thieves.* Unpublished paper.

West, D. J. 1963. *The Habitual Prisoner.* London: Macmillan

Wexler, D. B. 2001. "Robes and Rehabilitation: How Judges Can Help Offenders 'Make Good.'" *Court Review* 38: 18–23.

Wheeler, S. 1961. "Socialization in Correctional Communities." *American Sociological Review* 26: 697–712.

Wiggins, J. S. 1991. "Agency and Communion as Conceptual Coordinates for the Understanding and Measurement of Interpersonal Behavior," D. Cicchetti and W. Grove, eds., *Thinking Clearly about Psychology*, pp. 89–113. Minneapolis: University of Minnesota Press.

Wilkins, L. T. 1969. *Evaluation of Penal Measures*. New York: Random House.

Wilson, W. J., and Katherine M. Neckerman. 1987. "Poverty and Family Structure: The Widening Gap between Evidence and Public Policy Issues," S. H. Danziger and D. H. Weinberg, eds., *Fighting Poverty: What Works and What Doesn't*, pp. 232–259. Cambridge, MA: Harvard University Press.

Wines, E. C., dd. 1871. *Transactions of the National Congress on Penitentiary and Reformatory Discipline, 1870*. Albany, NY: Weed, Parsons.

Wormith, J. S. 1984. "Attitude and Behavior Change of Correctional Clientele: A Three Year Follow-Up." *Criminology* 22: 595–618.

Wormith, J. S., and Porporino, F. J. 1984. "The Controversy over the Effects of Long-Term Incarceration." *Canadian Journal of Criminology* 26: 423–438.

Zamble, E., and Porporino, F. J. 1988. *Coping Behavior and Adaptation in Prison Inmates*. New York: Springer-Verlag.

Zamble, E., and Porporino, F. J. 1990. "Coping with Imprisonment." *Criminal Justice and Behavior* 17: 53–70.

Zamble, E., and Quinsey, V. L. 1997. *The Criminal Recidivism Process*. Cambridge, UK: Cambridge University Press.

7

Communities and Reentry

CONCENTRATED REENTRY CYCLING

Todd R. Clear, Elin Waring, and
Kristen Scully

It is easy to view reentry through the lens of the individuals who are personally involved. *Coming home* from prison, as Joan Petersilia (2003) has termed it, is an intense personal experience. To come home is to rejoin the lives of families, associates, and other intimates. The personal issues that arise for the ex-prisoner coming home pose weighty challenges for the individual and his or her close associates, and it is not difficult to see why they matter. A growing literature now examines the significance of reentry for the individuals who experience it.

Yet the focus of this chapter is reentry as a community (rather than an individual) phenomenon. It is less obvious how reentry manifests itself at the community level, although its impact on communities is worthy of special attention. Reentry, because it is highly stigmatizing as well as concentrated among people already troubled by poverty and exclusion, can be a significant factor of community life – one that transcends the sum of individual experiences. We also consider the effects of incarceration. Incarceration sets the stage for reentry, affecting the same communities that reentry does and thereby compounding the effects of reentry in poor communities that have high rates of residents cycling in and out of prison. We have referred to these intertwined processes as "reentry cycling" and their impact on the community as "coercive mobility" (Clear, Rose, Waring, and Scully 2003). The shift in focus from individual-level analyses to community-level analyses is illustrated by a simple comparison. Faced with a criminally

This chapter was prepared under a grant from the Harry Frank Guggenheim Foundation. Opinions are those of the authors and do not necessarily reflect opinions of the Harry Frank Guggenheim Foundation.

active defendant, the rational citizen might well consider that removing this person from the street would make the streets safer. Conversely, a rational citizen should be troubled at the prospect of a community in which upwards of one-fifth of the parent-aged males[1] are "missing" (incarcerated) on any given day, and the majority of those remaining have been "missing" at some point in the last few years (Lynch and Sabol 2001).

In this chapter, we consider the straightforward problem of public safety for communities in which reentry occurs, but we also consider other ways in which communities are affected by reentry. We describe how reentry is closely related to community processes and how its impact cannot be adequately measured by aggregating its effect on individual-level processes. We begin by discussing evidence for community influences on local crime rates. Second, we argue that the immediate impact of reentry cycling is the weakening of informal social controls, which serve as the basis for public safety and community quality of life. Finally, with data from neighborhoods in Tallahassee, Florida, we illustrate how reentry is closely linked to the initial removal of the prisoner from the community and how both phenomena combine to create reentry cycling, which adversely affects the community. This reentry cycling is concentrated in poor neighborhoods, especially in areas where the majority of residents are people of color. The concentration of returning prisoners amplifies the impact of reentry because it exacerbates the effects of poverty, exclusion, and social alienation with which these communities already struggle. Thus, we conclude that high rates of incarceration and reentry, concentrated in poor places among people of color, serve to further weaken – rather than strengthen – the community capacity of these neighborhoods.

The aggregate impact of the various individual level effects is a principal pathway through which reentry cycling affects community life. To understand the aggregate impact, the reader might take the various topics addressed in this volume – employment, criminality, and families – and multiply the findings by the 630,000 people who will leave prison this year. But reentry also operates at the community level in indirect ways. Community cohesion is deeply challenged when reentry is a widespread experience for community residents. Reentry is, again, a story not only of individuals but of community as well.

---

[1] The phrase "parent-aged males" refers to men aged 20–44.

Defining Community

Today's sociologists enjoy pointing out the elusiveness of the term *community*. Some of this has to do with a world growing ever smaller, with every part now connected to every other. And some of this has to do with today's unprecedented mobility, in which people change their residences frequently over a lifetime or live in one place and work in various others. Some of it has to do with the weakening of racial and ethnic boundaries that used to keep people apart. *Community*, as we might imagine it in a description of small-town America, is not a very accurate descriptor in today's world.

Yet "place" matters in some ways as much or more than ever. And community identities remain critical aspects of social definition and experience. Place matters, much recent research tells us, in many more ways than we might have imagined. Studies using geo-coded social data show us again and again that the variable "neighborhood" (even if only a rather arbitrary line drawn to separate one place from another) often has a direct effect on social indicators and just as often has a moderating effect on the relationships between important variables.

Increasingly, studies report that there are place effects on crime. Recent examples include Bellair (1997), who showed that "getting together with neighbors" had a negative impact on burglary, auto theft, and robbery in 60 urban neighborhoods. His related analysis (Bellair 2000) found that greater amounts of informal property surveillance by neighbors reduced some types of crime. Analyzing the British Crime Survey, Markowitz and his colleagues (2001) found that lower neighborhood cohesion predicts greater crime and disorder. Studies of Chicago neighborhoods (Morenoff and Sampson 1997) suggest that informal social controls – voluntary associations, kin/friend networks, and local organizations – can reduce crime.

There is also reason to think that neighborhood-level effects may not always be linear. Nonlinear models may help explain why seemingly contradictory theories might be useful to explain relationships at the community level. Regoezci (2002), for example, showed how density produces social withdrawal in a curvilinear fashion. Clear and his colleagues (Clear et al. 2003) have shown a similar curvilinear impact of incarceration on crime.

The growing body of literature on place as a context for social problems affirms the quantitative importance of community characteristics for individual experiences within those places. A contrast to the statistical importance of place in understanding social relations is the illuminating fact that the *definition* of place is not as critical. Empirical investigations use census block groups, census tracts, indigenous "neighborhoods" defined by voluntary associations of neighbors living within them, and state-created political boundaries. In each case, the division is typically useful in sorting out some social indicator, and in at least one study the particular boundary used was largely immaterial (Wooldredge 2002).

So although it is useful to spend some time thinking about just what is meant by the term *community* in the content of studying a social phenomenon, it is just as important not to get caught up in a definitional red herring. There is value in pondering the importance of community with regard to a problem such as reentry even if there is a certain fuzziness regarding just what is meant by the term. Communities are places where people live (or work) and where the nature of the places is such that the variance on certain measures *within* the community is less than the variance *between* that community and others nearby. Communities provide concentrations of certain experiences and the proximity of certain people who are alike, and the similarity is noticeable because, somewhere nearby, circumstances are comparatively different.

Reentry, Removal, and Concentrated Reentry Cycling

Reentry is the process by which a former prisoner rejoins his or her community as a free citizen. It is a process of powerful emotional significance and practical challenges, as the chapters in this volume attest. From the perspective of community life, reentry has two important additional qualities. First, it is concentrated in certain locations. Second, it is a natural part of a cycling process involving removal of relatively large numbers of residents from the community and relocation to prisons, return to the community from the prison, and (often) removal to the prison once again, what we are calling concentrated reentry cycling.

Ex-prisoners do not reenter communities randomly. They return to the communities from which they came or go to places that are very similar. Because the people who go to prison are overwhelmingly poor and disproportionately persons of color, they are drawn from and return to characteristically poor, ethnic neighborhoods. For example, one study (Clear and Rose 2003) shows that in Brooklyn neighborhoods that are overwhelmingly African American, the incarceration rate of adult males is 12.4 per 1,000; by contrast, in predominantly white Brooklyn neighborhoods the rate is 2.7 per 1,000.

Reentry must be thought of as a cyclical process in two ways: (1) every reentry was preceded by a removal and (2) many (or most) reentries will be followed by a removal. Some analysts have called this process *churning*[2] to emphasize the high rate of return among recent prison and jail releases. But the term *churning* places emphasis solely on the return to prison or jail, suggesting that the original removal is not equally important. We refer to reentry cycling to include the equal numbers of removals. The idea of reentry cycling describes the mutual processes of removal for imprisonment, return after the sentence has been served, and high risk of eventual removal for failure to succeed during reentry.

Disruptive Effects of Reentry Cycling

There appears to be little research on reentry as a community-level phenomenon. Conversely, an interest in the impact of incarceration has begun to emerge, as a growing number of critics of incarceration policy have noted the concentrated impact of incarceration among poor people of color (see Meares 1998; Braman 2003; Ritchie 2003; Clear and Rose 2003). There is scant evidence of both the aggregate individual-level community effects of reentry cycling and the transcendent community-level effects (Lynch and Sabol 2004). Few studies of reentry have been reported, and fewer still address community-level impacts of reentry. Much of this chapter, therefore, is the recounting of plausible impacts that might be expected based on various studies of community life not directly concerned with reentry. The few attempts to assess empirically the way incarceration policy – both removal and reentry – affects communities are nonetheless instructive. In this section, some of these studies are briefly reviewed as a basis for opening a broader discussion of the impacts of incarceration policy on communities.

The first empirical investigation of the impact of place on reentry was reported by Gottfredson and Taylor in 1988. They developed a model of rearrest for ex-prisoners in Baltimore using personal characteristics and neighborhood characteristics. They found that when they controlled for personal characteristics (risk), the neighborhood (zip code) to which the ex-prisoner returned had a significant impact on the probability of reentry failure. They speculated that their results uncovered neighborhood-level

---

[2] See for example Lynch and Sabol 2004; Blumstein and Beck, this volume.

processes, such as job and drug markets, that affect the chances of released prisoners "making it."

Surprisingly, the provocative nature of this finding spawned little in the way of follow-up research. To date, there are four sets of studies assessing the impact of levels of incarceration on communities. Lynch and Sabol (2001) analyzed neighborhood-level, longitudinal data from Baltimore to determine the effect of incarceration on voluntary participation, collective efficacy, and fear at the community level. They found that incarceration rates affect collective efficacy and voluntary associations by affecting community offense levels, which rise as incarceration increases. However, a direct effect was not found.

Later, in two national-level studies, Lynch and Sabol deepened their investigation of this phenomenon. In the first (2003), they found that higher rates of both removal and return of males contributed to higher rates of female-headed households among African Americans. In the second (2004), they again showed the negative impact of incarceration rates on family structure for blacks but this finding did not appear for whites (for similar evidence, see also Myers 2000; Darity and Myers 1994). Their latter study also found marginal evidence of a deleterious impact of incarceration on employment.

The Lynch and Sabol articles provide substantial evidence that incarceration practices can exacerbate social problems, especially among people of color. Two caveats must be raised about their work, however. First, because these studies investigate counties, they have modeled the impact of incarceration for geographic areas much larger than neighborhoods, and so may underestimate the impact of imprisonment on more localized areas, such as neighborhoods. Second, because they treat the effects of incarceration as linear – that is, as consistent for all levels of incarceration – they do not address the coercive-mobility thesis, which proposes that there are special effects of concentrated incarceration in poor communities that are different from the effects of limited levels of incarceration in other locations.

Jeffrey Fagan and his colleagues have conducted a longitudinal analysis of the impact of incarceration in New York City neighborhoods between 1985 and 1996. Modeling the effect of incarceration in 1 year on various community measures in the following year, they find that as incarceration rates in 1 year increase, crime rates in the following year increase (Fagan, West, and Holland 2003). Later analyses (Fagan, West, and Holland 2004; see also Piquero, West, Fagan, and Holland 2005) show that increases in incarceration rates result in higher crime and compromised informal social control at the neighborhood level. They argue that most of this effect is a product of the enforcement of drug laws.

The Fagan studies, like those of Lynch and Sabol, address the localized social effects of incarceration across all locations and levels of incarceration. Our argument is that the level and nature of incarceration in poor places – especially places of color – is substantively different under current policy and has substantively different collective effects that go beyond the individual problems that occur at lower levels of incarceration in less-troubled communities. Clear et al. (2003) analyzed the impact of 1996 incarceration in Tallahassee, Florida, neighborhoods, on 1997 crime rates in those neighborhoods, controlling for crime in 1996 and various neighborhood social problems. This study found evidence of a "tipping point" past which the effects of removing residents for incarceration in 1 year did not reduce crime in the subsequent year but instead increased it. This study also found a constant effect of a neighborhood's reentry rates in 1 year, increasing crime rates in the following year. The upshot of this work is that the poorest neighborhoods with the highest rates of reentry cycling suffer two hardships – crime rates are increased *both* by the level of reentry and the level of removal, as separate but linked phenomena.

Other community- and family-level effects have been studied using a variety of methodologies. Rose, Clear, and Ryder (2002) interviewed residents of two high-incarceration neighborhoods in Tallahassee and found that families of those who have been incarcerated report withdrawing from community life and reducing participation in community institutions such as churches. Fishman (1990) documented that partners of incarcerated men in Vermont experienced severe financial hardship as a consequence of that incarceration. St. Jean (forthcoming 2006) interviewed residents of poor neighborhoods in Chicago and found that their need to balance the bond to family members who are incarcerated with their desire for order and safety led to a cynicism about the system and a detachment from positive strategies of social control. Thomas (2003) has speculated that sexually transmitted diseases increase as the proportion of previously incarcerated men in the community increases. He has argued that incarceration destabilizes intimate relationships in ways that exacerbate the spread of disease by increasing the prevalence of high-risk sexual encounters. Uggen and Manza (2002) has shown that incarceration changes political participation and may reduce the perceived legitimacy of political processes. Moreover, he has shown that incarceration affects the outcomes of elections by changing the rates of voter participation of black males.

These studies approach the problem of the community effects of incarceration from a variety of standpoints. Most consider how the level of incarceration in a neighborhood affects other attributes of individuals who live there, such as family structure, political opinion, or willingness to vote. Some studies investigate theoretically meaningful locations such as neighborhoods, others aggregate data by zip codes, census block groups, or even at the county level. The use of controls for alternative effects is weaker in some studies (interviews) and stronger in others (statistical longitudinal path models). Although each study has complex findings, all suggest the plausibility of a link between the growth of incarceration and the exacerbation of community-level problems. Taken as a group, they provide evidence that the incarceration rate of one's neighbors is a factor in one's community life.

What does it mean to say that the rate of a place's reentry cycling – the removal and return of its residents – affects community life? Why does reentry cycling affect community life, and how are those effects manifested? The answer to these questions begins with a grounded understanding of the relationships between community, reentry, and public safety.

Communities, Reentry, and Public Safety

Communities comprise a multiplicity of characteristics, almost any of which will arguably have at least some relevance for reentry. A community's housing will affect the availability of accommodations for those in reentry; its job market will affect the availability of employment. In discussing public safety in the context of community life, five constructs provide significant insights for understanding how differences among communities contribute to differences in public safety: human capital, social networks, social capital, collective efficacy, and informal social control. In the discussion below, each is defined and its relevance for community processes and public safety is described.

Human Capital

The basic building block of community well-being is *human capital*. Human capital refers to the personal resources an individual brings to the social and economic marketplace. Typical forms of human capital are education and job skills that potential employers might value. Others include intelligence and ease in social situations. People with generous endowments of human capital have personal talents and attributes upon which to call to advance their personal interests, especially in the realm of the competitive marketplace: a good education, a solid job history, an array of skills, and so forth.

Human capital is a quality of individuals, not communities. Places whose residents possess good amounts of human capital will tend to be more successful communities, if only because the people who live there are themselves more successful. They will tend to be safer, if only because people who experience greater social accomplishment are less likely to be involved in street crime.

But human capital is not a community-level attribute, and places in which there is a wealth of human capital may struggle to be effective communities when residents attribute little importance to community life. For example, people of wealth and social status may enjoy only superficial connections to those who live near them; conversely, places whose residents are bereft of human capital may generate a strong social basis for collective action. In either case, however, the endowment of human capital enjoyed by a place's residents will serve as a constraint on community life. Even so, places where there is great human capital will tend to enjoy a degree of safety, even if community life does not thrive, because those with human capital would not live there otherwise. In this way, collectives rich in human capital tend to be places where street crime is rare.

As a group, ex-prisoners are substantially lacking in human capital. The existence of a criminal conviction is itself a debilitating factor for the ex-prisoner, because a felony conviction can make ex-prisoners ineligible for a broad array of housing assistance, welfare, and certain types of employment (Petersilia 2003). But the criminal conviction is only a marker on a population already bereft of human capital. Only about half have graduated from high school (Hughes, Wilson, and Beck 2001). Nearly three fourths have drug or alcohol abuse histories (Beck 2000), almost one third have substantial physical or mental illness histories (Marcuschak and Beck 2001), and nearly one third were unemployed at the time of their arrest (Petersilia 2003). The people who end up going to prison have such poor job prospects to begin with that the impact of imprisonment on the employment prospects through the life course is not large, though the negative impact of incarceration on lifetime earnings from employment is quite substantial (Nagin and Waldfogel 1998; Western, Kling, and Wieman 2001). Ex-prisoners started out as intermittently employed in unskilled daily-wage jobs, and they tend to stay that way. Thus, ex-prisoners bring to their communities deficiencies

187

in human capital, and their return from prison sustains the generally low level of human capital that characterizes the neighborhoods in which reentry is concentrated.

Table 7.1 displays the correlations among measures of human capital and reentry rates for 80 neighborhoods in Tallahassee. It shows that reentry is significantly related to concentrated disadvantage and racial concentration at the neighborhood level but not to mobility and heterogeneity (two measures of social disorganization).[3] These data indicate that the neighborhoods with deficits in human capital receive the most returning prisoners.

Social Networks

People use their human capital to compete for goods and services, but they rely on their *social networks* to accomplish goals otherwise unattainable through human capital alone. Social networks are essentially the array of relationships in which a person lives, works, and engages in recreation. For most of us, the dominant social networks are composed of family members and people in our workplace. Social networks can also contain friendship relations, attenuated or even distant acquaintanceships, and other atypical interpersonal relationships. The unit of analysis of the social network is the "tie" – the nature of the bond between the person and the other member of the network.

Poor people tend to have what is referred to as "strong" ties, that is, ties that are mostly reciprocal and are formed within tight networks. These kinds of ties are very useful for meeting needs of intimacy and mutuality, but they are not very useful for activating sources of support from outside the network. For example, strong ties do not help people learn of jobs that are about to come available or help people find services to deal with problems. "Weak" ties, by contrast, tend to generate contacts outside the close interpersonal network. These ties are capable of bringing new resources into the person's life by expanding the network (Granovetter 1993).

Ex-prisoners tend to have sparse networks that are dominated by strong ties rather than weak ones. Because they have been away from their networks for some time, the networks are often reduced to a few people who have kept close associations. These are strong ties, limited in scope, and restricted

---

[3] The lack of significant relationship to census measures of mobility is probably due to the fact that the people who live in high-reentry neighborhoods are stuck there and cannot move–most of the mobility is of a coercive nature, instigated by the state through incarceration.

Table 7.1. *Correlations among Measures of Human Capital, Removal and Reentry Rates, and Total Crime, Tallahassee*

	Correlations and Significance Levels ($n = 80$)							
	Total Crime	Total Removals	Total Returns	Poverty	Percent Black	Mobility	Concentrated Disadvantage	Heterogeneity
Total Crime	1.00000	0.56560 <.0001	0.58770 <.0001	0.75008 <.0001	0.37814 0.0005	0.39345 0.0003	0.50104 <.0001	0.26391 0.0180
Total Removals	0.56560 <.0001	1.00000	0.89664 <.0001	0.64336 <.0001	0.75370 <.0001	0.18766 0.0955	0.74203 <.0001	0.02609 0.8183
Total Returns	0.58770 <.0001	0.89664 <.0001	1.00000	0.57621 <.0001	0.70001 <.0001	0.11197 0.3227	0.72030 <.0001	0.09698 0.3921
Poverty	0.75008 <.0001	0.64336 <.0001	0.57621 <.0001	1.00000	0.37405 0.0006	0.49560 <.0001	0.57147 <.0001	0.24338 0.0296
Percent Black	0.37814 0.0005	0.75370 <.0001	0.70001 <.0001	0.37405 0.0006	1.00000	0.01457 0.8979	0.86998 <.0001	−0.00098 0.9931
Mobility	0.39345 0.0003	0.18766 0.0955	0.11197 0.3227	0.49560 <.0001	0.01457 0.8979	1.00000	0.12539 0.2709	0.20973 0.0619
Concentrated Disadvantage	0.50104 <.0001	0.74203 <.0001	0.72030 <.0001	0.57147 <.0001	0.86998 <.0001	0.12539 0.2709	1.00000	0.09385 0.4107
Heterogeneity	0.26391 0.0180	0.02609 0.8183	0.09698 0.3921	0.24338 0.0296	−0.00098 0.9931	0.20973 0.0619	0.09385 0.4107	1.00000

189

in their potential to generate material support outside of what is directly available from those in the network. Because ex-prisoners lack so much in the way of human capital, they are a potential drain on the support capacities of the few strong ties upon which they can rely in reentry. One of the most pressing tasks facing the ex-prisoner is to develop social ties that will marshal the new resources needed for a better life: a job, a place to live, and educational skills. At least initially, the ex-prisoner who can rely on his or her family for these supports does so.

When ex-prisoners return to their communities, they experience existing arrays of social networks in one of two general ways. Many are extremely isolated from these networks. As a consequence of their criminal behavior, they may have alienated their families. As a consequence of their desire to stay out of trouble, they may have isolated themselves from former associates. This kind of reentry can be a lonely process, devoid of support systems and detached from social connections. Yet this is highly visible to the community: many idle ex-prisoners spend their nights sleeping in public places and loiter on street corners during daylight hours; they take their place in the various social service lines, waiting for work, health care, and public assistance; they add to the numbers of people who are disconnected from the broader social and economic forces of society.

Others who return from prison are more fortunate, for they enter kinship networks ready to welcome them back. But these ex-prisoners strain those relationships, even when they receive warm welcomes. Because they typically have such limited human capital to offer employers and other social contacts, they are forced to rely on their families for help, especially in the beginning. These families, usually also poor and with few available resources to divert to the ex-prisoner's needs, are typically systems of strong ties. Whatever can be done to ease the transition process is usually drawn from within the family and acquaintanceship unit; few new resources can be brought from outside the existing family system. When families welcome ex-prisoners home, they are forced to devote sometimes considerable resources to making the transition succeed. Mothers, siblings, or others may give ex-prisoners money to cover expenses until a job is secured; children may shift their time to be with the returned parent; room may be made for the ex-prisoner to sleep and to spend waking hours; and always, there is the potential for conflict when people whose lives are already stressful make room for a new set of demands.

For the latter type of reentry, it is important to recognize that these demands disrupt the homeostasis that had developed in response to the

190

person's original removal to prison. Removing young people of parenting age who are in their early years of adulthood removes parents, income-earners, and interpersonal supports. People who had ties to the person who is sent to prison are affected by that removal, and they find ways to reorganize their lives to make up for the absence of the prisoner. The return of the ex-prisoner changes this new interpersonal homeostasis and forces a new negotiation of expectations and relations. This, too, absorbs resources of the network.

When these family networks are composed of strong ties, which is typical, the new arrival may be difficult to absorb into the tightly coupled system. New intimacies will have developed while the prisoner was away, and events will have affected the family in ways that produce new facts of life to which the ex-prisoner must become accustomed. Even when reentry is less challenging, it still places stress on the family unit and demands valuable emotional and interpersonal resources.

Social Capital, Collective Efficacy, and Informal Social Control

Although human capital refers to the capacity of individuals to compete in the marketplace, *social capital* refers to the capacity of a person to call upon personal ties (usually within social networks) to advance some personal interest. Social capital can be activated to solve a myriad of problems. It can be the ability to use friends and acquaintances to find out about job openings and gain access to a potential employer in an advantageous way. Social capital can also mean access to health care resources or helpful information about housing and child care, as well as contacts to obtain this kind of care. Social capital and social networks are closely related. Social networks define the underlying structure of interpersonal relationships that hold the capacity for providing social capital; social capital is the capacity of networks to provide goods for people within these networks.

Places in which poor people are concentrated are typically places in which social networks offer little in the way of social capital (Wilson 1987; Hagan 1993). Relationships are dominated primarily by networks of strong ties. Contacts that extend outside the immediate set of intimates are scarce, and they cannot be called upon for much in the way of support. Because social capital is limited, people struggle to meet their needs. They look to the state for assistance in meeting basic needs, and they assume that needs not met by government agencies will not be readily overcome through collective action.

191

Ex-prisoners are in a particularly poor position with regard to social capital. They are not trusted by many of those around them, and they are legally barred from taking advantage of the various sources, albeit limited, of social capital on which others in their community rely. For example, ex-prisoners might lose their eligibility to receive public benefits such as public housing and welfare, and some forms of employment become prohibited. They have paid their social debt but they have not reconstituted their social bank account.

Collective efficacy is the capacity of a group of people who live in the same vicinity to come together to solve problems or otherwise take action that affects their collective circumstances. Collective efficacy is a normative concept. It assumes a shared understanding of what is a collective problem and what is needed to solve the problem, and it relies on the community sense that people share an interest in each other's prospects. Studies have demonstrated that collective efficacy is a factor in crime rates (Sampson, Raudenbush, and Earls 1997).

In many of the most economically disadvantaged places where reentry cycling is concentrated, normative dissensus exists. Anderson's study (1996) of poor inner-city neighborhoods describes the normative conflict between the older leaders and the younger males in the community, and exposure to the criminal justice system has been shown in some studies to be associated with lack of confidence in authority (Tyler 1990). To the extent that collective efficacy is built on a normative foundation, areas where reentry is a recurrent phenomenon may lack that normative foundation. Many of the people who live in these places may have had the kind of experience with legal authority, as represented by the criminal justice system, that undermines belief in conventional authority. The mix of experiences may lead to a mix in the regard for authority and so may serve as a poor collective normative foundation.

For people to come together in collective efficacy also requires a degree of stability to undergird the shared normative views. The original work of Shaw and McKay (1942) articulating the problem of social disorganization defines the problem of residential mobility and documents its importance. Places that lack a stable population have difficulty developing the interpersonal relationships that promote collective efficacy. As noted above, though, the places where reentry is concentrated today may be places where there is a degree of traditional residential stability, but only because people stay in these areas because they are unable to move elsewhere (Wilson 1987). Voluntary mobility out of undesirable areas is replaced by the coercive mobility of incarceration, however, which means there is turnover in population despite the inability of residents to find other places to live. There is also a tendency toward withdrawal among people who live in these undesirable places. This isolation has several sources. People who fear crime withdraw from their neighbors (Skogan 1990), as do people who struggle to find time to meet family obligations. Those who have family members in prison report responding to this circumstance by isolating themselves from others (Rose et al. 2002).

The most powerful source of public safety is the array of *informal social controls* that suppress deviance. These are the forces that sustain order and compliance with norms that are outside the formal agency of the state. There are principally two levels of informal social control (Hunter 1985). *Private* social control is the influence exerted by families and loved ones to get people to conform to social expectations (in particular, not to break laws or violate norms). Private social control is typically the result of strong ties. *Parochial* social control is the influence of nonintimate social relations to get people to conform to voluntary social groups, employers, religious institutions, and so forth. Weak ties are the basis of parochial social control.

Informal social control capacities are strained by reentry (Clear, Rose, and Ryder 2001). This is in large part because families, the main source of private social control, are directly challenged to become a part of an ex-prisoner's adjustment. In high-volume reentry communities, this can become a dominant problem in the community. As people turn attention to the resuscitation of their strong networks, weak ties are neglected and become even less capable of providing support.

It is for these reasons that reentry cycling poses a challenge to the public safety capacities of collective efficacy and informal social control. When oversubscribed social networks are forced to accommodate a newly returning ex-prisoner, they become even less likely to shift attention to collective action at the community level. When locations absorb large numbers of ex-prisoners who do not return to welcoming family systems, the capacity for meaningful collectivity is even more burdened. In both cases of reentry – the particularly challenging and also the relatively smooth experience – the normative consensus and interpersonal connectedness that are the foundation of collective efficacy are undermined.

Therefore, informal social control struggles in the face of reentry cycling. Residents come to distrust authority, and they become alienated from basic political institutions. Family units redirect their resources to adjust first to the removal of family members and then to their return. Little capacity exists for the formation of or participation in informal organizational entities – social clubs, religious institutions, and neighborhood associations – that serve as the main source of parochial social control. Increasingly, residents turn to the formal agencies of the state for what they need – the police, welfare systems, and public health agencies. Community life as a force of order deteriorates.

The same dynamic applies to social capital. As discussed, the impoverished neighborhoods to which ex-prisoners return lack social capital. The ex-prisoner's arrival does nothing to augment this deficiency, and the complex needs of many ex-offenders magnify the effects of limited social capital. Ex-prisoners come to places devoid of social capital, and their arrival reinforces residents' sense that sociopolitical isolation is warranted.

Community characteristics – human capital, social networks, social capital, collective efficacy, and informal social control – serve as mediating forces of public safety. Neighborhoods in which street crime thrives are typically places where residents lack human capital and where social networks fail to produce much social capital. These are locations where challenges to community life arise in various forms: racial disadvantage, poor employment prospects, housing inadequacies, political alienation, family discontinuity, and health problems. The limited capacity for collective efficacy exacerbates the impact of these social problems, and minimal human capital limits the capacity of informal social control. People must devote much of their time and attention to the struggle to "make ends meet," and they lack the time and opportunity to develop and sustain relationships that transcend the struggle. Moreover, when people in poor communities remain isolated from one another – staying in their residences out of fear and alienation – street crime is more likely to flourish (Skogan 1986). Under these conditions, social networks cannot be nourished and informal social controls cannot be bolstered.

The Cycling of Removal and Return in Tallahassee

In this section, we use Tallahassee data to illustrate patterns of reentry cycling and coercive mobility. Figure 7.1 shows the distribution of returning prisoners among Tallahassee neighborhoods in a single year.[4] Almost one

---

[4] Discrepancies in numbers of removals and returns are due primarily to missing addresses for return data. Descriptions of the Tallahassee data may be found in Clear, Rose, Waring, and Scully (2003).

Figure 7.1 Number of Releases in 80 Tallahassee Neighborhoods, 1997

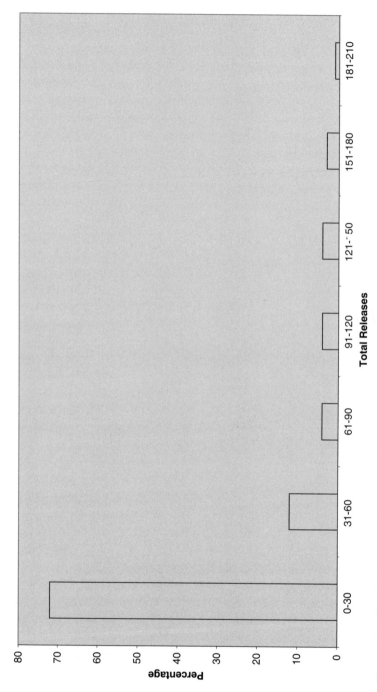

Figure 7.2 Total Releases as a Percentage of Tallahassee Neighborhoods, 1994–2002

third of the 80 neighborhoods in Tallahassee had no influx of ex-prisoners in 1997, and over half had one or fewer ex-prisoners reenter that year (more than two thirds had two or fewer in reentry). By contrast, in more than 10 percent of Tallahassee's neighborhoods, returning ex-prisoners accounted for 1 percent or more of its total residential population. The implication of this concentration reveals the disparate impact reentry can have at the community level. The potential effects of concentrated reentry are more severe if these patterns are generally consistent over time.

For example, Figure 7.2 shows the distribution of releases to Tallahassee neighborhoods for the 9-year period between 1994 and 2002. Almost three fourths of Tallahassee's neighborhoods received fewer than 30 released prisoners during that period (however, most only received a few). Noteworthy is the 5 percent of neighborhoods that received more than 5 times as many prison releases during this same period. Taking into consideration the population size of Tallahassee neighborhoods, those with the highest rate of reentry experienced one prison return for every 10 residents. Similar calculations in Brooklyn in 1998 found that in some areas one resident was removed to prison or jail for every eight males of parenting age (CASES 1998). Rose, Clear, and Ryder (2002) report that in two Tallahassee communities in which they conducted extensive interviews, almost every resident had experienced or expected to experience the return of a family member from prison.

Just as poor communities are disproportionately affected by prisoner reentry, they are similarly affected by incarceration (i.e., removal to prison). Figure 7.3 shows rates of admission to prison for Tallahassee neighborhoods in 1997. In that year, nearly half of Tallahassee's neighborhoods had no residents removed to prison. By contrast, the most intensely affected neighborhood had 2 percent of its resident population removed that year. Figure 7.4 presents this skewed pattern of admissions over the 9-year period between 1994 and 2002. Two thirds of the neighborhoods had 15 or fewer residents removed during this period, whereas the three neighborhoods most affected by prisoner removal had 10 times more residents removed. This skewed pattern has been reported by others who have studied incarceration at the community level (CASES 1998; Lynch and Sabol 2004; Lynch, Sabol, and Shelley 1998). Such studies provide estimates of one-day incarceration rates in these communities of up to one in seven black males in their 20s and 30s. Lynch and Sabol (2004) estimate that 48 block groups in Cleveland receive between 350 and 700 ex-prisoners per year, excluding those released from jail.

Figure 7.3 Number of Prison Admissions from Tallahassee Neighborhoods, 1997

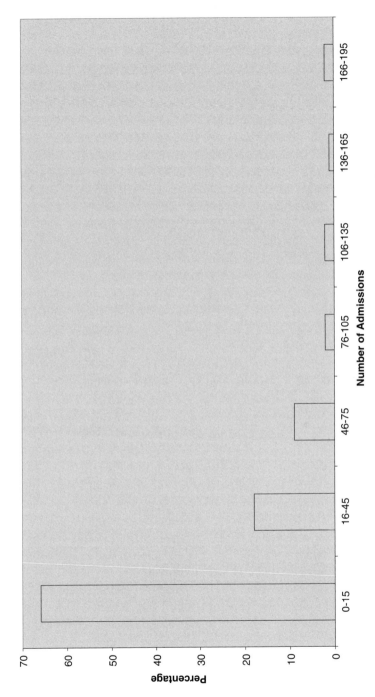

Figure 7.4 Total Admissions as a Percentage of Tallahassee Neighborhoods, 1994–2002

Table 7.2. *Total Number of Removals and Returns per Offender in Tallahassee,
1994–2002*

Returns	Removals						
	0	1	2	3	4	5	Total
0	0	1517	89	10	1	0	1617
1	1482	1210	285	25	2	0	3004
2	91	126	251	75	3	0	546
3	12	5	42	50	11	0	120
4	0	1	3	12	10	4	30
5	0	0	0	1	1	1	3
6	0	0	0	0	0	1	1
Total	1585	2859	670	173	28	6	5321

Examining the dual dynamics of removal and return that is concentrated
in certain neighborhoods, Table 7.2 shows the total number of removals
and returns for each offender for Tallahassee neighborhoods between 1994
and 2002. There were 5,321 people who experienced either removal or
return during that period. Of these people, 56 percent were "one-cycle"
experiences, that is, they experienced only a single removal or return during
the entire 9-year period. Of the remainder, 15 percent had *at least* two
removals *and* two returns during that period. (Bear in mind, these figures
apply only to felony-sentenced Florida residents who received sentences to
be served in prison; misdemeanor removals and returns are not included.)

Figure 7.5 illustrates coercive mobility, the cumulative impact of these
cycles of removal and return. In 1997, one neighborhood alone accounted
for more reentry cycling (37 admissions and releases) than the 35 neighborhoods with the lowest levels of reentry cycling combined. Further, more
than 1 in 30 residents in this neighborhood were in some form of reentry
cycling in that year. In Tallahassee, 21 percent of communities had neither
removals from the community nor releases from prison, whereas 44 percent
had both. One community had 37 events, and another had 27, well over 10
percent of the population of each neighborhood.

These data suggest that the effects of reentry cycling result from the
concentrated and *overlapping* nature of removal and reentry in already poor
neighborhoods *over time*. The concentration of effects over time means
that numbers that might appear on the surface to be small turn out, when
repeated across multiple years, to have more substantial impacts. The fact
that removal and reentry rates coincide explains why there may be a limited

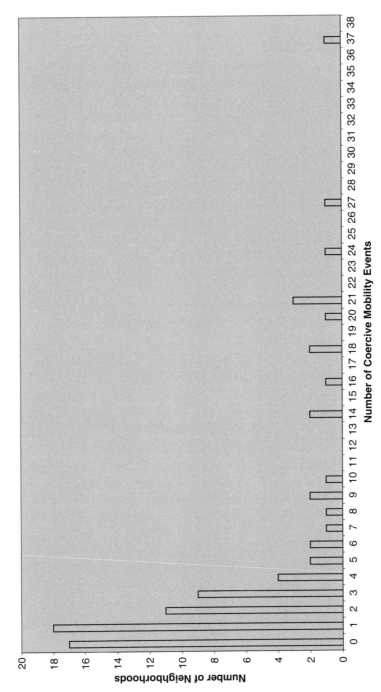

Figure 7.5 Sum of Admissions and Releases in 80 Tallahassee Neighborhoods, 1997

crime-reduction effect of removing active offenders – in any given year, some residents are sent to prison but others – perhaps an equivalent number – return from prison (see Rosenfeld et al., this volume). Rather than a noticeable drop in crime, then, what happens is a homeostasis of "missing people." On any given day, about the same number of people are behind bars, though the membership of the incarcerated cohort is variable.

It is this homeostasis of missing people that affects both formal and informal social control. The effects are complicated and multidirectional. Removing criminally active residents assuredly reduces crime to some extent. Returning them undermines that effect. Having some proportion of residents in flux destabilizes social relationships in ways that undercut informal social control. The net result is that, at a high-enough level, reentry cycling can result in considerable social disruption and produce the very problems that incarceration is meant to ameliorate. The fact that this pattern is sustained over time means that diminished social control capacity can become a semistable characteristic of poor neighborhoods.

Understanding Communities and Reentry Cycling

A recent summary of the literature on collateral impacts of incarceration on communities (Lynch and Sabol 2004) argues that the level of evidence on the question of communities and reentry cycling is limited by the lack of high-quality empirical studies. It is true that there have been too few studies of this phenomenon. And there are other methodological problems that make the study of neighborhood effects difficult. Many of the effects are simultaneous, and so cross-sectional models are unable to disentangle causes from effects. Even the largest cities have a limited number of neighborhoods, and most community characteristics are not distributed equally across neighborhoods, complicating the analysis.

Given these problems, Lynch and Sabol emphasize the need for multiyear data and replication models. This suggestion is based on the recognition that all theories of neighborhood and community-level effects are theories of cumulative effects over time. Although this general call for research is important, it should be narrowed so that the research addresses five specific issues. First and foremost, we need to investigate further the precise relationship between concentrated reentry cycling and neighborhood dynamics. Clear and Rose have shown both theoretically (Rose and Clear 1998) and empirically (Clear et al. 2003) that reentry cycling can produce detrimental community-level effects, but this is far from a proven case. Some new evidence will be provided by the Collaborative Project on Concentrated Incarceration,[5] now underway at John Jay College, which investigates the impact of concentrated incarceration and removal on various community dynamics in ten U.S. cities. But more studies are needed to determine if this phenomenon is limited to certain locations or is widespread and consistent.

Second, to understand better how reentry cycling occurs, it is important to clarify how removal and reentry cycles work their way through neighborhoods over time. Figure 7.6 shows the variation in reentry cycling across a 9-year period for Tallahassee's neighborhoods. Each neighborhood's highest, lowest, and median annual rate of reentry and removal (total coercive mobility) is plotted. This figure shows that almost every Tallahassee neighborhood has some reentry cycling during the period 1994–2002, but the variance among neighborhoods in that period augments a variance that occurred within neighborhoods as well. Neighborhoods with very high median rates had years in which the annual rate was quite low, approximating other locations.

This raises important questions about the dynamics of reentry cycling across time and place. Most prison releases go to the places from which they were removed, but this is certainly not a universal pattern. The fact that some neighborhoods may be net exporters to the prison system and others net importers raises important questions about the significance of the differences. What makes a neighborhood gain more residents than it loses, and how does this fact affect the neighborhood over time? Why do some prisoners return to places from which they did not enter prison? What are the consequences of this asymmetrical pattern?

Third, there is a need for micro-level studies of incarceration. A few ethnographic studies have been reported, and these are enormously informative of the way people adapt to the circumstances of incarceration in their lives. In addition to this kind of study, we think systematic studies of social network formation and change in response to incarceration are needed. The theory of coercive mobility is built on a foundation of hypothesized effects on social networks. The existence of these effects needs to be determined through empirical investigation. Such studies would follow networks of association during periods of incarceration and reentry and document how networks changed during these periods.

---

[5] Funded cooperatively by The Open Society Institute and the JEHT Foundation.

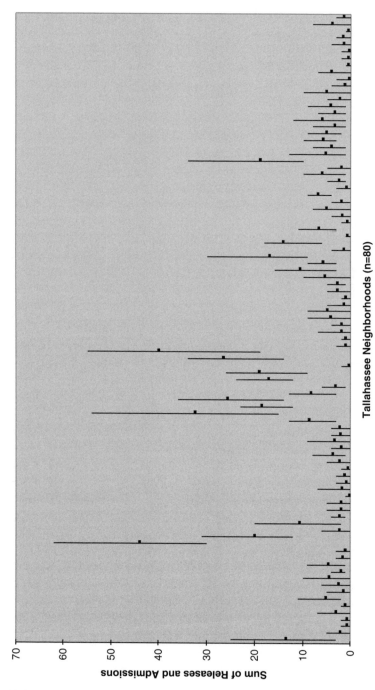

Tallahassee Neighborhoods (n=80)

Figure 7.6 High, Low, and Median Coercive Mobility Events in Tallahassee Neighborhoods, 1994–2002

204

Fourth, the effects of reentry cycling for males and females are probably different, for several reasons. Men and women go to prison for different offenses, stay there different lengths of time, and leave different arrays of relationships behind. Although men recycle at much higher levels than women, women occupy more significant positions in community, family, and associational networks than men. Moreover, a focus on women opens the door to the problem of intergenerational cycling through the criminal justice system. The intergenerational effect is well documented (Hagan and Dinovitzer 1999), but little is known about how it comes about.

Finally, we need to develop a practical understanding of community-level effects by studying the impact of programs that are designed to ameliorate them. If community-level effects are important, then ways of combating them need to be strengthened. These would most likely take the form of partnerships between the community and the justice system. Evaluations of these partnerships would help to inform the best ways to confront the public-safety problems of reentry for communities.

References

Anderson, Elijah. 1996. *The Code of the Street: Decency, Violence, and the Moral Life of the Inner City*. New York: Norton.

Beck, Alan J. 2000. *State and Federal Prisoners Returning to the Community*. Washington, DC: Bureau of Justice Statistics.

Bellair, Paul E. 1997. "Social Interaction and Community Crime: Examining the Importance of Neighbor Networks." *Criminology* 35: 677–704.

Bellair, Paul E. 2000. "Informal Surveillance and Street Crime." *Criminology* 38: 137–170.

Braman, Donald. 2003. "Families and Incarceration," Marc Mauer and Meda Chesney-Lind, eds., *Invisible Punishment: The Collateral Consequences of Mass Incarceration*, pp. 117–135.

New York: The New Press. CASES. 1998. *The Community Justice Project*. New York: Center for Alternative Sentencing and Employment Services.

Clear, Todd R., and Dina R. Rose. 2003. "Individual Sentencing Practices and Aggregate Social Problems," D. F. Hawkins, S. Myers, and R. Stone, eds., *Crime Control and Criminal Justice: The Delicate Balance*. Westport, CT: Greenwood.

Clear, Todd R., Dina R. Rose, and Judith A. Ryder. 2001. "Incarceration and Community: The Problem of Removing and Returning Offenders." *Crime and Delinquency* 47: 335–351.

Clear, Todd R., Dina R. Rose, Elin Waring, and Kristen Scully. 2003. "Coercive Mobility and Crime: A Preliminary Examination of Concentrated Incarceration and Social Disorganization." *Justice Quarterly* 20: 33–64.

Darity, William, and Samuel Myers. 1994. *The Black Underclass: Critical Essays on Race and Unwantedness*. New York: Garland.

Fagan, Jeffrey, Valerie West, and Jan Holland. 2003. "Reciprocal Effects of Crime and Incarceration in New York City Neighborhoods." *Fordham Urban Law Journal* 30: 1551–1602.

Fagan, Jeffrey, Valerie West, and Jan Holland. 2005. "Neighborhood, Crime, and Incarceration in New York City." *Columbia Human Rights Law Review* 36:.

Fishman, Laura. 1990. *Women at the Wall*. Albany: State University of New York Press.

Gottfredson, Stephen D., and Ralph B. Taylor. 1988. "Community Contexts and Criminal Offenders," Tim Hope and Margaret Shaw, eds., *Communities and Crime Reduction*. London: Her Majesty's Stationary Office.

Granovetter, Mark. 1993. "Strength of Weak Ties." *American Journal of Sociology* 78: 1360–1380.

Hagan, John. 1993. "The Social Embeddedness of Crime and Unemployment." *Criminology* 31: 465–492.

Hagan, John, and Ronit Dinovitzer, 1999. "Collateral Consequences of Imprisonment for Children, Communities, and Prisoners," M. Tonry and J. Petersilia, eds., *Prisons: Crime and Justice*, vol. 26. Chicago: University of Chicago Press.

Hughes, T. D., Wilson, D. J., and Alan J. Beck. 2001. *Trends in State Parole, 1990–2000*. Washington, DC: Bureau of Justice Statistics.

Hunter, A. J. 1985. "Private, Parochial and Public Social Orders: The Problem of Crime and Incivility in Urban Communities," G. D. Suttles and M. N. Zald, eds., *The Challenge of Social Control: Citizenship and Institution Building in Modern Society*, pp. 230–242. Norwood, NJ: Aldex.

Lynch, James P., and William J. Sabol, 2001. *Crime, Coercion, and Communities: The Effects of Arrest and Incarceration Policies on Informal Social Control in Neighborhoods*. Final Report. Washington, DC: National Institute of Justice. Lynch, James. P., and William. J. Sabol. 2003. "Assessing the Longer-Run Consequences of Incarceration: Effects on Families and Employment," D. F. Hawkins, S. Myers, and R. Stone, eds., *Crime Control and Criminal Justice: The Delicate Balance*. Westport, CT: Greenwood.

Lynch, James P., and William J. Sabol. 2004. "Assessing the Effects of Mass Incarceration on Informal Social Control in Communities," M. Pattillo, D. Weiman, and B. Western, eds., *Imprisoning America: The Social Effects of Mass Incarceration*. New York: Russell Sage.

Lynch, James P., William J. Sabol, and Mary Shelley. 1998. *Spatial Patterns of Drug Enforcement Policies in Metropolitan Areas: Trends in the Prevalence and Consequence of Incarceration*. Paper presented to the American Society of Criminology, Washington, DC, November 11.

Markowitz, F., Paul Bellaire, Allen Liska, and Jiao Liu. 2001. "Extending Social Disorganization Theory: Modeling the Relationship between Cohesion, Disorder and Fear." *Criminology* 39: 293–320.

Maruschak, L., and Alan J. Beck. 2001. *Medical Problems of Inmates, 1997*. Washington, DC: Bureau of Justice Statistics.

Meares, Tracey. 1998. "Social Organization and Drug Enforcement." *American Criminal Law Review* 35: 191–215.

Morenoff, J. D., and Robert J. Sampson. 1997. "Violent Crime and the Spatial Dynamics of Neighborhood Transition: Chicago, 1970–1990." *Social Forces* 76: 31–64.

Myers, Samuel. 2000. *Unintended Consequences of Sentencing Reforms.* Paper presented to the American Sociological Association, Washington, DC, August 13.

Nagin, Daniel, and Joel Waldfogel. 1998. "The Effect of Conviction on Income Through the Life Cycle." *International Review of Law and Economics* 18: 25–40.

Petersilia, Joan. 2003. *When Prisoners Come Home: Parole and Prisoner Reentry.* Chicago: Oxford University Press.

Piquero, Alex R., Valerie West, Jeffrey Fagan, and Jan Holland. 2005. "Neighborhood, Race, and the Economic Consequences of Incarceration in New York City, 1985–1996. John Hagan, Laurie Krivo, and Ruth Peterson, eds., The Many Colors of Crime: Inequalities of Race, Ethnicity and Crime in America. New York: New York University.

Regoeczi, Wendy C. 2002. "The Impact of Density: The Importance of Nonlinearity and Selection on Flight and Fight Responses." *Social Forces.* 81: 505–530.

Ritchie, Beth. 2003. "The Social Impact of Mass Incarceration on Women," Marc Mauer and Meda Chesney-Lind, eds., *Invisible Punishment: The Collateral Consequences of Mass Incarceration,* pp. 136–149. New York: The New Press.

Rose, Dina R., and Todd R. Clear. 1998. "Incarceration, Social Capital and Crime: Examining the Unintended Consequences of Incarceration." *Criminology* 36: 441–479.

Rose, Dina, Todd R. Clear, and Judith Ryder. 2002. *Drugs, Incarcerations, and Neighborhood Life: the Impact of Reintegrating Offenders into the Community.* Final Report. Washington, DC: National Institute of Justice.

Sampson, Robert J., Steven Raudenbush, and Felton Earls 1997. "Neighborhoods and Violent Crime: A Multilevel Study of Collective Efficacy." *Science* 277: 918–924.

Shaw, Clifford R., and Henry D. McKay. 1942. *Juvenile Delinquency and Urban Areas.* Chicago: University of Chicago Press.

Skogan, Wesley. 1986. "Fear of Crime and Neighborhood Change," Albert J. Reiss, Jr., and Michael Tonry, eds., *Communities and Crime.* Chicago: University of Chicago Press.

Skogan, Wesley. 1990. *Disorder and Decline: Crime and the Spiral of Decay in American Neighborhoods.* New York: Free Press.

St. Jean, Peter K. B. 2006. *Pockets of Crime: A Closer Look at Street Crimes, Broken Windows and Collective Efficacy Theories.* Forthcoming, Chicago: University of Chicago Press.

Thomas, James. 2003. Proposal to the National Science Foundation.

Tyler, Tom. 1990. *Why People Obey the Law.* Chicago: University of Chicago.

Uggen, Christopher, and Jeff Manza. 2002. "Democratic Contraction? The Political Consequences of Felon Disenfranchisement in the United States." *American Sociological Review* 67: 777–803.

Western, Bruce, Jeffrey Kling, and David Weiman, 2001. "The Labor Market Consequences of Incarceration." *Crime and Delinquency* 47: 410–438.

Wilson, William Julius. 1987. *The Truly Disadvantaged: The Inner City, The Underclass, and Public Policy*. Chicago: University of Chicago.

Wooldredge, John. 2002. "Examining the (ir)Relevance of Aggregation Bias for Multi-Level Studies of Neighborhoods and Crime with an Example Comparing Census Tracts to Official Neighborhoods in Cincinnati." *Criminology* 40: 681–710.

8

Work and Family Perspectives on Reentry

Christopher Uggen, Sara Wakefield, and
Bruce Western

Employment and marriage play central roles in standard analyses of recidivism, and a long line of research suggests that ex-offenders who find good jobs and settle down in stable marriages threaten public safety much less than those who remain single and unemployed. Successful prisoner reentry thus involves the linked processes of reintegration into social institutions such as work and family and desistance from crime. Therefore, research on reentry and recidivism often aims to identify factors that place people at risk of joblessness and marital disruption – low education, impulsive behavior, drug abuse and so on. From this perspective, the job of public policy is to remedy these preexisting defects in ex-offenders, thereby promoting employment, marriage, and ultimately reducing crime.

In this chapter we reexamine the roles of employment and marriage in prisoner reentry. Although we certainly agree that good jobs and strong marriages assist successful reentry and reduce recidivism, we try to extend the usual analysis in three ways. First, we adopt a life course perspective in which the timing of work and marriage emerge as critical for desistance from crime. This perspective suggests that age-graded public policy interventions are needed to normalize the life course trajectories of ex-offenders. Second, we consider whether the criminal justice system – particularly corrections – might negatively affect the employment opportunities and marriage prospects of ex-offenders. In this case, public policy should also work to remedy the damage caused by official criminal justice processing or to seek alternatives to incarceration that may be less costly to public safety in the long term. Finally, in discussing the problem of prisoner reentry, we examine the social contexts to which prisoners are returning. We find that marriage and labor markets now appear significantly worse than in the early 1980s, suggesting that small improvements in the behaviors and skills of individual ex-offenders are only part of a comprehensive reentry strategy.

Our analysis departs from the customary emphasis on the importance of marriage and employment by enlisting broader institutional and social contexts as key influences on prisoner reentry and recidivism. In addition to the now-familiar, and still extraordinary, difficulties faced by a disadvantaged high-risk group of men trying to establish work and family lives, we argue that public policy must also face the challenge that crime in the current period may be partly a product of the prison boom. Beyond the collateral consequences of incarceration (Mauer and Chesney-Lind, 2002), successfully reducing crime may ultimately await improvements in labor and marriage markets that are well beyond the reach of criminal justice policy.

Work

For our purposes, "work" involves individual employment status and the presence and quality of jobs available to ex-prisoners, as well as labor markets and macroeconomic conditions that may affect overall recidivism rates. Although the relationship between crime rates and unemployment rates remains the subject of debate, a long line of research has tied macroeconomic conditions to fluctuations in crime and imprisonment (Britt 1997; Sampson 1987; Western 2002; Western and Beckett 1999). In recent decades, the disappearance of jobs from depressed urban areas has concentrated disadvantage and crime in certain communities, most notably in neighborhoods with a preponderance of racial minority residents (Kasarda 1989; Massey and Denton 1993; Morenoff and Sampson 1997; Wilson 1996). Rising income inequality and the diminishing quality of employment in the secondary sector of the labor market are likely to have had especially strong effects on the criminal involvement and incarceration rates of African American males (Blau and Blau 1982; Crutchfield and Pitchford 1997; Harer and Steffensmeier 1992; Western, Kleykamp, and Rosenfeld 2003; Western and Pettit 2000). As we detail, inmates are thus often characterized by problematic labor market histories prior to entering prison. Although employment may offer an important opportunity for offenders to change their lives and leave crime behind, there are many barriers that inhibit the development of marketable job skills during periods of incarceration (see, e.g., Uggen and Wakefield 2003).

The Work Histories of Returning Prisoners

As a result of changing historical conditions and the social distribution of disadvantage, convicted felons often enter prison with a history of unemployment, low educational attainment, and few marketable job skills. Figure 8.1 compares educational attainment, employment, and family status at time of arrest for state and federal prison inmates with comparable data on males aged 25–34 in the general population – the median age range for inmates (U.S. Bureau of the Census 1998; U.S. Department of Justice 2001). Only one third of the inmates held a high school diploma or equivalency, relative to almost 90 percent of young adult men in the general population. The differences in employment status are also striking, with only 55 percent of inmates employed full time at the time of their most recent arrest. Although no directly comparable self-reported data are available for the general population, the proportion of inmates reporting mental, emotional, and physical disabilities suggests additional barriers to employment for returning prisoners. Finally, prison inmates are much less likely to be married and far more likely to be divorced or separated (separations comprise an additional 6 percent of the inmate population, not shown in Figure 8.1) than young men in the general population of the United States.

How Is Work Reintegration Related to Desistance from Crime?

Criminological theories and commonsense understandings of crime and conformity underscore the importance of work as the setting for social reintegration. Individuals with a history of joblessness are at high risk for criminal involvement and locating stable, high-quality work can provide an important pathway out of crime. Connections made through work are likely to serve as "informal social controls" that inhibit criminal behavior (Sampson and Laub 1990, 1993; Laub, Nagin, and Sampson 1998). Strong work and family connections also have the capacity to alter the social networks of offenders and increase social capital by replacing criminally involved friends with co-workers, supportive family members, and law-abiding peers (Coleman 1990; Granovettor 1973; Hagan 1993). For example, Elijah Anderson's (1992, 1999) ethnographic research on changes in urban African American neighborhoods suggests the importance of social networks in obtaining good jobs and forming strong families. Anderson emphasizes the role of older working adults (labeled "old heads" by

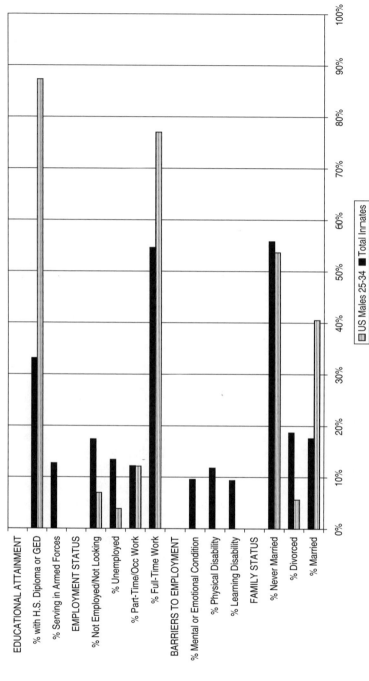

Figure 8.1 Employment, Education, and Family Status of State and Federal Inmates, 1997 (*Source*: authors' analysis of USDOJ 2001)

Anderson) and viable job opportunities in reducing crime, describing African American neighborhoods of the past in which those engaged in legitimate employment provided opportunities for younger residents. Today, these "old heads" are in short supply, particularly in high-poverty, minority communities where incarceration has become a normative life course experience (Pettit and Western 2003; Rose and Clear 1998).

In the absence of job opportunities and the presence of economic disadvantage, adolescents are increasingly likely to become "embedded" in criminal social networks (Hagan 1993) and "knifed off" from more conventional work and family opportunities (Caspi and Moffitt 1995). Criminal embeddedness tends to restrict later educational attainment and work opportunities, thereby making continued involvement in crime more likely. Figure 8.2 presents the educational and work background of prison inmates with reference to their criminal histories. The figure distinguishes between first-time offenders, who report higher levels of education and employment rates, and recidivists, who are less educated and less likely to have been employed full time when they were arrested. Violent recidivists appear to have even greater barriers to employment than nonviolent recidivists, with those convicted of multiple violent offenses reporting the highest rates of mental or emotional conditions, physical disabilities, and learning disabilities.

Beyond the simple presence of a job, some studies have established a gradient in which high-quality jobs are especially important to the processes of criminal involvement, desistance, and reintegration (Allan and Steffensmeier 1989; Sampson and Laub 1993; Uggen 1999). Allan and Steffensmeier (1989) find that inadequate employment, as well as unemployment, increases arrest rates among young adults. Neal Shover points to jobs paying a decent income and jobs offering opportunities to exercise creativity and intelligence as facilitating desistance from crime (1996, p. 127). Uggen (1999) finds that former prisoners who obtain jobs ranked high in quality are less likely to reoffend than those who obtain lower-rated jobs, net of the process of self-selection into employment. Thus, a diverse body of research suggests a link between high-quality work opportunities and cessation from crime, even when adjustments are made for potential biases arising from the selection process that sorts workers into particular jobs.

Employment may encourage desistance by altering the social networks of offenders and increasing the informal social controls to which they are subject. Laub and Sampson (2003), for example, emphasize how employment is linked to changes in routine activities and the ways in which employers, like spouses, provide social control. Work involvement may also help

213

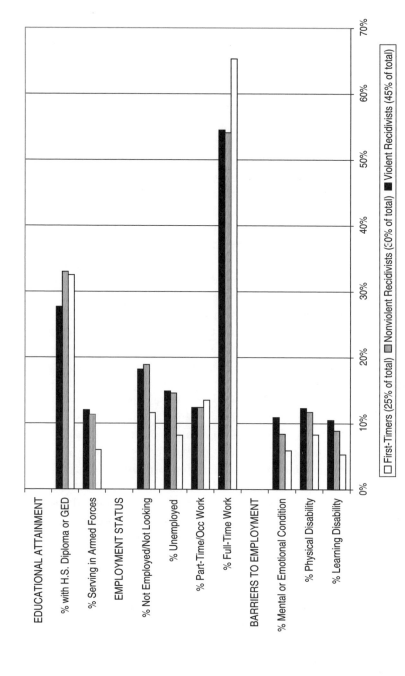

Figure 8.2 Employment and Educational Characteristics of Inmates by Criminal History, 1997 (*Source:* authors' analysis of USDOJ 2001)

former prisoners develop identities as law-abiding citizens. From a symbolic-interactionist perspective, Matsueda and Heimer (1997) describe desistance as a process of adopting prosocial work and family roles (see also Maruna 2001; Uggen, Manza, and Behrens 2003). Ex-offenders who find quality work are likely to develop prosocial identities that may supplant or overshadow the salience of existing identities as rule-violators, troublemakers, or criminals. Taken as a whole, this literature suggests that one avenue for reducing recidivism and increasing public safety would involve helping offenders find work and gain the education and training needed to obtain work of higher quality.

The literature on desistance also suggests that arrest may have greater deterrent effects for working offenders relative to those who are unemployed. Several studies suggest that those engaged in work and family life have more to lose from continued criminal involvement and may therefore be less likely to reoffend. Sherman and Smith (1992), for example, find that the deterrent impact of arrest for domestic violence is larger for working offenders. Similarly, Kruttschnitt, Uggen, and Shelton (2000) find that sex offender treatment is more effective among those with stable employment histories. In sum, ex-offenders with a "stake in conformity" (Toby 1957) are less likely to continue in crime and are embedded in social networks that may provide a viable alternative to criminal involvement.

Family

As with educational attainment and employment status, most people enter prison with a number of disadvantages in their families of origin and are delayed on markers of family formation as adults. Moreover, family deficits as children and delays in family formation as adults are strongly associated with criminal involvement. As a result, former prisoners who develop strong family ties and overcome earlier familial disadvantages are also likely to broaden their social networks, adopt prosocial identities, and ultimately leave crime behind.

Like unemployment, the prevalence of single parenthood and poverty is linked to higher crime rates (Sampson 1987). In adulthood, the development of strong family ties may reduce recidivism among former inmates by offering them a multitude of prosocial roles, including those as involved parents or supportive spouses. A high-quality marriage may also exert informal social controls on the lives of offenders and reduce their tendencies to associate with criminal peers (Laub, Nagin, and Sampson 1998; Warr

1998). As is the case with employment, some studies suggest that the quality and commitment of marriage, rather than the mere presence of a marital union, is critical to inhibiting subsequent crime. Horney, Osgood, and Marshall (1995) report that cohabitation, in the absence of marriage, may even increase offending. Additionally, spouses who are involved in crime themselves are unlikely to reduce crime in their mates and may present a barrier to desistance for their reentering partners (Giordano, Cernkovich, and Rudolph 2002).

The Family Histories of Returning Prisoners

The impact of family on criminal desistance represents three processes. First, disadvantage in the family of origin may encourage crime in children raised in these families. Second, delays in family formation as a result of earlier disadvantage and criminal involvement are likely to render desistance from crime more difficult. Finally, to the extent that incarceration disrupts existing family bonds, former prisoners face greater difficulties in establishing stable family lives. Figure 8.3, describing the family background of inmates in state and federal correctional facilities (U.S. Department of Justice 2001), demonstrates high levels of early life disadvantage. Almost 13 percent of inmates experienced severe disruptions in their living arrangements as children, reporting that they spent some time in a foster home or institutional agency during childhood. Childhood poverty and economic disadvantage were high among inmates. Approximately 45 percent of black inmates, 22 percent of white inmates, and 33 percent of Hispanic inmates reported that their parents received public assistance. Similarly, about 6 percent of white inmates and 28 percent of black inmates reported living in public housing as children. Almost one third of all inmates also reported that their parents abused alcohol or illegal drugs.

Racial differences among inmates are apparent on the measures of socioeconomic disadvantage, parental alcohol and drug abuse, and disrupted living arrangements. White inmates were more likely to have spent time in a foster home and report parents with substance abuse problems, whereas black inmates were much more likely to have lived in public housing and received public assistance as children. Finally, roughly 18 percent of all inmates report that at least one parent spent time in prison or jail during their childhood. Recent research suggests that parental incarceration has far-reaching consequences for children. Children of incarcerated parents suffer economically from the removal of the parent's legal (and illegal)

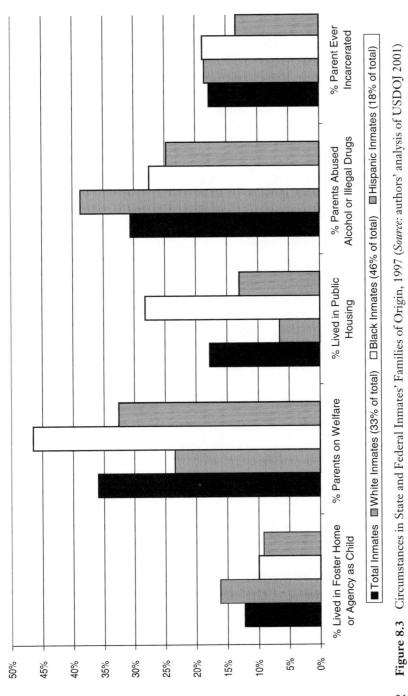

Figure 8.3 Circumstances in State and Federal Inmates' Families of Origin, 1997 (*Source*: authors' analysis of USDOJ 2001)

217

income (Hagan and Dinovitzer 1999), may be at greater risk of precocious exits from adolescence (Hagan and Wheaton 1993), and are especially vulnerable to involvement in the criminal justice system themselves (Hagan and Palloni 1990).

Criminal history is also related to delays in family formation in adulthood. John Hagan's "criminal embeddedness" model suggests that juvenile offenders become involved in delinquent social networks that delay family formation, schooling, and occupational attainment. Figure 8.4 describes prison inmates in relation to their criminal history. Clear differences are observed in the family situations of first-time offenders, nonviolent recidivists, and violent recidivists for all measures except spousal incarceration. Violent recidivists report the highest levels of parental incarceration, parental substance abuse, public assistance, and disrupted living arrangements whereas first-time offenders report the lowest levels on these characteristics. Similarly, violent recidivists report the highest levels of delays in family formation as adults. Violent recidivists are less likely to have children and least likely to be married. These reports from inmates suggest that public safety may be enhanced by addressing childhood disadvantage and assisting offenders in family formation and reintegration as adults. Because most inmates are already parents, assisting them in playing a more supportive and responsible parental role may help foster their own prosocial identities, regardless of whether they will ultimately gain or regain custody of their children. It may also reduce crime in the future by lessening the disadvantages experienced by their children.

Overall, the literature on work and family suggests that disadvantage in the labor market, poor employment histories, and early family life disadvantages make criminal involvement more likely. Our review of the characteristics of prison inmates supports this conclusion, with inmates exhibiting high levels of disadvantage across a number of domains. Incarceration is likely to exacerbate these deficits, rather than merely preserve them, because imprisonment removes offenders from any existing positive social networks and carries a number of consequences after release, including stigma and legal barriers to work, educational training, and public assistance.

The Effects of Incarceration on Work and Family

Although job and family instability are linked to crime, research also shows that the experience of imprisonment diminishes the ability of former prisoners to find work and maintain family relationships. The negative effects

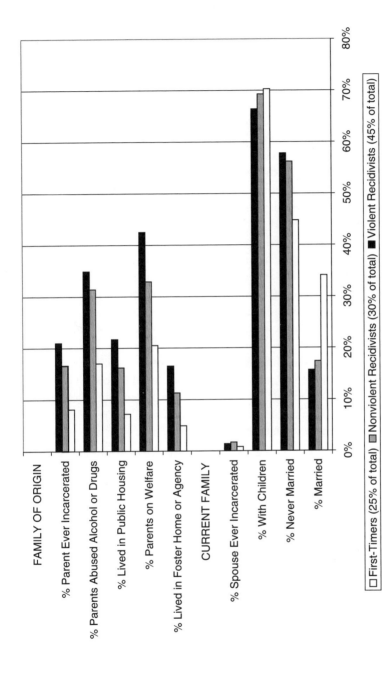

Figure 8.4 Family Characteristics of State and Federal Inmates by Criminal History, 1997 (*Source*: authors' analysis of USDOJ 2001)

219

of incarceration have been estimated with data on wages and employment in the labor market and rates of marital dissolution in the marriage market.

Ex-prisoners face two challenges to obtaining steady employment. First, the stigma of criminal conviction makes them unattractive job candidates. Second, incarceration may erode job skills and social ties to those who could provide employment opportunities. The stigma of criminal conviction can be seen in survey data, social experiments, and the law. Holzer's (1996, p. 59) survey of four large cities found that only 33 percent of employers would hire an applicant with a criminal record, compared to over 80 percent who would hire a welfare recipient or 70 percent who would hire the long-term unemployed. Pager's (2003) experimental results are even more striking. Her audit study sent young black and white men to apply for randomly selected entry-level jobs. The men were randomly assigned a resume showing evidence of a criminal record. Employers called back white applicants without records 34 percent of the time, compared to a callback rate of just 17 percent for whites with a criminal record. Blacks applicants without records received callbacks from employers 14 percent of the time (less frequently than whites *with* records), whereas blacks presenting criminal records were called back only 5 percent of the time. These results provide strong evidence of differential treatment by employers of young men with criminal records; moreover, the penalty of criminal conviction seems especially large for African American men. In most jurisdictions, the stigma of conviction takes on a legal significance. A felony record can temporarily or permanently disqualify employment in licensed or professional occupations. These prohibitions typically extend beyond the professions to include jobs in the health care industry and skilled trades. Felony status in several states can also prevent public sector employment (Office of the Pardon Attorney 1996).

If stigma attaching to criminal justice contact reduces earnings, we might expect little difference in the effects of arrest, conviction, probation, or incarceration. From the employer's viewpoint, each intervention carries similar information about the trustworthiness of a prospective worker. Some work has distinguished the effects of juvenile delinquency from arrest, probation, and adult incarceration (Freeman 1992; Grogger 1995; Western and Beckett 1999). Incarceration effects are relatively large for this research, suggesting that other mechanisms in addition to stigma might be operating.

In addition to stigmatizing ex-offenders, incarceration may also erode job skills and social networks. Social networks are important for providing job seekers with information about employment opportunities. Spending

time in prison or jail weakens these social contacts. If juvenile delinquency embeds young offenders in criminal social networks, incarceration
may strengthen such networks, replacing social connections to legitimate
employment. Job skills are also undermined by imprisonment. Time out
of employment prevents the acquisition of skills obtained by others who
remain continuously employed. The experience of incarceration may limit
an inmate's capacity to maintain regular employment after release (Western,
Kling, and Weiman 2001). Preexisting mental or physical illnesses may
be exacerbated by prison time. Moreover, behaviors that are adaptive for
survival in prison are likely to be inconsistent with work routines outside
(Irwin and Austin 1997, p. 121). These effects may be especially large in the
recent period of declining support for training, drug treatment, and health
care.

These economic effects of incarceration are intertwined with the negative effects of imprisonment on marriage and family life. The decision
of low-income mothers to marry or remarry depends in part on the economic prospects, social respectability, and trustworthiness of their potential
partners (Edin 2000). Incarceration undermines all these qualities. Labor
market research shows that male ex-inmates earn less and experience more
unemployment than comparable men who have not been to prison or jail
(Western, Kling, and Weiman 2001). If ex-inmates are stuck in low-wage
or unstable jobs, their opportunities for marriage will likely be limited.
Ethnographers find that the stigma of incarceration makes single mothers
reluctant to marry or live with the fathers of their children if those fathers
have prison or jail records (Edin 2000; Waller 1996). Ecological analysis
yields similar results. Sabol and Lynch (1998) report that large numbers of
female-headed families are found in counties receiving the most returning
prisoners. In short, the stigma and collateral consequences of incarceration
shrinks the pool of possible marriage partners.

Incarceration is also destabilizing for intact relationships. The experience
of imprisonment can produce strong feelings of shame and anger, both for
inmates and their families, providing a source of marital stress after release
(Hagan and Dinovitzer 1999, pp. 126–127). The stigma of incarceration
may be diminished in communities with high incarceration rates, but prison
or jail time is still massively disruptive. Research on veterans finds that long
periods of enforced separation during military service significantly raises the
risk of divorce (e.g., Pavalko and Elder 1990). Similar results are reported
for men who have served time in prison. Analysis of a sample of new fathers
shows that men who have served time in prison or jail are only half as likely

to be married a year after their child's birth as similar men who have not been incarcerated (Western, Lopoo, and McLanahan 2002). Just as civil disabilities limit employment opportunities, bars on public housing and welfare eligibility among ex-felons also create significant impediments to the formation of stable unions among poor couples. Furthermore, to the extent that incarceration raises involvement in crime or retains ex-inmates in crime-involved peer networks, marriage and other parental relationships will also be strained.

The effects of incarceration on marriage may also spill over to affect the children of parents who go to prison. A growing research literature details significant consequences for the children of incarcerated parents. In a recent article on the consequences of rising incarceration rates, John Hagan and Ronit Dinovitzer argue that the impact of incarceration on children "may be the least understood and most consequential implication of the high reliance on incarceration in America" (1999, p. 122). In 1999, more than 700,000 inmates were parents to 1.5 million children under the age of 18 and 22 percent of these children were under the age of five (Mumola 2000). The actual number of children who have ever had a parent incarcerated is much higher because the available estimates of the number of children affected by incarceration represent only a snapshot in time that is based on the current prison population (see, e.g., Mumola 2000; U.S. Department of Justice 2002).

About 55 percent of state prison inmates and 63 percent of federal inmates are parents. Almost one fourth of inmate parents have three or more children (Mumola 2000). And, though the majority of prison inmates are male, the number of incarcerated women has been rising steadily for quite some time. The era of sentencing guidelines and the concurrent war on drugs have had a particularly unfortunate impact on female offenders with children. Prior to sentencing guidelines at the federal and state level, many judges sentenced mothers to probation sentences to avoid disrupting their families, particularly in cases where no suitable relative was available to care for the children. Today, family obligations are not an acceptable reason for departure from the guidelines and greater gender equity in sentencing has increased the percentage of incarcerated females who are also mothers (Hagan and Dinovitzer 1999).

Imprisoned offenders are disproportionately from impoverished backgrounds, which places them at greater risk for early and nonmarital parenthood. Early transitions to parenthood are clearly linked to later instability in marriage and relationships (Western, Lopoo, and McLanahan 2002) and

222

welfare dependency (Hogan and Astone 1986). Incarceration is likely to exacerbate existing delays in family formation and the disadvantages that characterize the backgrounds of prison inmates raise questions about the ability of former inmates to form healthy families as adults. Figure 8.5 displays characteristics of inmate parents at the time of their arrest. Less than half of all inmate parents attained a high school diploma or GED. Although 62 percent of incarcerated fathers reported being employed full time (compared to 55 percent of all inmates), only 42 percent of mothers were working full time and 32 percent were not looking for work. Although both fathers and mothers in prison are concentrated in the lower income categories, mothers earned substantially less than fathers did in the month prior to their arrest. Most inmate parents have never married or are currently divorced. Additionally, 15 percent of incarcerated mothers were homeless at the time of their arrests. Unemployment and homelessness rates of this magnitude are not unusual among the prison population, yet the numbers suggest that many of these parents, especially mothers, may have experienced great difficulty supporting their children immediately prior to entering prison. Although these figures demonstrate that inmate parents were disadvantaged prior to entering prison, the experience of incarceration imposes additional constraints on the resources and qualities needed to serve as successful fathers and mothers. Moreover, parental incarceration may in turn place the succeeding generation of children at greater risk of incarceration in the future.

Relatively few programs dedicated to successful family reintegration for offenders have been rigorously evaluated, although debates about the wisdom of reuniting children with criminally involved parents are common. Surprisingly, there have been few empirical studies to date on the impact of children on the criminal offending of their parents; most of the research on recidivism has focused on marriage and cohabitation to the neglect of research on child-rearing and parental deviance. Thus, it is difficult to know whether offenders who become parents are more likely to desist from crime than nonparents or the extent to which the parenting skills of former inmates change over time.

Though most incarcerated parents were living with their children prior to imprisonment (Mumola 2000), children may benefit from the removal of a parent heavily engaged in crime. Kandel, Rosenbaum, and Chen (1994) report that crime and drug use by mothers contributes to problem behaviors in children through increased marital disruption and poor parenting skills. Because many imprisoned parents had their children early and

223

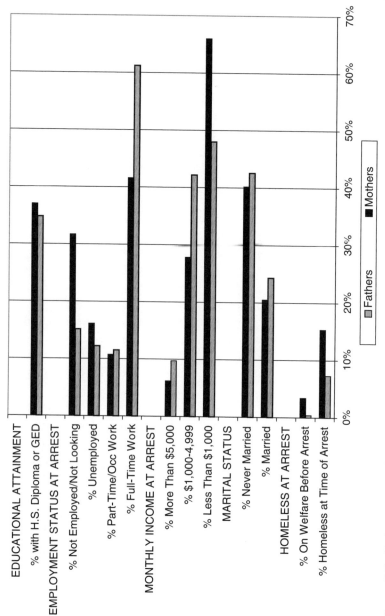

Figure 8.5 Socioeconomic Characteristics of Incarcerated Parents, 1997 (*Source*: authors' analysis of USDOJ 2001)

outside of marriage, early parenthood is common for their children as well. Children of young and unmarried parents are also at substantial risk of economic deprivation, educational deficits, unstable family living arrangements, serious behavioral problems, and, more generally, a problematic transition to adulthood (Aquilino 1991; Bumpass and McLanahan 1989; Furstenberg, Brooks-Gunn, and Chase-Landale 1989; Lerman and Ooms 1993; McLanahan and Bumpass 1988; McLanahan and Sandefur 1994; Michael and Tuma 1985; Resnick, Chambliss, and Blum 1993; Wu and Martinson 1993).

Though some children may benefit from the removal of an abusive, drug-dependent, or mentally ill parent to prison, there is some evidence that criminally involved parents may contribute positively to the rearing of their children. In a study of nonresident fathers, Irwin Garfinkel and colleagues note that "while many young fathers have trouble holding a job and may even spend time in jail, most have something to offer their children" (1998, p. 8). The authors argue further that "the overwhelming impression of these young men conveyed by the literature is one of immaturity and irresponsibility rather than pathology or dangerousness (1998, p. 8; also quoted in Hagan and Dinovitzer 1999). Additional studies demonstrate that nonresident fathers and mothers spend time with their children and attempt to contact them regularly (Stewert 1999), contribute positively toward their children's development and wellbeing (Amato and Rivera 1999; Furstenberg 1993), and contribute informally to their financial support (Edin and Lein 1997; Western and McLanahan 2000). It is likely that, at least for some children, the loss of a parent to prison contributes negatively to the child's development, financial stability, and sense of well-being. Moreover, because nonresident parents have the capacity to substantially improve the lives of their children through a number of supports, the loss of even a *nonresident* parent to incarceration may have a significant impact on their children.

Though about 12 percent of inmate mothers and 20 percent of inmate fathers never contact their children (Mumola 2000), most inmate parents attempt to stay in touch with their children on a regular basis. Figure 8.6 presents information on the level and type of contact between incarcerated parents and their children. Following the literature on nonresident parents more generally, incarcerated parents maintain a surprising level of contact with their children, especially in light of the difficulties introduced by the prison environment. Because prison space for women is scarce and facilities are often located in remote areas, incarcerated mothers can expect to spend their time behind bars far away from their children (Hagan and

226

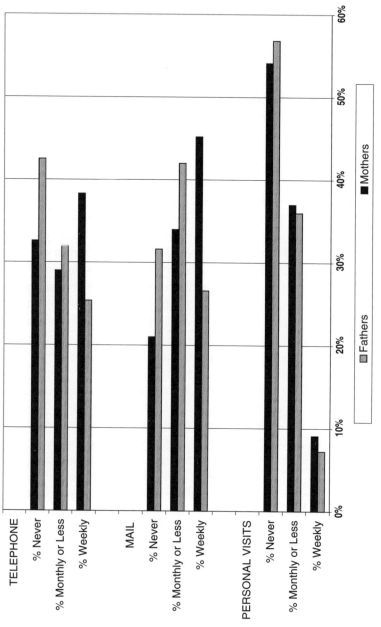

Figure 8.6 Contact between Incarcerated Parents and Their Children, 1997 (*Source*: adapted from Mumola 2000)

Dinovitzer 1999; Travis and Visher 2005). Moreover, security concerns often take precedence over the needs of inmates to maintain contact with their families, so meager funding and few personnel are available to monitor visits and telephone calls (Travis and Visher 2005). As a result, the most frequent form of contact for parents who communicate with their children regularly is through the mail. Still, more than 80 percent of state prison inmates and 90 percent of federal prison inmates contacted their children from prison (Mumola 2000). As Figure 8.6 illustrates, contact with children is quite high among incarcerated parents, offering some encouragement to the idea that familial reintegration may provide one cornerstone of a comprehensive reentry program.

Figure 8.7 presents information on the current living arrangements of children who have a parent in prison. The figure shows striking differences between mothers and fathers in reporting their child's current living arrangement.[1] Almost 90 percent of incarcerated fathers report their children as living with the biological mother, whereas less than 30 percent of mothers report their children as living with the biological father. Instead, over half of incarcerated mothers report that their children are living with a grandparent. Additionally, among mothers whose children are not living with a grandparent, living with father barely places as the second most common living arrangement: 28 percent of mothers report their children as living with their fathers, relative to 26 percent who report their children as living with other relatives. Based on these data, relative to children with incarcerated fathers, children whose mothers are in prison are more likely to be living with a grandparent and or to be placed in homes where they are unrelated to any of the inhabitants (such as a foster home or with family friends).

Reentry and the Life Course

We have so far tried to expand the standard analysis of the effects of employment and marriage on crime by considering evidence for the negative effects of incarceration on economic opportunity and family life. We can go a step further by trying to place the experience of incarceration in a life course perspective. The life course perspective identifies key transition markers of adult status such as moving out of the home of origin, completing an

---

[1] Because parents reported living arrangements for each of their children, the sum of all categories of child living arrangements is greater than 100%.

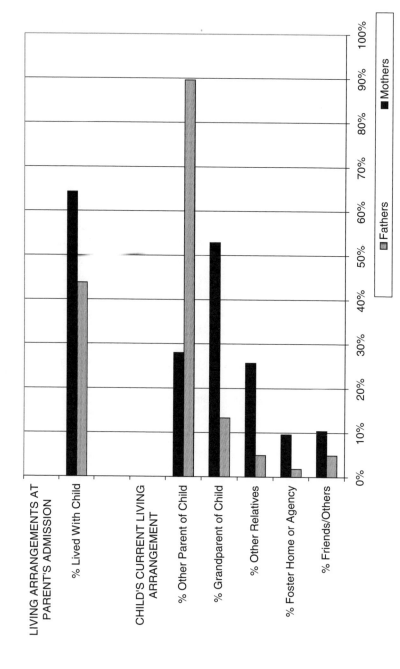

Figure 8.7 Current Living Arrangements of Children with Parents in State Prisons, 1997 (adapted from Mumola 2000)

education, finding stable work, getting married, and becoming a parent (Hogan 1981; Shanahan 2000). Today, the age at which particular life course events occur is increasingly compressed (Shanahan 2000). At the same time, young people have greater agency in structuring their lives, as evidenced by the increasing variability in the transition to adulthood (Buchmann 1989).

Becoming an adult is not only a matter of achieving the markers of adult status but also of obtaining them in reasonable sequence at a socially pre-scribed or normative age. Moreover, the timing of life course transitions is culturally specific and structurally determined. For example, becoming a parent for the first time at approximately age 25 is currently considered nor-mative behavior in the contemporary United States. However, becoming a parent at age 14 renders a teenage mother "off-time" in relation to her age cohort. Off-time events often have consequences long after they occur and hold the potential to delay or disrupt later transitions. Early pregnancy, for example, is likely to impact later educational and occupational attainment.

The life course perspective has several implications for thinking about the effects of employment and marriage on prisoner reentry. Most young people enter the criminal justice system lagging far behind their age cohort in employment status, socioeconomic attainment, marriage formation, establishment of an independent residence, and other markers of adult-hood. Incarceration is likely to increase delays and render them more visible for returning prisoners. Although many prisoners gain marginal increases in human capital while incarcerated, such as the attainment of a General Equivalency Diploma, the vast majority of inmates will reenter their com-munities with these deficits intact. A number of life course perspectives link delayed transitions and off-time events to involvement in crime, suggesting that inmates who leave prison off-time in the transition to adulthood may be those most likely to continue in crime.

The life course perspective also suggests that marriage and employment may be central to redirecting the life paths of ex-offenders. This view sug-gests that the disruption of imprisonment will be largest for older prisoners approaching midlife, when the costs of being off-time in the marriage and labor markets will be greatest. Thus the earnings penalty of conviction and incarceration increases with age (Bushway 1996; Western 2002). Because the costs of being off-time will be most transparent for ex-prisoners in their 30s and 40s who compare themselves to others of similar age with steady jobs and families, older men may be especially motivated get on-track in terms of the modal life trajectory. This motivation is suggested by research finding age-graded effects of labor market success on criminal desistance.

Among adolescents, intensive work is associated with increased crime or minor delinquency (Bachman and Schulenberg 1993; Staff and Uggen 2003). Among adults, however, legitimate work is linked to reductions in criminal behavior. In an analysis of an experimental program that provided a basic job opportunity to recently released prisoners, Uggen (2000) found that supported employment significantly enhanced the likelihood of desistance among offenders aged 27 and older but had little impact on younger offenders. Similarly, an early experiment that provided transitional financial assistance to released prisoners suggested stronger program effects among older releasees (Mallar and Thornton 1978). Although a simple job opportunity is unlikely to induce desistance among younger offenders, other studies suggest this group may be especially amenable to intensive training and educational programs (Schochet, Burghardt, and Glazerman 2000).

Because most inmates were involved in their children's lives prior to being incarcerated, imprisonment of a parent constitutes a major disruption in the early lives of many children. Such disruption affects their individual development, but also poses a long-term threat to public safety. For example, Aquilino (1991) found that children who live with a grandparent when no parent is present had lower educational attainment than children in other living situations. In light of the dominance of this type of living situation for children with incarcerated mothers, these findings suggest that children whose *mothers* are in prison may be at particular risk. More generally, children of incarcerated parents experience temporal instability in living arrangements that is linked to problems in behavioral adjustment during adolescence and young adulthood (Hagan and Wheaton 1993).

Incarceration can have substantial consequences on the family, but there are good reasons to believe that ex-prisoners can be good parents and supportive spouses if they are able to overcome the economic disadvantages that characterize their lives prior to incarceration. In our discussion of work and family, we have offered several potential avenues of reintegration for former inmates and offered a variety of interpretations for research findings. Former offenders who marry or find work are less likely to reoffend because spouses and employers reduce contact with criminal peers and act as informal social controls (Horney et al. 1995; Laub et al. 1998; Sampson and Laub 1990; Warr 1998). Roles as supportive spouses, active parents, and skilled employees can also foster formation of a noncriminal prosocial identity that is linked to desistance from crime.

In sum, the experience of incarceration may directly aggravate existing disadvantages for many inmates and their families. Unfortunately, the causal sequencing of work and family disadvantages, criminal involvement, and consequences of incarceration is difficult to disentangle. Yet the life course perspective suggests that merely the loss of time and opportunities will negatively impact the probability of desistance for ex-prisoners, particularly if prison time is not used to increase educational training or reduce the barriers to employment associated with substance abuse problems or mental illness. Overall, however, public safety is increased and the risk of incarceration to inmates and their children is reduced only to the extent that offenders can overcome earlier disadvantages and assume stable work and family roles. The current historical context suggests that such tasks may be more difficult in the contemporary era. We next discuss how the social environment to which ex-prisoners return may impact their ability to establish stable work and family connections once they leave prison.

The Social Context of Reentry

Research and policy discussion of the problem of prisoner reentry commonly focuses on the deficits of offenders that place them at risk of unemployment, marital instability, and subsequent offending. However, we seldom ask how the communities to which prisoners are returning might affect the likelihood of obtaining a steady job, reestablishing family ties, and staying out of prison. Table 8.1 provides information about these receiving communities by showing trends in criminal justice, labor markets, and marriage markets.

There is clear evidence that the criminal justice context has become more punitive and police and correctional authorities are now more deeply involved in the lives of those at greatest risk for incarceration – young black men with little education. At the end of the 1990s, incarceration rates for black men in their 20s who have failed to graduate from high school exceeded 40 percent, substantially higher than the incarceration rate for this same group in the early 1980s and orders of magnitude higher than the incarceration rate for the general population. In contrast to this trend of increasing incarceration, rates of drug use and criminal victimization have declined. In the early 1980s, about 8 percent of African Americans reported using cocaine in the past 12 months. By the late 1990s, this number had fallen to 1.9 percent. Today, returning prisoners are at much greater risk of reincarceration due to parole violations relative to 20 years ago (see also Blumstein and Beck, this volume). These trends in crime and social control efforts suggest that the risks of reincarceration are much higher in

231

Table 8.1. *The Changing Social Context of Reentry in the 1970s, 1980s, and 1990s*

	1974–1982	1983–1996	1997–2000
Context of crime and punishment			
Incarceration rate, black male H.S. dropouts, aged 22–30[1]	15.0%	25.8%	40.1%
Per Capita Justice System Expenditures[7]	$155	$267	$442
Number of Inmates Incarcerated for Drugs[2]	20,681	46,881	124,079
Drug offenders in state prison (percent)[2]	10.0%	8.6%	11.0%
Percentage of State Prison Admissions who are Parole Violators[8]	15%	24%	34%
Self-Reported Cocaine Use by the U.S. Population (Age 12+) in the last 12 months[3]	5.5%	4.1%	1.7%
Self-Reported Cocaine Use by African American Males in the U.S. Population (Age 12+) n the last 12 months[3]	8.1%	6.3%	1.9%
Socioeconomic context			
Jobless rates, black male H.S. dropouts, aged 22–30[4]	35.5%	45.9%	49.1%
Weekly earnings, black male H.S. dropouts, aged 20–40[5]	$345.35	$354.3	$350.62
African Americans below the Poverty Level[6]	31.3%	31.3%	22.0%
Family context			
Percentage Married among African American Adult Males[5]	54.6%	49.2%	46.7%

Note:

[1] 1974–82 column uses 1980–82 data, 1997–2000 column uses 1997–1999 data.
[2] 1974–82 column uses 1974 data, 1983–96 column uses 1988 data, 1997–2000 column uses 1997 data.
[3] 1974–82 column uses 1979 data, 1983–96 column uses 1988 data, 1997–2000 column uses 1999 data.
[4] 1974–82 column uses 1980 data, 1983–96 column uses 1986 data, 1997–2000 column uses 1999 data.
[5] 1974–82 column uses 1980 data, 1983–96 column uses 1990 data, 1997–2000 column uses 2000 data.
[6] 1974–82 column uses 1975 data, 1983–96 column uses 1985 data, 1997–2000 column uses 2000 data.
[7] 1974–82 column uses 1982 data, 1983–96 column uses 1988 data, 1997–2000 column uses 1999 data.
[8] 1974–82 column uses 1979 data, 1983–96 column uses 1987 data, 1997–2000 column uses 1998 data.

Sources: Adapted from Uggen and Thompson (2003). **Jobless rate:** Western and Pettit (2002); **Incarceration rate:** Western and Pettit (2002); **Drug incarceration:** *Sourcebook of Criminal Justice* (1976 and 2000) and *Correctional Populations in the U.S.* (1988) data; **Parole Violation:** Bureau of Justice Statistics. *Prisoners Sentenced to More Than One Year Admitted to State or Federal Prison and Conditional Release Violators Sentenced to More Than One Year.* Accessed online (www.oip.usdoj.gov/bjs/prisons.html). **Expenditures:** *Justice Expenditures and Employment Abstracts* (1992–2002). **Self-Reported Drug Use:** The U.S. population data were taken from the National Household Survey on Drug Abuse, conducted by the National Institute on Drug Abuse. The online data analysis was conducted using the 1979, 1988, and 1999 data (www.icpsr.umich.edu/SAMHDA/nhsdasda.html); **Joblessness:** Western and Pettit (2002); **Earnings:** authors' calculations, Current Population surveys; **Poverty:** U.S. Census Bureau Current Population Reports.

the current period than in the early 1980s simply because the justice system is so much larger and more reliant on imprisonment than in the past.

The low-skill urban labor markets that supply large numbers of state and federal prisoners have also steadily deteriorated. Due largely to structural changes in the U.S. economy, the urban manufacturing jobs that provided black noncollege men with steady jobs have largely moved to the suburbs of southern and sunbelt states or abroad. These structural shifts in employment are reflected in increasing jobless rates for young black dropouts. Although the jobless rate for young black male dropouts hovered around 35 percent in the early 1980s, joblessness had climbed to nearly 50 percent by the late 1990s when unemployment in the labor market as a whole fell to historically low levels. The real weekly earnings of young black dropouts also remained stagnant during this time. In short, these labor market indicators suggest a chronic shortage of economic opportunity in communities with the highest incarceration rates and the largest numbers of returning prisoners.

Marriage markets have also weakened through the 1980s and 1990s. Marriage rates have declined significantly across the population, although the decline in marriage has been particularly pronounced among African Americans. Marriage rates among black men fell from nearly 55 percent to around 47 percent in the 2 decades following 1980. In families with low levels of education, fertility and marriage decisions became detached. Low-education women continued to have children at relatively young ages, whether married or not. Thus the fall in marriage rates is also connected to rapid growth in the nonmarital birth rate among low-education black women over the past 20 years. Ellwood and Jencks (2002) report that about 35 percent of low-education women, aged 25–34, were single parents in 1970, in contrast to over 50 percent by 2000. Table 8.1, which shows little change in male fertility among low-education African Americans but a clear decline in marriage rates, also suggests the growth in the number of low-education unmarried parents. It is not clear what role mass incarceration in the contemporary era may have played in the decline of marriage rates among African Americans. Imprisonment may play a direct role on marriage markets by removing potential marriage partners from the community. Alternatively, incarceration may reduce marriage even among ex-prisoners because stigma and work barriers resulting from imprisonment make ex-prisoners less attractive marriage partners. It is likely that both processes are operating to reduce marriage, particularly among African Americans who are at high risk of imprisonment.

In sum, although we would ideally like returning prisoners to find jobs, get married, and avoid reincarceration, they face substantial hurdles that are much higher now than 20 or 30 years ago. Criminal justice supervision has intensified. There appear to be fewer second chances today than in the past. Jobless rates are extremely high and relatively insensitive to general improvements in labor market conditions. Family life is now characterized by low marriage rates and mounting numbers of female-headed households. In the poor urban communities that supply most of the penal population, passing the usual markers of adulthood seems hard enough, even without the added burdens of a prison record.

Policy Implications

This discussion suggests that measures that promote steady employment and stable marriages among ex-prisoners can ultimately improve public safety by contributing to criminal desistance. Clearly, education and training programs can at least raise the levels of schooling, functional literacy, and cognitive skill among prisoners. By increasing human capital, such programs may make offenders more competitive in the labor market.[2] Our review of the literature, however, suggests that work programs must be targeted toward specific groups of offenders. Older offenders might benefit from simple job placement services or the provision of a basic work opportunity that pays a living wage. Conversely, younger offenders may be more likely to respond to intensive educational programs. With these programs in place, the evidence suggests that both groups of offenders will be more likely to desist from crime.

Work can encourage desistance through a number of mechanisms. First, work subjects former prisoners to greater informal social control by employers and co-workers. Second, work may reduce the associations with criminal peers by expanding social networks to include more law-abiding citizens. Third, work offers a powerful opportunity to adopt a prosocial role and leave criminal identities behind. Finally, and most simply, work may decrease crime by providing an alternate source of financial support. In a study of

---

[2] One intriguing (but potentially dangerous) idea is to involve some offenders in public safety efforts themselves – such work would facilitate the development of prosocial orientations and identity, and could provide a degree of guardianship in their communities. There are, of course, risks to such strategies (see, e.g., Marris and Rein 1973 on the Mobilization for Youth program), including the resistance of professionals in the social services and criminal justice system (Maruna 2001, 118).

234

within-person change in legal and illegal earnings, Uggen and Thompson (2003) report that that employment and monthly legal earnings reduce the amount that offenders earn illegally. For all types of offenders, programs that are targeted toward their particular needs are likely to enhance attainment in the labor market and result in increased public safety.

Men with jobs will be more attractive marriage partners and perhaps better parents, even more so if they are sober and nonviolent. Treatment for addiction and behavioral problems might also improve marriage prospects. Figure 8.8 presents mental health and substance-abuse statistics for parents in state prisons in 1997. A majority of parents (both mothers and fathers) were using drugs in the month prior to their most recent arrest. Additionally, more than 30 percent of fathers and 40 percent of mothers were using drugs at the time of their most recent offense. A large number of parents also report a history of alcohol dependence or were drunk at the time of their most recent offense. Though these numbers are actually lower than those for the general inmate population, they indicate that a great number of parents reported alcohol and other substance abuse problems. Incarcerated parents also report much lower rates of mental health problems than the general inmate population, but over 20 percent of incarcerated mothers nonetheless report a diagnosed mental illness. For parents with mental health and substance-abuse issues, programs directed only at improving job prospects or increasing educational attainment are unlikely to succeed. Similarly, programs aimed at teaching offenders to become better parents or supportive spouses will fail if they do not address the systemic economic disadvantages that impact this population. Some combination of job training, work opportunity, family support, and substance-abuse counseling may therefore be needed for former prisoners facing multiple barriers to successful postrelease adjustment.

Although these suggestions to renew commitments to prison education and postrelease services are well motivated by social science research, they are also wholly unrealistic in a policy climate that has cut prison programming and expanded the prison population fourfold in 30 years. There is little political will to improve public safety by reducing the propensity to commit crime by at-risk men. Given this constraint, are cheap policy interventions available? Our discussion highlights two possibilities. First, eliminating punitive civil disabilities will improve the access of ex-felons to employment opportunities, welfare benefits, and political rights. Removing some of the formal barriers to employment and job training would further the goal of offender reintegration. Unfortunately, public policy has

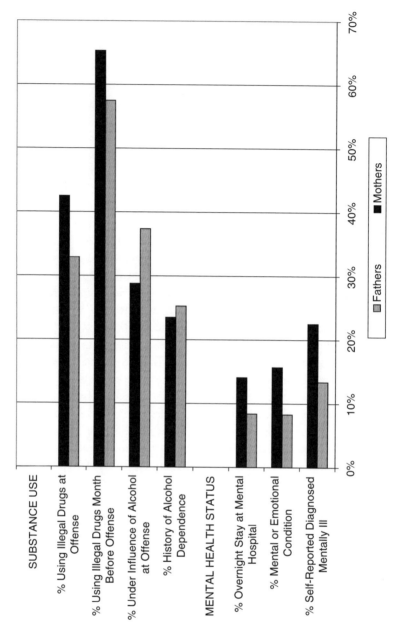

Figure 8.8 Mental Health and Substance Abuse Problems of Incarcerated Parents (adapted from Mumola 2000)

recently moved in the direction of erecting even greater formal restrictions on employment for former inmates. Barriers to educational funding, receipt of public assistance, and access to certain jobs further restrict the labor market opportunities for an already disadvantaged population. Although barring certain sex offenders from work in child-care facilities may make good sense, for example, it remains to be seen whether shutting minor drug offenders out of educational training is in any way related to increased public safety or reduced recidivism. Similarly, driving former inmates out of public housing may further disrupt their ability to support themselves on income from legitimate employment and encourage activity in the illegal economy.

Second, because imprisonment negatively affects marital stability and employment after release, there will be some advantage in diverting at least some offenders from prison. The incarceration of drug offenders, for example, has been found to have little crime-reducing effect (DiIulio and Piehl 1991; Piehl, Useem, and DiIulio 1999). Experiences of incarceration may turn such offenders to crime by reducing their opportunities for employment and marriage. For these and perhaps other offenders, diversion may contribute more to public safety than incarceration.

Finally, many of the challenges faced by reentering prisoners are well beyond the control of criminal justice agencies. The deterioration of low-skill urban labor markets, racial discrimination, punitive sentiment among voters and lawmakers, and anxiety among employers about hiring ex-offenders all create substantial obstacles to successful prisoner reintegration. Correctional administrators, police, and parole officers have little influence in these areas. Their responsibility for recidivism is accordingly limited. These significant obstacles also suggest that able and well-motivated ex-offenders will have difficulty holding down a job, building a stable family life, and staying out of crime with these forces arrayed against them.

There are at least two policy implications derived from our knowledge about these barriers to reentry. First, our measures of policy success should be calibrated by the standards of the poor communities that supply the prisoners. If an employment program cannot improve job retention, this may be due in part to low rates of job retention in secondary labor markets rather than program failure. If a substance abuse program cannot maintain the sobriety of its clients, this may be partly due to high rates of drug use among peers and the plentiful supply of cheap drugs in the neighborhood. Second, the massive problem of prisoner reentry and recidivism is the product of a prison boom that may require many different social service agencies to solve. Although correctional authorities have accumulated expertise in maintaining the care, custody, and control of criminal offenders, there is little they can do about employer discrimination, weak demand for unskilled workers, or high nonmarital birth rates. A large pool of ex-prisoners exacerbates these social problems, but solutions must ultimately lie outside of the criminal justice system. Building sound communities with strong families and steady jobs will improve public safety, but such a policy goal must ultimately enlist those in the fields of education, workforce development, and family services as well as criminal justice. Voters and lawmakers are deeply concerned about crime, yet quadrupling the incarceration rate has not made citizens feel significantly safer. A systemic approach to public safety may help renew public support for social service agencies and provide a more coherent model of crime control than the current approach that relies overwhelmingly on incarceration. Such an approach acknowledges the key roles of marriage and employment in criminal desistance and the costs to public safety of maintaining a large and burgeoning correctional population.

References

Allan, Emilie Anderson, and Darrell J. Steffensmeier. 1989. "Youth, Underemployment, and Property Crime: Differential Effects of Job Availability and Job Quality on Juvenile and Young Adult Arrest Rates." *American Sociological Review* 54 (1): 107–123.

Anderson, Elijah A. 1999. *Code of the Street*. New York: Norton.

Anderson, Elijah A. 1992. *Streetwise: Race, Class, and Change in an Urban Community*. Chicago: University of Chicago Press.

Amato, Paul R., and Fernando Rivera. 1999. "Paternal Involvement and Children's Behavioral Problems." *Journal of Marriage and the Family* 61: 375–384.

Aquilino, William. 1991. "Family Structure and Home-Leaving: A Further Specification of the Relationship." *Journal of Marriage and the Family* 53: 999–1010.

Bachman, Jerald G., and John Schulenberg. 1993. "How Part-Time Work Intensity Relates to Drug Use, Problem Behavior, Time Use, and Satisfaction Among High School Seniors: Are These Consequences or Merely Correlates?" *Developmental Psychology* 29: 220–235.

Blau, Judith R., and Peter M. Blau. 1982. "The Cost of Inequality: Metropolitan Structure and Violent Crime." *American Sociological Review* 47 (1): 114–129.

Blumstein, Alfred, and Allen J. Beck. 2005. "Reentry as a Transient State between Liberty and Recommitment," Jeremy Travis and Christy Visher, eds., *Prisoner Reentry and Crime in America*. Cambridge: Cambridge University Press.

Britt, Chester L. 1997. "Reconsidering the Unemployment and Crime Relationship: Variation by Age Group and Historical Period." *Journal of Quantitative Criminology* 14(4): 405–428.

Buchmann, Marlis. 1989. *The Script of Life in Modern Society: Entry into Adulthood in a Changing World*. Chicago: University of Chicago Press.

Bumpass, Larry, and Sara McLanahan. 1989. "Unmarried Motherhood: Recent Trends, Composition, and Black-White Differences." *Demography* 26: 279–286.

Bushway, Shawn D. 1998. "The Impact of an Arrest on the Job Stability of Young White American Men." *Journal of Research in Crime and Delinquency* 35(4): 454–479.

Caspi, Avshalom, and Terrie E. Moffitt. 1995. "The Continuity of Maladaptive Behavior: From Description to Understanding in the Study of Antisocial Behavior," Dante Cicchetti and Donald J. Cohen, eds., *Developmental Psychology, Volume 2: Risk, Disorder, and Adaptation*, pp. 472–511. New York: Wiley.

Coleman, James. 1990. *Foundations of Social Theory*. Cambridge, MA: Harvard University Press.

Crutchfield, Robert D., and Susan R. Pitchford. 1997. "Work and Crime: The Effects of Labor Stratification." *Social Forces* 76: 93–118.

DiIulio, John, Jr., and Anne Morrison Piehl. 1991. "Does Prison Pay? The Stormy National Debate Over the Cost-Effectiveness of Imprisonment." *Brookings Review* Fall: 28–35.

Edin, Kathryn. 2000. "How Low-Income Single Mothers Talk About Marriage." *Social Problems* 47(1): 112–133.

Edin, Kathryn, and Laura Lein. 1997. *Making Ends Meet*. New York: Russell Sage Foundation.

Ellwood, David T., and Christopher Jencks. 2002. "The Spread of Single-Parent Families in the United States Since 1960." Kennedy School of Government Working Paper No. RWP04–008. Harvard University.

Furstenberg, Frank. 1993. *Young Fathers in the Inner City: The Sources of Parental Involvement*. Center for the Advanced Study in the Behavioral Sciences Palo Alto, California.

Furstenberg, Frank, Jeanne Brooks-Gunn, and P. Chase-Landale. 1989. "Teenaged Pregnancy and Childbearing." *American Psychologist* 44: 313–320.

Freeman, Richard B. 1992. "Why Do So Many Young Men Commit Crimes and What Might We Do About It?" *Journal of Economic Perspectives* 10: 22–45.

Garfinkel, Irwin, Sara McLanahan, and Thomas L. Hanson. 1998. "A Patchwork Quilt of Nonresident Fathers." Working Paper no. 98–25. Princeton, NJ: Princeton University.

Giordano, Peggy C., Stephen A. Cernkovich, and J. L. Rudolph. 2002. "Gender, Crime, and Desistance: Toward a Theory of Cognitive Transformation." *American Journal of Sociology* 107(4): 990–1064.

Granovettor, Mark S. 1973. "The Strength of Weak Ties." *American Journal of Sociology* 78: 1360–1380.

Grogger, Jeffrey T. 1995. "The Effect of Arrests on the Employment and Earnings of Young Men." *Quarterly Journal of Economics* 110(1): 51–72.

Hagan, John. 1993. "The Social Embeddedness of Crime and Unemployment." *Criminology* 31: 465–492.

Hagan, John, and Ronit Dinovitzer. 1999. "Children of the Prison Generation: Collateral Consequences of Imprisonment for Children and Communities." *Crime and Justice* 26: 121–162.

Hagan, John, and Alberto Palloni. 1990. "The Social Reproduction of a Criminal Class in Working Class London, Circa 1950–1980." *American Journal of Sociology* 96(2): 265–299.

Hagan, John, and Blair Wheaton. 1993. "The Search for Adolescent Role Exits and the Transition to Adulthood." *Social Forces* 71(4): 955–980.

Harer, Miles D., and Darrell Steffensmeier. 1992. "The Differing Effects of Economic Inequality on Black and White Rates of Violence." *Social Forces* 70(4): 1035–1054.

Hogan, Dennis P. 1981. *Transitions in the Lives of American Men*. New York: Academic Press.

Hogan, Dennis P., and Nan Marie Astone. 1986. "The Transition to Adulthood." *Annual Review of Sociology* 12: 109–130.

Holzer, Harry J. 1996. *What Employers Want: Job Prospects for Less-Educated Workers*. New York: Russell Sage Foundation.

Horney, Julie, Wayne D. Osgood, and Inke Haen Marshall. 1995. "Criminal Careers in the Short-Term: Intra-Individual Variation in Crime and Its Relation to Local Life Circumstances." *American Sociological Review* 60(5): 655–73.

Irwin, James, and John Austin. 1997. *It's about Time: America's Imprisonment Binge*. Belmont, CA: Wadsworth.

Kandel, Denise B., Emily Rosenbaum, and Kevin Chen. 1994. "Impact of Maternal Drug Use and Life Experiences on Preadolescent Children Born to Teenage Mothers." *Journal of Marriage and the Family* 56: 325–340.

Kasarda, John. 1989. "Urban Industrial Transition and the Urban Underclass." *Annals of the American Academy of Political and Social Sciences* 501: 26–47.

Kruttschnitt, Candace, Christopher Uggen, and Kelly Shelton. 2000. "Predictors of Desistance among Sex Offenders: The Interaction of Formal and Informal Social Controls." *Justice Quarterly* 17: 61–87.

Laub, John H., Daniel S. Nagin, and Robert J. Sampson. 1998. "Trajectories of Change in Criminal Offending: Good Marriages and the Desistance Process." *American Sociological Review* 63: 225–238.

Laub, John H., and Robert J. Sampson. 2003. *Shared Beginnings, Divergent Lives: Delinquent Boys to Age 70*. Cambridge, MA: Harvard University Press.

Lerman, R., and T. Ooms. 1993. *Young Unwed Fathers: Changing Roles and Emerging Policies*. Philadelphia, PA: Temple University Press.

Mallar, Charles, and Craig V. D. Thornton. 1978. "Transitional Aid for Released Prisoners: Evidence from the LIFE Experiment." *Journal of Human Resources* 13: 208–236.

Marris, Peter, and Martin Rein. 1973. *Dilemmas of Social Reform: Poverty and Community Action in the United States*. Chicago: Aldine.

Maruna, Shadd. 2001. *Making Good: How Ex-Convicts Reform and Rebuild Their Lives.* Washington, DC: American Psychological Association Books.

Massey, Douglas S., and Nancy Denton. 1993. *American Apartheid.* Cambridge, MA: Harvard University Press.

Matsueda, Ross, and Karen Heimer. 1997. "A Symbolic Interactionist Theory of Role-Transitions, Role-Commitments, and Delinquency," Terence B. Thornberry, ed., *Developmental Theories of Crime and Delinquency.* New Brunswick, NJ: Transaction Press.

Mauer, Marc, and Meda Chesney-Lind. 2002. *Invisible Punishment: The Collateral Consequences of Mass Imprisonment.* New York: The New Press.

McLanahan, Sara, and Larry Bumpass. 1988. "Intergenerational Consequences of Family Disruption." *American Journal of Sociology* 94: 130–152.

McLanahan, Sara, and Gary Sandefur. 1994. *Growing Up with a Single Parent: What Hurts, What Helps.* Cambridge, MA: Harvard University Press.

Michael, R., and Nancy Tuma. 1985. "Entry Into Marriage and Parenthood by Young Men and Women: The Influence of Family Background." *Demography* 22: 515–544.

Morenoff, Jeffrey, and Robert J. Sampson. 1997. "Violent Crime and the Spatial Dynamics of Neighborhood Transition: Chicago, 1970–1990." *Social-Forces* 76(1): 31–64.

Mumola, Christopher J. 2000. *Incarcerated Parents and Their Children.* Bureau of Justice Statistics Special Report. Washington, DC: Government Printing Office.

Office of the Pardon Attorney. 1996. *Civil Disabilities of Convicted Felons: A State-by-State Survey.* Washington, DC: U.S. Department of Justice.

Pager, Devah. "The Mark of a Criminal Record." 2003. *American Journal of Sociology* 108: 937–975.

Pavalko, Eliza K., and Glen H. Elder. 1990. "World War II and Divorce: A Life Course Perspective." *American Journal of Sociology* 95: 1213–1234.

Pettit, Becky, and Bruce Western. 2003. "Inequality in Lifetime Risks of Imprisonment." Unpublished manuscript.

Piehl, Anne Morrison, Bert Useem, and John J. DiIulio Jr. 1999. *Right Sizing Justice: A Cost Benefit Analysis of Imprisonment in Three States.* New York: Manhattan Institute.

Resnick, Michael D., Stephanie A. Chambliss, and Robert W. Blum. 1993. "Health and Risk Behaviors of Urban Adolescent Males Involved in Pregnancy." *Families in Society* 74: 366–374.

Rose, Dina R., and Todd R. Clear. 1998. "Incarceration, Social Capital, and Crime: Implications for Social Disorganization Theory." *Criminology* 36: 441–479.

Sabol, William J., and James P. Lynch. 1998. *Assessing the Longer-Run Consequences of Incarceration: Effects on Families and Unemployment.* Paper presented at the 20th Annual Research Conference of the Association for Public Policy Analysis and Management, New York.

Sampson, Robert J. 1987. "Urban Black Violence: The Effect of Male Joblessness and Family Disruption." *American Journal of Sociology* 93(2): 348–382.

Sampson, Robert J., and John H. Laub. 1993. *Crime in the Making: Pathways and Turning Points through Life.* Cambridge, MA: Harvard University Press.

Sampson, Robert J., and John H. Laub. 1990. "Crime and Deviance over the Life Course: The Salience of Adult Social Bonds." *American Sociological Review* 55(5): 609–627.

Schochet, P., J. Burghardt, and S. Glazerman. 2000. *National Job Corps Study: The Short-Term Impacts of Job Corps on Participants' Employment and Later Outcomes.* Princeton. NJ: Mathematica Policy Research, Inc.

Shanahan, Michael. 2000. "Pathways to Adulthood in Changing Societies: Variability and Mechanisms in Life Course Perspective." *Annual Review of Sociology* 26: 667–692.

Sherman, Larry, and Douglas Smith. 1992. "Crime, Punishment, and Stake in Conformity: Legal and Informal Social Control of Domestic Violence." *American Sociological Review* 57: 680–690.

Shover, Neal. 1996. *Great Pretenders: Pursuits and Careers of Persistent Thieves.* Boulder, CO: Westview Press.

Staff, Jeremy, and Christopher Uggen. 2003. "The Fruits of Good Work: Job Quality and Adolescent Deviance." *Journal of Research in Crime and Delinquency* 40: 263–290.

Stewert, Susan D. 1999. "Nonresident Mothers' and Fathers' Social Contact with Children." *Journal of Marriage and the Family* 61: 894–907.

Toby, Jackson. 1957. "Social Disorganization and Stake in Conformity: Complementary Factors in the Predatory Behavior of Hoodlums." *Journal of Criminal Law, Criminology, and Police Science* 48: 12–17.

Travis, Jeremy, and Christy Visher. 2005. "Prisoner Reentry and Pathways to Adulthood: Policy Perspectives," Wayne D. Osgood, Mike Foster, and Connie Flanagan, eds., *On Your Own without a Net: The Transition to Adulthood for Vulnerable Populations.* Chicago: University of Chicago Press.

Uggen, Christopher. 1999. "Ex-Offenders and the Conformist Alternative: A Job Quality Model of Work and Crime." *Social Problems* 46: 127–151.

Uggen, Christopher. 2000. "Work as a Turning Point in the Life Course of Criminals: A Duration Model of Age, Employment, and Recidivism." *American Sociological Review* 65(4): 529–546.

Uggen, Christopher, Jeff Manza, and Angela Behrens. 2003. "Less Than the Average Citizen: Stigma, Role Transition, and the Civic Reintegration of Convicted Felons," Shadd Maruna and Russ Immarigeon, eds., *After Crime and Punishment: Ex-Offender Reintegration and Desistance from Crime.* Albany: State University of New York Press.

Uggen, Christopher, and Melissa Thompson. 2003. "The Socioeconomic Determinants of Ill-Gotten Gains: Within-Person Changes in Drug Use and Illegal Earnings." *American Journal of Sociology* 109: 146–185.

Uggen, Christopher, and Sara Wakefield. 2003. "Young Adults Returning to the Community From the Criminal Justice System: The Challenge of Becoming an Adult," D. Wayne Osgood, Mike Foster, and Connie Flanagan, eds., *On Your Own without a Net: The Transition to Adulthood for Vulnerable Populations.* Chicago: University of Chicago Press.

U.S. Bureau of the Census. 1998. *Statistical Abstract of the United States.* Washington, DC: U.S. Government Printing Office.

U.S. Department of Justice. 2002. *Prisoners in 2001*. Washington, DC: Bureau of Justice Statistics, U.S. Government Printing Office.

U.S. Department of Justice. 2001. *Survey of Inmates in State and Federal Correctional Facilities, 1997*. [Computer file]. Compiled by U.S. Dept. of Commerce, Bureau of the Census. ICPSR ed. Ann Arbor, MI: Inter-university Consortium for Political and Social Research [producer and distributor].

Waller, Maureen R. 1996. *Redefining Fatherhood: Paternal Involvement, Masculinity, and Responsibility in the "Other America."* Ph.D. dissertation. Princeton, NJ: Princeton University.

Warr, Mark. 1998. "Life-Course Transitions and Desistance from Crime." *Criminology* 36(2): 183–216.

Western, Bruce. 2002. "The Impact of Incarceration on Wage Mobility and Inequality." *American Sociological Review* 67(4): 526–546.

Western, Bruce, and Katherine Beckett. 1999. "How Unregulated is the U.S. Labor Market? The Penal System as a Labor Market Institution." *American Journal of Sociology* 104(4) 1030–1060.

Western, Bruce, Meredith Kleykamp, and Jake Rosenfeld. 2003. "Crime, Punishment, and American Inequality." Unpublished manuscript.

Western, Bruce, Jeffrey R. Kling, and David F. Weiman. 2001. "The Labor Market Consequences of Incarceration." *Crime and Delinquency* 47: 410–427.

Western, Bruce Leonard M. Lopoo, and Sara McLanahan. 2002. "Incarceration and Bonds among Parents in Fragile Families," Mary Patillo, David Weiman, and Bruce Western, eds., *The Impact of Incarceration on Families and Communities*. New York: Russell Sage Foundation.

Western, Bruce, and Sara McLanahan. 2000. "Fathers Behind Bars: The Impact of Incarceration on Family Formation," Mike Benson and Greer Litton Fox, eds., *Families, Crime, and Criminal Justice: Charting the Linkages*, pp. 307–322. Stamford, CT: JAI Press, Inc.

Western, Bruce, and Becky Pettit. 2000. "Incarceration and Racial Inequality in Men's Employment." *Industrial and Labor Relations Review* 54: 3–16.

Western, Bruce, and Becky Pettit. 2002. *Inequality in Lifetime Risks of Imprisonment*. Paper presented at the 2001 Annual Meetings of the American Sociological Association, Anaheim, CA.

Wilson, William Julius. 1996. *When Work Disappears: The World of the New Urban Poor*. Chicago: The University of Chicago Press.

Wu, Lawrence, and Brian C. Martinson. 1993. "Family Structure and the Risk of Premarital Birth." *American Sociological Review* 58: 210–232.

9

Considering the Policy Implications

Jeremy Travis and Christy Visher

Introduction

This book was initiated during a time when the American public, policy-makers at all levels of government, and researchers in a number of disciplines were focused on the issue of prisoner reentry. This heightened interest in the causes and consequences of the annual flow of individuals leaving the nation's prisons was certainly overdue. The cycle of arrest, removal, incarceration, and return of large numbers of people, mostly men, who are disproportionately drawn from minority urban communities, constitutes one of the most profound social developments in modern America. Anyone interested in the well-being of these communities surely benefits from an understanding of the impact of America's expanded reliance on imprisonment as a response to crime.

Yet, although understandable, the new interest in prisoner reentry is somewhat perplexing. What, after all, is new? The fourfold increase in the rate of incarceration in America since the early 1970s has been the topic of considerable public and academic discussion. The fact that, with few exceptions, most prisoners are released to return home is well known. The phenomenon of prisoner reentry is not a sudden development – on the contrary, the size of the annual reentry cohort has been growing steadily since the early 1970s. But, for some reason, the national discussion of crime and punishment over the past three decades has not paid sufficient attention to the formidable consequences of the unprecedented growth in incarceration.

The issue of public safety has played a role in both the noteworthy lack of interest in prisoner reentry over the past 30 years and the sudden, unexpected, and swift appearance of interest in this topic at the turn of the century. The buildup of America's prison population has been justified, in

244

large part, on the argument that higher rates of incarceration are a necessary response to crime (Bennett, DiIulio, and Walters 1996). This was especially true during the second half of the 1980s, when the country experienced sharp increases in crimes of violence, particularly those involving guns and young people (Blumstein and Wallman 2000). A variety of punitive sentencing reforms were adopted – including mandatory minimums, truth-in-sentencing, three-strikes laws, parole abolition, and sentencing guidelines – because, according to their advocates, they would enhance public safety. In this environment, when political leaders were averse to being labeled "soft on crime," there was little to be gained by advocating for policies that would meet the needs of individuals leaving prison or consideration of more complex solutions to public safety problems.

With the stunning decline in rates of violent crime that began in the early 1990s, the political and policy environment has shifted noticeably. Now, violent crime in America, as recorded by the National Crime Victimization Survey, is at the lowest level since the early 1970s, when the first victimization survey was conducted. America is also experiencing the lowest property crime rate in a generation. This dramatic turn of events has taken "crime" off the top of the list of public concerns, thereby making it somewhat easier for the nation to focus on the issue of prisoner reentry.

Thus, in an interesting way, the heightened concerns about rising crime rates in America impeded a sustained inquiry into the consequences of the new incarceration policies that resulted from those concerns. Now, by contrast, the nation's low crime rates have provided an opening in the public discourse for a focus on the results of this dramatic growth in America's prison population.

As the country's interest in prisoner reentry has grown, the public safety issue has occasionally influenced the national conversation. In some cities around the country, rates of violent crime have started to increase after years of steep decline. Police chiefs in those jurisdictions have occasionally pointed to the large number of returning prisoners as the reason for the uptick in violence. Some law enforcement agencies have instituted crackdowns on parolees as part of their crime control strategies. A few journalistic accounts of prisoner reentry have painted a picture of large numbers of hardened, bitter ex-cons put away during the violent 1980s suddenly being released from prison, with the implication that they will trigger a new crime wave. But these voices linking public safety concerns to the phenomenon of prisoner reentry have not dominated the public discourse. In fact, they may have increased the interest in prisoner reentry.

The contributors to this book hope that the analysis found in these chapters will add to the state of knowledge about the nexus between prisoner reentry and crime in America at this important time when public policies are still in development and public understanding is increasing. The chapters in this book have shed light on the extent of the public safety risk posed by returning prisoners, the effectiveness of programs and policies on both sides of the prison walls in reducing the safety risk, and the intersection among prisoners, their families, and communities in terms of recidivism and safety. Others have addressed the related issue of the impact of incarceration on declining crime rates in America (Rosenfeld 2000; Spellman 2000). Yet we wanted to examine an issue that should be at the heart of the national interest in prisoner reentry, namely the connection between returning prisoners, the safety risks they pose, and the private and public institutions available to reduce those risks.

Defining the Scope of the Public Safety Risk

A threshold question confronting any inquiry into the nexus between prisoner reentry and public safety is the scope of the safety risk itself. Measures of recidivism tell part of the story. The Bureau of Justice Statistics completed two recidivism studies, at different points in time during the prison buildup, with remarkably similar results. The BJS examination of prisoners released from 11 states in 1983 found that 62.5 percent of them were rearrested for either a felony or serious misdemeanor within 3 years (Beck and Shipley 1989). A similar study of a 1994 cohort of prisoners released from 15 states found that 67.5 percent were rearrested within 3 years (Langan and Levin 2002). Rates of reconviction for prisoners released in the two studies were also quite similar (46.8 percent vs. 46.9 percent), as were rates of return to prison or jail for new convictions or other parole violations (41.4 percent for the 1983 study vs. 51.8 percent for the 1994 study).[1]

But a comparison of recidivism rates only tells part of the story of the shifting relationship between prisoner reentry and public safety. The most important change, of course, has been the increase in the size of the reentry cohort. In 1980, the state and federal prisons held 319,598 prisoners

---

[1] The 51.8 percent return to prison rate is heavily affected by the inclusion of California; when California is excluded the return-to-prison rate falls to 40.1 percent (Langan and Levin 2002: 13).

and released 144,000. Twenty-two years later, in 2002, nearly 1.4 million individuals were held in a greatly expanded network of state and federal prisons. That year, approximately 630,000 individuals were released (Harrison and Karberg 2003). So, at a minimum, with the shift in incarceration policies, the effects of recidivism are amplified by a much larger number of released prisoners.

But the composition of the reentry population has also changed significantly over this time period. As Blumstein and Beck (1999) point out, the incarceration rate for drug offenses (i.e., prisoners per 100,000 persons) has grown dramatically – by almost 900 percent between 1980 and 1996 – far outstripping the growth for murder (164 percent), sexual assault (300 percent), robbery (54 percent), assault (257 percent), and burglary (81 percent). Overall, nonviolent offenders accounted for three fourths of the growth in prison admissions during this period. As a result, today's reentry cohort contains a much greater percentage of individuals held on drug convictions than at any earlier time.

Blumstein and Beck (this volume) document a second important shift in the composition of the reentry cohort, namely the longer prison sentences served by those now returning from prison. As a result of sentencing reforms such as truth-in-sentencing, combined with increased use of parole revocations, prisoners are serving substantially longer periods of time behind bars. According to BJS, during the 1990s, when the prison population nearly doubled, the average length of time served by the release cohort increased by 27 percent, from an average of 22 months for those released in 1990 to 28 months for those released in 1998 (Beck 2000). Over roughly the same period of time, the proportion of soon-to-be-released prisoners who had served 5 years or more almost doubled, rising from 12 percent in 1991 to 21 percent in 1997 (Lynch and Sabol 2001).

These changes in the profile of the reentry cohort are likely to have important public safety consequences, although the exact dimensions are not fully understood. For example, although it is clear that current drug enforcement policies have significantly increased the rate of incarceration for drug offenses, particularly drug selling (Maxwell 1999; Tonry 1999), it appears that the incarceration of drug offenders has little effect on reducing crime (DiIulio and Piehl 1995; Piehl, Useem, and DiIulio 1999). But little is known about the effects of these drug enforcement policies on drug markets themselves (Reuter 1997), nor has research determined the impact of releasing large numbers of drug offenders back into the community.

Perhaps, consistent with a deterrence theory, released drug offenders are less likely to reconnect with drug activities; however, with little money in their pockets and stronger connections to drug dealers as a result of their time in prison, perhaps they are more likely to engage in those activities. Furthermore, the fact that many leave prison under parole supervision may make them an easy target for law enforcement, meaning that their rate of arrest is not an accurate representation of their underlying criminal behavior.

By contrast, the research base is more robust on the public safety effects of longer prison sentences. Some scholars believe that recidivism rates increase with longer prison terms (Hagan and Dinovitzer 1999). They suggest that the attenuation of ties to family, work, and social networks – combined with the development of new networks of criminal associates while in prison – result in a weakening of social capital and a greater likelihood that the prisoner will become "embedded" in criminal behaviors. So, ironically, the criminal justice policies that have increased the rates of incarceration, particularly the length of prison sentences, may have had the unanticipated and unintended effect of increasing the public safety risks posed by those sent to and released from prison. However, Rosenfeld et al. (this volume) find no difference in recidivism connected to time served in prison, controlling for other influences. More research is clearly required to understand better the public safety implications of longer prison sentences.

The past two decades have borne witness to another critical change in the profile of the reentry population, namely the sharp increase in the number of individuals sent back to prison on parole revocations. In 1980, about 17 percent of all admissions to America's prisons were parole violators, individuals sent back to prison for failing to adhere to the conditions of their release. By 1999, that rate had doubled – 35 percent of those coming into prison were parole violators. And, because this higher percentage was applied to a larger population of incoming prisoners, the absolute number of parole revocations had increased more than 7 times, from 27,000 in 1980 to 203,000 in 2000 (Travis and Lawrence 2002). Called *churning* by Lynch and Sabol (2001), *reentry cycling* by Clear, Waring, and Scully (this volume), and a *transient state* between liberty and recommitment by Blumstein and Beck (this volume), this movement of large numbers of individuals in and out of prison within a relatively short period of time reflects an important new reality. Rearrests for new crimes constitute an important measure of the safety risk posed by reentry, and returns to prison for parole violations reflect a second measure of reentry failures.

A final metric of the nexus between prisoner reentry and public safety is the relationship between crimes by the reentry cohort and the overall levels of crime in the communities receiving the returning prisoners. Rosenfeld, Wallman, and Fornango (this volume) determined that, for the years 1994 to 1997, in the 13 states in the BJS recidivism study, prisoners who had been released in the 3 preceding years accounted for between 13 and 16 percent of the states' arrests. They also projected this ratio between arrests of returning prisoners and all arrests for the years between 1995 and 2001, assuming the same recidivism rate found in the 1994 cohort, and estimated that, by 2001, the arrests of recently released prisoners accounted for over 20 percent of all arrests. The rearrest ratio differed substantially by crime type – in 2001, according to these estimates, released prisoners accounted for 30 percent of arrests for violent crime compared to 18 percent for property crime and 20 percent for drug offenses.

This analysis points out a critical connection between reentry, crime and safety. Today, as America experiences the highest levels of prisoner reentry and the lowest levels of crime in a generation, recently released prisoners are contributing to the nation's crime problem more than ever before. This is true not because recidivism rates have changed, but instead because the size of the reentry population is growing and at the same time the number of arrests among the population is declining, reflecting lower crime rates.

These measures of the intersection between prisoner reentry and public safety create new challenges for policymakers. More prisoners are being released than at any earlier time in the nation's history, with a higher percentage having previously been incarcerated for drug offenses and parole violations. Although, on average, they present rearrest risks not significantly higher than those documented in the first study 10 years earlier, they are now more likely to be returned to prison for parole violations. And, perhaps most striking, the cohort of returning prisoners are responsible for a substantial share of all arrests, increasing from 13 percent of arrests in 1994 to an estimated 20 percent in 2001. This shift has been particularly pronounced for crimes of violence, nearly doubling from 15 percent in 1994 to an estimated 28 percent 7 years later.

In short, if law enforcement officials, policymakers, and community leaders wish to keep crime rates low, they would be well advised to focus resources and attention on the risks posed by returning prisoners. Stated differently, the development of policies that promote successful reentry could yield substantial gains in public safety.

Assessing the Policy Options

The historic increase in the nation's incarceration rates and the concomitant rise in the reentry population pose new challenges to policymakers interested in developing effective crime control strategies. One school of thought, of course, holds that the nation should reduce its reliance on imprisonment as a preferred policy choice and invest some of the savings in crime-prevention programs. Pursuing this option would have a number of social and economic benefits. States could save money that they currently spend on prisons, a highly attractive result in today's era of fiscal constraints. Individuals and their families would not suffer the disruption that prisons impose. Communities would experience reductions in the dislocation of residents sent to prison, what Clear and Rose have called "coercive mobility" (Clear and Rose 1999). But, although the rate of growth in America's prison population has slowed somewhat (Glaze and Palla 2004), the overwhelming political reality seems to lead to persistently high rates of imprisonment.

The country's experiment in "mass imprisonment" (Mauer and Chesney-Lind 2002) also provides a focus on an age-old issue, namely whether prisons themselves are criminogenic. This inquiry is quite distinct from determining whether prisons reduce crime because of their incapacitation effects or their specific deterrence effects. The reentry perspective adopted in this volume raises the question whether the large number of individuals moving through America's prison system are more or less likely to engage in criminal activity postrelease. Over a decade ago, Gendreau, Goggin, and Cullen (1999) provided a bracing answer to that question: "The sad reality is that so little is known about what goes on inside the 'black box' of prisons and how this relates to recidivism."

The state of knowledge on this critical question has not advanced significantly since that bleak assessment was rendered (Maruna and Toch, this volume). Yet Maruna and Toch, in their discussion of corrections practices and relevant criminological theory, point to several innovative policies that might turn prisons into institutions that reduce the reoffending rates of their graduates. If prisons have the effect of attenuating the social bonds that may guard against recidivism, then perhaps prisons should embrace the mission of strengthening (or at least maintaining) those bonds for the incarcerated population. In this view, prisons should actively foster strong family ties, rather than simply allow inmates visiting privileges. They should encourage, not impede, the involvement of volunteers, mentors, faith representatives, employers, and positive peer groups in the life of the inmates.

In crafting an even bolder suggestion, Maruna and Toch suggest that the system of prison governance should be fundamentally restructured, giving inmates substantially more control over the rules governing prison life. In other contexts, this kind of attention to "procedural justice" has resulted in greater respect for the rule of law, enhanced legitimacy in the imposition of sanctions against rule-violators, and reductions in antisocial behavior (Tyler 1988, 1990). Similarly, prisons could sequence the offering of programs designed to raise levels of educational attainment, literacy and numeracy, job skills, and social functioning so that the prison term more closely resembles a systematic effort to improve human capital rather than a menu of haphazard interventions. In this view, prisons should be expected, at a minimum, to "do no harm," but better yet to actively promote the processes of desistance (Farrall 2002). Although the research evaluating these innovations is sparse – and, in the classic evaluation of the Butner prison experiment, disappointing to those who hoped for recidivism reductions – the idea that prisons should be evaluated on their effectiveness at reducing recidivism rates seems particularly compelling at a time when so many people are passing through these institutions, many of whom go on to commit future crimes.

The more traditional policy prescription is to offer inmates programs that will reduce their subsequent crime risks. Certainly the profile of prisoners is one of substantial deficits in essential knowledge and skills. As Petersilia points out (this volume), 2 in 5 (41 percent) exiting state prisoners do not have a high school diploma or a GED, almost 2 in 3 (59 percent) report using drugs in the month before they committed their crime, 1 in 5 (20 percent) were under the influence of alcohol alone at the time of their crime, and 1 in 10 (9 percent) reported mental or emotional problems. Their work history prior to incarceration was scant. One third (33 percent) reported that they were unemployed in the month before their arrest. In its survey of prisoners released to Baltimore, the Urban Institute found that nearly half (45 percent) had been fired from a job at least once (Visher, Kachnowski, La Vigne, and Travis 2004). These characteristics define the prison population as deficient with respect to human capital.

Providing programs designed to improve the human capital of prisoners makes sense from a public safety perspective. In recent years, a number of meta-analyses of prison program evaluations have arrived at a similar conclusion: prison programs can reduce recidivism rates (Andrews, Zinger, Hoge, Bonta, Gendreau, and Cullen 1990; Cullen and Gendreau 2000; Gaes, Flanagan, Motiuk, and Stewart 1999). Of particular importance when considering policy options for addressing the safety risks of the reentry population is the finding that prison programs are most effective when they link interventions inside the prison walls to those outside (Gaes et al 1999; Inciardi et al 1997). These programs respond to the realities of the high risk of recidivism in the first months following release, and provide critical supports during this crucial period of transition from incarceration to freedom.

But even this viewpoint should be tempered by important qualifications before it is embraced fully by policymakers and practitioners. For example, the research design of the evaluations contained in these meta-analyses does not always meet the highest standards of experimental design with random assignment to treatment and control groups. For this reason, in part, it is difficult to determine the role of the individual prisoner's motivation to change in the observed reductions in recidivism. More important, the evaluated programs are typically stand-alone interventions. Were the prison environment restructured to support desistance, along the lines suggested by Maruna and Toch, the program effects might be far greater. Finally, the programs operate within the current context of postrelease supervision. Were supervision reorganized to promote desistance, then the power of the intervention might be further enhanced.

In addition to the policy challenge of reorienting the prison experience to promote desistance, thereby enhancing public safety, another clear policy option is to construct a system of postrelease supervision that also reduces crime rates. Ever since Maconochie (see Morris 1990) introduced the idea of "tickets of leave" for prisoners who had earned the right to early release from prison under community supervision, this component of the criminal justice system, typically called parole, has been a mainstay of sentencing practice. Today, about 4 in 5 released prisoners are placed on some form of supervision, for periods of time ranging from a few months to several years – even for life. In 2003, there were 774,588 adults on parole in America (Glaze and Palla 2004).

Viewed from a public safety perspective, it is remarkable that so little is known about the effectiveness of this standard criminal justice practice in reducing recidivism rates of returning prisoners. As Piehl and LoBuglio point out (this volume), the mechanisms of supervision that might reduce crime rates can be clearly stated. First, the services provided to parolees might stabilize their lives so that they are better connected to institutions such as work, family, and positive support systems. This enhanced connectedness, or reintegration, might hasten desistance. In addition, the surveillance function inherent in any supervision system might deter criminal behavior. Finally, early detection of misconduct, if followed by increased surveillance or a return to prison, might be a very effective form of deterrence.

Yet the research literature contains few studies examining the crime control consequences of these mechanisms of postrelease supervision. Ideally, we would construct a study that would follow prisoners randomly assigned to supervision and no supervision – better still, a study that assigned participants to different kinds of supervision with varying mixes of surveillance and services. The study closest to this ideal was carried out by the RAND corporation, which received funding from the National Institute of Justice to assess the effectiveness of intensive supervision programs (ISP). These programs swept the nation during the 1980s, with ISP proponents arguing that smaller caseloads, tighter surveillance, and more referrals to services would surely reduce recidivism rates and cut prison costs. In effect, the ISP movement was founded on the belief that because supervision was good, more supervision would be better. The RAND evaluation, using a random assignment design, certainly did not confirm these high hopes (Petersilia and Turner 1993). Rearrest rates in the experimental and comparison groups were about the same. But substantially more of the ISP participants (65 percent) than the controls (38 percent) were found in violation of a technical condition of their supervision. And program participants were sent back to prison at a higher rate (27 percent) than those receiving regular supervision (19 percent). It appears that the main accomplishment of supervision is to "produce" opportunities for violators rather than deter them.

In the absence of a stronger evidence base, it is difficult to argue that postrelease supervision reduces crime. Rosenfeld, Wallman, and Fornango (this volume) find lower recidivism among parolees than prisoners subject to mandatory supervision, or no supervision, controlling for a number of other influences. However, this finding is based on observational data rather than the controlled experimentation needed for definitive conclusions. Yet we have witnessed a sharp shift in supervision practices toward a crime control, surveillance model. Drug testing is now routinely ordered in many jurisdictions. The use of electronic bracelets has increased. Parole officers are philosophically more aligned with their law enforcement counterparts than with their colleagues in the human services. Just as incarceration rates have increased in response to the public's concerns about crime, so too has the operating philosophy of parole taken a more punitive turn (Petersilia 2003).

In essence, the American criminal justice system has created a system of "back-end" sentencing that sends hundreds of thousands of people back to prison each year. The public safety benefits of this "back end" sentencing have not been determined. Under one interpretation of this new reality, the American system of supervision has become highly efficient at detecting those who present the highest risk of criminal conduct, particularly through new technologies such as drug testing, and a policy of rapidly, preemptively returning these high risk individuals to prison averts large numbers of crimes. It is certainly plausible that incarcerating the population identified as likely to reoffend will have a significant crime reduction effect. However, Blumstein and Beck (this volume) point out that even this supposition leaves important questions unanswered. Could another combination of sanctions and incentives yield the same result, perhaps at a lower cost? Is this the most efficient way to allocate scarce prison space to achieve crime reduction? And, perhaps most important, once the prisoner has served time for the parole violation and is returned to the community, has the risk to the public been reduced at all, has the antisocial behavior only been deferred for a few months, or perhaps has the prisoner emerged even more likely to offend than before?

In both of these policy arenas – the use of supervision following prison and the use of parole revocations as a response to parole violations – we have seen substantial shifts in practice toward a more punitive posture, but without a research basis for concluding that these shifts have enhanced public safety. What is clear, however, is that the costs are high, as both intensive supervision and aggressive revocation policies have fueled, from the back end, the costly growth of America's prison population.

Yet the policy responses to the safety risks posed by returning prisoners are not limited to the mechanisms available to the criminal justice system. Efforts to reduce recidivism rates would be incomplete if they only included strategies to improve the capabilities of prisons and supervision to enhance the desistance process. As Uggen, Wakefield, and Western suggest (this volume), policies that promote employment and marriage for the returning prisoner population would likely encourage desistance from crime. The workplace itself, with its inherent behavioral requirements and supervisory structures, provides a form of social control (Laub and Sampson 2003). The literature on desistance highlights the role that families can play in supporting prosocial behavior. Marriage, for example, particularly a marriage demonstrating a high level of commitment, can be a powerful force in the desistance process (Horney, Osgood, and Marshall 1995).

254

The operations of the American system of incarceration, release, and reentry seem designed to weaken prisoners' connections to work and relationships. Of the nearly 1.1 million state and federal prisoners deemed eligible for work in 2000, only 53 percent currently had a work assignment. Most of them (43 percent) performed institutional maintenance, and only 7 percent were employed making goods available for general consumption (Atkinson and Rostad 2003). These activities do little to prepare prisoners for the world of work in the community. Also troubling is the finding that state and federal prisons are doing less to improve the human capital of returning prisoners. Between 1991 and 1997, the share of prisoners nearing their release date who reported having participated in vocational programs declined from 31 to 27 percent and from 43 to 35 percent for education programs (Lynch and Sabol 2001). During this era of mass incarceration, correctional policies that emphasize preparation for work during the incarceration period and connections to work upon release could have two desirable results: (1) improvements in lifetime earnings and (2) reductions in the recidivism rates of former prisoners.

Similarly, correctional policies can undermine connections between prisoners and their families. A majority (62 percent) of state prisoners are held in facilities more than 100 miles from their homes (Mumola 2000), making family visits difficult and costly. A number of states have entered into financial arrangements with telephone service providers, whereby families of inmates pay inflated fees for collect calls, with the prison receiving a portion of the payment (Petersilia 2003). This translates into an expensive reality for poor families that pay large portions of their budgets to remain in contact with their loved ones (Braman 2002). Prison visiting procedures create additional obstacles to constructive interactions between inmates and their families. There is little attention to reforms that could mitigate the negative impact on the children who visit their parents in prison (Women's Prison Association 1996). At the time of release, few corrections agencies work with the inmate's family members to help all involved adjust to the changes incarceration brings to these relationships. Correctional policies that place a priority on maintaining, where possible, strong family ties during incarceration, and particularly during reentry, could have multiple benefits. And stronger families would be valuable, both as social institutions that support productive citizens and as institutions that support the processes of desistance.

These observations about the role of work, marriage, and family lead to a larger policy recommendation. Is it possible to imagine a world in which the agencies of the justice system – corrections, police, courts, and parole – work together with other public and private institutions – housing providers, workforce development agencies, drug treatment providers, foster care agencies, and churches and other faith institutions – to systematically reduce the risk of failure around the time of reentry? What if these entities adopt the goal of significantly reducing recidivism rates for the reentry cohort? What would such a strategy look like?

These new institutional arrangements would scarcely resemble today's approach to prisoner reentry. In this new approach, every prisoner would be assessed for his or her safety risk prior to release, including both the risk of offending and the risk of victimization. And a plan would be developed to reduce that risk. If the prisoner is mentally ill and requires medication, then connections would be made to community mental health providers. If the prisoner has a history of addiction and faces a high risk of relapse, then connections to drug treatment would be established, on either an inpatient or outpatient basis. If the prisoner posed a risk to a specified individual, victim service agencies would develop safety plans for that potential victim, perhaps including orders of protection, electronic monitoring to keep a safe distance between the individuals, or relocation of the threatened party. If the prisoner's prior gang involvement presents a risk of retaliation upon release, then police officers working in the gang unit could be deployed to cool the dispute.

At the same time, this consortium of reentry agencies would work with families, employers, local residents, community organizations and ex-offender groups to create "concentric circles of support" for returning prisoners (Travis 2005). This approach would be based on the recognition that improvements in the circumstances of individual prisoners are necessary but not sufficient ingredients in a strategy to produce significant reductions in failure rates. Strengthening the relationships that constitute informal social control is also required.

Implementing such a strategy would require new alignments of agencies and institutions. Perhaps the recognition that, at the beginning of the 21st century, returning prisoners account for approximately 30 percent of all arrests for violence in this country will mobilize the political will to carry out these realignments. This strategy would certainly benefit from the expenditure of new resources, both public and private – but realistically, those resources are already subject to fierce competition. Alternatively, a policy following the simple dictum that public safety resources should be allocated according to public safety risk would revolutionize the nation's approach to reentry management. The risk of rearrest is highest in the months immediately following release from prison, but resources are not allocated to be most intense at that time. If parole services were front-loaded, and corrections transition assistance was concentrated in the months before and after release, the reentry process would unfold quite differently. If drug treatment slots, transitional housing units, health care appointments, and foster care determinations were all aligned with the moment of release – the moment of greatest risk – then those existing public resources might amplify their public safety impact.

This new strategy would also require articulation of a new policy goal – and a new system of accountability. Rather than measure the effectiveness of programs simply in terms of their overall impact on recidivism rates often after several years, programs would be assessed on their contributions to reductions in failure rates immediately following release from prison. Then, at the community level, the consortium of reentry managers brought together to enhance public safety would be held accountable for reducing the risks in the days, weeks, and months immediately after the prison gates open and a prisoner makes the difficult journey home. Of course, this change in focus would also have a long-term impact on recidivism and would improve the chances of a prisoner's successful reintegration into free society.

We believe the new national attention on prisoner reentry, when refracted through the prism of public safety, could lead to new models for managing the transition from prison. These new models place the agencies of justice, particularly corrections, parole, and police, in new roles as brokers of services, conveners of stakeholders, and advocates for public safety. Adoption of these new roles will require strong leadership, rigorous testing of new approaches, and a willingness to accept risk that has not historically characterized corrections, police and parole. But now, with the reentry population at historically high levels, and the crime rates at historically low levels, there is a window of opportunity for new thinking and new leadership to implement this new vision.

References

Andrews, D., Zinger, I., Hoge, R., Bonta, J., Gendreau, P., and Cullen, F. 1990. "Does Correctional Treatment Work? A Clinically Relevant and Psychologically Informed Meta-Analysis." *Criminology* 28: 369–404.

Atkinson, Robert D., and Knut A. Rostad. 2003. *Can Inmates Become an Integral Part of the U.S. Workforce?* Paper prepared for the Urban Institute Reentry Roundtable, New York, May 19–20.

Beck, Alan. 2000. *State and Federal Prisoners Returning to the Community: Findings from the Bureau of Justice Statistics.* Paper presented at the First Reentry Courts Initiative Cluster Meeting, Washington, DC, April 13, 2000.

Beck, Alan, and B. E. Shipley. 1989. *Recidivism of Prisoners Released in 1983.* Washington, DC: U.S. Department of Justice, Office of Justice Programs, Bureau of Justice Statistics.

Bennett, William J., John J. DiIulio, and John P. Walters 1996. *Body Count: Moral Poverty – and How to Win America's War Against Crime and Drugs.* New York: Simon and Schuster.

Blumstein, Alfred, and Allen J. Beck. 1999. "Population Growth in U.S. Prisons, 1980–1996," Michael Tonry and Joan Petersilia, eds., *Prisons: Crime and Justice,* vol. 26, pp. 17–61. Chicago: University of Chicago Press.

Blumstein, Alfred, and Joel Wallman. 2000. *The Crime Drop in America.* New York: Cambridge University Press.

Braman, Donald. 2002. "Families and Incarceration," Marc Mauer and Meda Chesney-Lind, eds., *Invisible Punishment: The Collateral Consequences of Mass Imprisonment.* New York: The New Press.

Clear, Todd, and D. Rose. 1999. "When Neighbors Go to Jail: Impact on Attitudes about Formal and Informal Social Control." *Research in Brief.* Washington, DC: U.S. Department of Justice, National Institute of Justice.

Cullen, Francis T., and Paul Gendreau. 2000. "Assessing Correctional Rehabilitation: Policy, Practice, and Prospects," J. Horney ed., *Criminal Justice 2000: Policies, Processes, and Decisions of the Criminal Justice System.* Washington, DC: National Institute of Justice.

DiIulio, John J., and Anne Piehl. 1995. "Does Prison Pay? Revisited: Returning to the Crime Scene." *Brookings Review* Winter: 21–25.

Farrall, Stephen. 2002. *Rethinking What Works with Offenders: Probation, Social Context and Desistance from Crime.* Devon, UK: Willan.

Gaes, G. T., T. Flanagan, L. Motiuk, and L. Stewart. 1999. "Adult Correctional Treatment," M. Tonry and J. Petersilia, eds., *Prisons, Criminal Justice: A Review of Research.* Chicago: University of Chicago Press.

Gendreau, P., Goggin, C., and Cullen, F. 1999. *The Eeffects of Prison Sentences on Recidivism.* A report to the Corrections Research and Development and Aboriginal Policy Branch, Solicitor General of Canada, Ottawa.

Glaze, Lauren E., and Seri Palla. 2004. *Probation and Parole in the United States, 2003.* Washington, DC: U.S. Department of Justice, Bureau of Justice Statistics. NCJ 205336.

Hagan, John, and Ronit Dinovitzer. 1999. "Collateral Consequences of Imprisonment for Children, Communities and Prisoners," M. Tonry and J. Petersilia, eds., *Prisons, Criminal Justice: A Review of Research.* Chicago: University of Chicago Press.

Harrison, Paige M., and Jennifer C. Karberg. 2003. *Prison and Jail Prisoners at Midyear 2002*. Washington, DC: U.S. Department of Justice, Bureau of Justice Statistics.

Horney, Julie, D. Wayne Osgood, and Ineke Haen Marshall. 1995. "Criminal Careers in the Short-Term: Intra-Individual Variability in Crime and Its Relation to Local Life Circumstances." *American Sociological Review* 60: 655–673.

Inciardi, James A., Steven S. Martin, Clifford A. Butzin, Robert M. Hooper, and Lana D. Harrison. 1997. "An Effective Model of Prison-Based Treatment for Drug-Involved Offenders." *Journal of Drug Issues*, 27(2): 261–278.

Langan, Patrick, and David Levin. 2002. *Recidivism of Prisoners Released in 1994*. Washington, DC: U.S. Department of Justice, Office of Justice Programs, Bureau of Justice Statistics.

Laub, John and Robert J. Sampson. 2003. *Shared Beginnings, Divergent Lives: Delinquent Boys to Age 70*. Cambridge, MA: Harvard University Press.

Lynch, James P. and William J. Sabol. 2001. *Prisoner Reentry in Perspective*. Crime Policy Report. Washington, D.C.: Urban Institute Press.

Maxwell, Sheila R. 1999. "Conservative Sanctioning and Correctional Innovations in the United States: An Examination of Recent Trends." *International Journal of the Sociology of Law* 27: 401–412.

Mauer, Marc, and Meda Chesney-Lind, eds. 2002. *Invisible Punishment: The Collateral Consequences of Mass Imprisonment*. New York: New Press.

Morris, Norval. 1990. *Between Prison and Probation: Intermediate Punishments in a Rational Sentencing System*. New York: Oxford University Press.

Mumola, Christopher. 2000. *Incarcerated Parents and Their Children*. Washington, DC: U.S. Department of Justice, Bureau of Justice Statistics.

Petersilia, Joan. 2003. *When Prisoners Come Home: Parole and Prisoner Reentry*. New York: Oxford University Press.

Petersilia, J. and S. Turner. 1993. "Intensive Probation and Parole." In Crime and Justice: An Annual Review of Research, M. Tonry (ed.), p. 281–335. Chicago: University of Chicago Press.

Piehl, Anne M., Bert Useem, and John J. DiIulio, Jr. 1999. *Right-Sizing Justice: A Cost-Benefit Analysis of Imprisonment in Three States*. New York: Manhattan Institute for Policy Research Center for Civic Innovation.

Reuter, Peter. 1997. Lecture at "Perspectives on Crime and Justice," lecture series sponsored by the National Institute of Justice. Washington, DC, February.

Rosenfeld, Richard. 2000. "Patterns in Adult Homicide: 1980–1995." Alfred Blumstein and Joel Wallman, eds. *The Crime Drop in America*. Cambridge, UK: Cambridge University Press.

Spelman, William. 2000. "The Limited Importance of Prison Expansion." Alfred Blumstein and Joel Wallman, eds. *The Crime Drop in America*. Cambridge, UK: Cambridge University Press.

Tonry, Michael. 1999. "Why Are U.S. Incarceration Rates So High?" *Crime and Delinquency* 45: 419–437.

Travis, Jeremy, and Sarah Lawrence. 2002. *Beyond the Prison Gates: The State of Parole in America*. Washington, DC: Urban Institute Press.

Travis, Jeremy. 2005. *But They All Come Back: Facing the Challenges of Prisoner Reentry*. Washington, DC: Urban Institute Press.

Tyler, Tom R. 1988. *The Social Psychology of Procedural Justice*. New York: Plenum.

Tyler, Tom R. 1990. *Why People Obey The Law*. New Haven, CT: Yale University Press.

Visher, Christy, Vera Kachnowski, Nancy G. La Vigne, and Jeremy Travis. 2004. *Baltimore Prisoners' Experiences Returning Home*. Washington, DC: Urban Institute Press.

Women's Prison Association. 1996. *When a Mother Is Arrested: How the Criminal Justice and Child Welfare Systems Can Work Together More Effectively*: Baltimore: Maryland Department of Human Resources.

Index

Index